AVID

READER

PRESS

The
Birds
That
Audubon
Missed

Discovery and Desire in the
American Wilderness

KENN KAUFMAN

Avid Reader Press

New York   London   Toronto   Sydney   New Delhi

AVID READER PRESS
An Imprint of Simon & Schuster, LLC
1230 Avenue of the Americas
New York, NY 10020

First Avid Reader Press hardcover edition May 2024

AVID READER PRESS and colophon are trademarks of Simon & Schuster, LLC

Simon & Schuster: Celebrating 100 Years of Publishing in 2024

For information about special discounts for bulk purchases,
please contact Simon & Schuster Special Sales
at 1-866-506-1949 or business@simonandschuster.com.

The Simon & Schuster Speakers Bureau can bring authors to your live event.
For more information or to book an event contact the
Simon & Schuster Speakers Bureau at 1-866-248-3049
or visit our website at www.simonspeakers.com.

Interior design by Ruth Lee-Mui

Manufactured in the United States of America

1   3   5   7   9   10   8   6   4   2

Library of Congress Cataloging-in-Publication Data
Names: Kaufman, Kenn, author.
Title: The birds that Audubon missed : discovery and desire
in the American wilderness / Kenn Kaufman.
Identifiers: LCCN 2023057178 (print) | LCCN 2023057179 (ebook) |
ISBN 9781668007594 (hardcover) | ISBN 9781668007594 (paperback) |
ISBN 9781668007617 (ebook)
Subjects: LCSH: Ornithology—United States—History. |
Birds—United States—Identification—History.
Classification: LCC QL672.73.U6 K38 2024 (print) | LCC QL672.73.U6
(ebook) | DDC 598.0973—dc23/eng/20240112
LC record available at https://lccn.loc.gov/2023057178
LC ebook record available at https://lccn.loc.gov/2023057179

ISBN 978-1-6680-0759-4
ISBN 978-1-6680-0761-7 (ebook)

To Kimberly Kaufman,
who brightens every day of the present for me

and to J. B. Kaufman,
who taught me how to look at the past with new eyes

Contents

A Note About Bird Names

For well over two centuries, U.S. scientists writing about birds have capitalized the English name of each species, and I follow that practice in this book. Readers unfamiliar with birding or ornithology may find all these capital letters jarring at first, but they help bring clarity when we're discussing the roughly eleven thousand known species of birds. There are many kinds of blue jays in the world, but the Blue Jay is a particular species living mainly in eastern North America. There are many sorts of egrets and a fan might say they're all great, but only one is officially the Great Egret (named for its size, not any judgment on quality). In a similar vein, we can write about "western ducks" and mean all the ducks in the West, but the capitals in "Western Sandpiper" signal that we mean just one species.

The official name of each bird in North America is standardized by a committee of the American Ornithological Society. In the early 1800s, before the committee was established, a bewildering variety of names might be applied to a bird by different authors—or even by the same author. In this book I refer to every species by the name that was current at the beginning of 2024, regardless of what it was called in the past, except when there's a reason to mention a specific old name.

Prologue: A Song in Labrador

The man was alone on the deck. It was before dawn, with only a gray hint of light on the eastern horizon, and it was cold, too, with a damp chill that seeped through his heavy coat. But he could not sleep, not now. Hunching his shoulders, he shivered and looked around.

Toward the north, he could just make out the shape of the wild shoreline looming above the mist: massive boulders and craggy cliffs fronting the sea, topped by a few conifer spires. The breeze, carrying a tang of salt and spruce, was barely enough to rustle the furled sails, or to drive wavelets lapping against the ship's wooden hull. A few hesitant notes of birdsong drifted in from somewhere on land, and the man strained to hear them more clearly. Even though it was the end of June, it was going to be another cold, dank day.

The man's companions were still below, wrapped in the peaceful sleep of hearty young men who have been working hard outdoors. And why not? They *were* young men, after all, with the luxury of believing they had plenty of time. He was working hard, too, but he didn't share their carefree sense of life stretching out ahead. He was older, and under pressure, and behind schedule. Anxiety gnawed at him with the same penetrating chill as the faint, icy breeze off the water.

He needed to succeed on this expedition—he needed to wrest new

1

discoveries from this cold wilderness. And up to this point, those discoveries had remained elusive.

What a long, strange voyage his life had been so far.

It was the summer of 1833. Three decades had passed since he had arrived in America, in 1803, as a brash teenager. His father, a prosperous French sea captain, had wanted to protect his son from being drafted into Napoleon's armies; so he'd sent the boy to spend time on a farm he had bought, as a business venture, in Pennsylvania. It was a temporary solution. The boy might have gone back to France for good if he hadn't fallen in love with his neighbor's daughter, Lucy.

Ah, Lucy. How he missed her now, as he did whenever he had to be away. How beautiful she had been when they met, when she was sixteen and he was eighteen. How beautiful she was still, in every way. Her steadfast heart had never wavered; she had never abandoned him, even in the worst of times. And he had had so many of those worst times. The stigma of the failure of his business ventures. The shame of debtors' prison. The indignity of begging for work, selling his talents for a pittance. And then what could have been the end of it, the crazy move that would have driven any normal wife to leave her husband: he had announced he was going to make his fortune by producing a monumental book about . . . birds.

Birds? You have failed as a shopkeeper, you have failed as a mill owner, you have barely kept afloat by painting portraits and teaching art lessons for bored wealthy patrons, and now you think you can achieve some great success by publishing a bird book?

But even then, miraculously, Lucy had stayed with him. For years, in the background behind his uneven attempts at business in Kentucky, the man had been stubbornly developing his ability to draw and paint. And eventually he was producing big, bold, beautiful portraits of birds, unlike anything the world had ever seen. Lucy might have known nothing about the history of ornithological illustration, but she had faith in the brilliance of her husband's work. In 1824, she had helped raise the money for him to travel from Louisiana to the city of Philadelphia. That was the center of science and printing in America at the time. There, he hoped he could find a publisher for his bird illustrations.

It hadn't worked out. Philadelphia had been the home of Alexander Wilson, author of the acclaimed *American Ornithology*, the first comprehensive work on North American birds. Wilson had died in 1813, but he was still revered by his followers in Philadelphia, and the man had made the mistake of offending them with rash denunciations of Wilson's character. Doors closed to him, and he would find no publisher in the United States.

In desperation, he had taken his portfolio of bird art to England. There, in a wild and improbable swing of events, he had found almost instant fame. Naturalists, scholars, artists, and nobles praised his illustrations. Within a few months, a team of engravers and printers and colorists had begun work on the first set of color plates, and subscribers had begun to sign up to receive installments of these grand illustrations as he produced them. He was going to be published after all.

Heady as this experience was, it was only the beginning of a task that would consume him for years. Between 1827 and 1838 he would produce and publish 435 magnificent color plates of birds. Between 1831 and 1839 he would publish five hefty volumes of text, with detailed accounts of all the birds depicted. These two great multipart works—*The Birds of America* and *Ornithological Biography*—would secure the fame of John James Audubon all over the world.

On that June morning in 1833, however, his success was far from certain. Only one-third of the color plates had been completed, only one of his five volumes of text written and published. His fame was growing; but among the scientific community in the United States, he couldn't touch the reputation of the late Alexander Wilson. Dead for twenty years, Wilson was still held up as the authority on North American birdlife, and the nine volumes of his *American Ornithology*—now being updated and reissued by others—were still regarded as the standard references.

Audubon sensed he was grappling with Wilson's ghost, and that was one of the two big forces that motivated him. He wanted to succeed for the sake of Lucy, to live up to the faith she had always had in him, and he wanted to succeed for the sake of his own vanity and his own competitive spirit, breaking out of Wilson's shadow at last.

To all appearances, he was trying to outdo Alexander Wilson in any way he could. His great work would be called *The Birds of America*, words that anyone could understand, avoiding the snooty tone of Wilson's *American Ornithology*. But just in case anyone wanted a more academic theme, his accompanying text would arrive under a more technical title, *Ornithological Biography*. His illustrations of birds would be bigger than Wilson's, with even the largest birds shown at life size, and with much more dramatic compositions.

And critically and essentially, he would treat *more different kinds* of birds than Wilson had.

He had recklessly promised his subscribers portraits of four hundred species of birds. But that promise put him in a bind, because he hadn't found that many yet. No one had. The known birdlife of eastern North America was still shy of four hundred full species, so if he were to illustrate that many, he would have to discover new ones.

The year before, he had arranged to travel to the wilds of southern Florida, turning up several birds not previously documented for the territory of the United States. Now he was traveling north. Labrador beckoned: the vast region, its boundaries still ill-defined at that time, occupying much of the northeastern mainland of Canada. Few naturalists had been anywhere near Labrador, but fishermen and explorers reported that those cold northern lands and waters teemed with birds. Among them, Audubon hoped, would be a host of new species—new subjects for his portraits, even species unknown to science.

So he had gathered an expeditionary force consisting of his younger son, John Woodhouse Audubon, then twenty years old, and four other lads of about the same age, energetic youths who were eager to experience the wilderness. He had chartered a two-masted schooner, the *Ripley*, with a skilled captain and a crew of nine. They had sailed from Eastport, Maine, on the sixth of June, navigating around the edge of Nova Scotia, stopping by the Magdalen Islands, and then heading north across the wide, stormy Gulf of St. Lawrence. They anchored off the wild coast of the land they called Labrador.

Today this stretch is included in the easternmost part of the province of Quebec. Not as isolated as it was, it's still remote. You can get to the edge of this region today by driving northeast and then east from Quebec City, tracing the north shore of the St. Lawrence River as it widens into the Gulf of St. Lawrence, following Route 138 for a thousand kilometers. Gradually the country grows wilder, the cities and towns become smaller and more widely spaced, and then the road ends at the small village of Kegaska, a short distance past the Natashquan River. For the next 450 kilometers eastward, the scattered towns and settlements can be reached only by ship or ferry.

When Audubon arrived on this coastline in 1833, there were no roads, of course, and hardly any settlements. He and his companions felt that they were explorers, and that great discoveries should be possible.

At first, though, their results were disappointing. To be sure, plenty of birds were around. Making daily excursions to the shore, the young men came back with many bird specimens. Some were of species that Audubon still needed to illustrate, so he was kept busy with sketching them in detail, at least on days when the seas were calm enough for him to sit at his drawing table in the ship's cabin. But as the days passed, every bird they found turned out to be one that Audubon recognized, from prior experience or from books or museum collections. Every bird they found was of a species already known, already described, already named.

But their luck was about to change. The expedition was just about to discover a new species. As recounted later, it was an exciting find. Here are John James Audubon's own words describing the day's adventure, as published the following year in the second volume of his *Ornithological Biography*.

We had been in Labrador nearly three weeks before this Finch was discovered. One morning while the sun was doing his best to enliven the gloomy aspect of the country, I chanced to enter one of those singular small valleys here and there to be seen. . . . But if the view of this favoured spot was pleasing to my eye, how much more to my ear were the sweet notes of this bird as they came thrilling on the sense, surpassing in vigour those of any American Finch with which I am acquainted, and forming a song which seemed a compound of those of the Canary and Wood-lark of Europe. I immediately shouted to my companions, who were not far distant. They came, and we all followed the songster as it flitted from one bush to another to evade our pursuit. No sooner would it alight than it renewed its song; but we found more wildness in this species than in any other inhabiting the same country, and it was with difficulty that we at last procured it. Chance placed my young companion, THOMAS LINCOLN, in a situation where he saw it alight within shot, and with his usual unerring aim, he cut short its career. On seizing it, I found it to be a species which I had not previously seen; and, supposing it to be new, I named it Tom's Finch, in honour of our friend LINCOLN, who was a great favourite among us. Three cheers were given him, when, proud of the prize, I returned to the vessel to draw it, while my son and his companions continued to search for other specimens.

It's a thrilling story of discovery—and it *was* a discovery, too, of a bird not previously documented by the strict Western or European standards of science. Two centuries later we still recognize Audubon as the original describer, and the bird is known officially as *Melospiza lincolnii*, or Lincoln's Sparrow.

This find was the kind of result Audubon needed: A brand-new species, another space filled in on the march to providing four hundred different birds for his subscribers. Another bird that had not secured a place in Alexander Wilson's *Ornithology*. Another unknown to George Ord, Thomas Nuttall, John Townsend, and anyone else who might challenge Audubon's standing in the field.

On the surface, the story seems straightforward. An expedition goes to a relatively little-known region. In these new surroundings, thanks

to the keen senses of the master naturalist, they discover a bird that
no scientist had seen before. Just the kind of result the expedition was
meant to achieve.

In reality, though, practically everything about this story is wrong
or misleading.

Lincoln's Sparrow does have a sweet and recognizable song, although not necessarily "surpassing in vigour" those of other American
species.* But did Audubon hear it first, as he related in this passage, and
direct his companions to it? Almost certainly not.

Why should we doubt the great man's own account of the discovery? After all, he wrote it within months after the fact, when presumably
it was all fresh. Unfortunately, Audubon has a legacy of stretching the
truth beyond the breaking point—sometimes exaggerating, sometimes
apparently making things up out of thin air. Flagrant examples of this
tendency were suspected by some, even during his lifetime; more have
continued to come to light as historians have looked critically at surviving documents of the era.

His published works and his letters often conveyed contradictory or
confusing claims about his life, as if he were trying to obscure his own
history. After his death in 1851, his family members and descendants,
far from attempting to set the record straight, just obscured it further.

Audubon had kept detailed journals during some periods of his
life, especially while traveling. We might expect these to capture a more
faithful version of daily events than the accounts he wrote later, self-
consciously, for publication. With that in mind, the two-volume *Audubon and His Journals*—edited by his granddaughter, Maria Audubon,
and published in 1897—should be a trove of original information, a
primary source we can trust. But it isn't.

Maria Audubon's editing of the journals and various letters had
clear aims: to burnish her grandfather's reputation and protect the

*The terms "sparrow" and "finch" were used almost interchangeably in that era, and dis-
tinct definitions for them would not be worked out until decades later, so there's nothing
surprising about the transition from "Tom's Finch" to "Lincoln's Sparrow."

family name. She admitted she had deleted large sections before publishing chosen excerpts, and then destroyed the originals. "I burned [them] myself in 1895. . . . I had copied from [them] all I ever meant to give to the public. . . . We thought that in view of the existing circumstances, fire was our only surety that many family details should be put beyond the reach of vandal hands."

Elliott Coues, a top ornithologist of the late 1800s, assisted Maria with editing the volumes. I'm just speculating here, but I think part of his role was to make sure the bird details were still plausible after her edits. Because she didn't just omit salacious bits of family drama. Even in John James's accounts of his expeditions, she apparently changed some passages and even added some.

In one striking example, Maria Audubon presented what were supposed to be quotes from her grandfather about his one western trip, up the Missouri River a decade after the Labrador journey. She has him writing about the vast herds of bison on the northern plains, and marveling at how their populations hold up despite the pressure from invading white hunters. Then: "But this cannot last; even now there is a perceptible difference in the size of the herds, and before many years the Buffalo, like the Great Auk, will have disappeared; surely this should not be permitted."

It seems impressive that Audubon, at that early date, was already making a plea to save the bison from following the Great Auk into extinction. There's a problem, though: in 1843, when this passage was supposedly written, the Great Auk was not extinct, nor suspected to be. The last definite known individuals were killed in 1844, but not until much later did anyone realize those had been the last ones; as late

opposite page: Lincoln's Sparrows by John James Audubon. An expedition to the wild coast of Labrador in summer 1833 turned up this species, previously unknown to Western science. Audubon wrote a dramatic account describing how he had discovered the bird by following its distinctive song, but there are reasons to believe the story is at least partly fictitious.

as 1860, the auks were rumored to be still nesting on a small island off Newfoundland. (Elliott Coues knew this, and it's surprising that he didn't stop Maria from including this clause.)

So there were reasons to be suspicious of this passage about bison. Those suspicions were confirmed after 2008, when writer Daniel Patterson discovered three partial transcripts from Audubon's Missouri River journals, fragments that had escaped Maria's burning spree. For the date in question—August 5, 1843—much of the wording in the newly discovered piece was the same as in Maria's published version. But it expressed more excitement about hunting and no concern about the future of the species; the "Great Auk speech," as Patterson called it, was absent. Evidently that flourish had been added by a dutiful granddaughter who wished to cast her ancestor as a visionary proto-conservationist.

What does this have to do with the discovery of Lincoln's Sparrow in Labrador? That was another case with more than one version of the same tale. The famous version, the long-accepted one, is the story I quoted above from *Ornithological Biography*, in which Audubon claimed credit for noting the sparrow first by its song. But as ornithologist and historian Matthew Halley has pointed out, the story doesn't quite add up.

In a collection of old manuscripts in the Delaware Museum of Nature & Science, Halley discovered a long-lost journal kept during the Labrador expedition by Thomas Lincoln himself—the young man for whom the sparrow was named. The find prompted Halley to look more closely at the bird's backstory.

In Maria Audubon's edited version of her grandfather's journals, June 27, 1833, is fixed as the date of the sparrow's discovery. But it's not presented as a highlight. The entry starts off describing the morning's fog and rain, then says the weather cleared and they went ashore. The text goes into some detail about Canada Jays and Ruby-crowned Kinglets before mentioning that "We shot a new species of Finch, which I have named *Fringilla lincolnii*." The descriptive notes that follow, supposedly scribbled down by Audubon on shipboard off the coast of Labrador, give a more accurate and insightful diagnosis of the bird than what was published the next year in the carefully composed text of the *Ornithological Biography*. In my opinion these first descriptive comments, far from being included in the original journals, were probably written decades later by Elliott Coues.* The entry for the day also claims that the party stayed onshore until dinnertime, contradicting Audubon's published claim that once he had the sparrow specimen in hand, "proud of the prize, I returned to the vessel to draw it."

As Halley pointed out, another transcript of some of Audubon's journals had appeared three decades before Maria's version. *The Life of John James Audubon, the Naturalist, edited by His Widow*, had been published in New York in 1869; it included Lucy's own personal observations as well as many journal excerpts. In that version, the account for June 27, 1833, started off with the same description of rainy and foggy weather, but then ended: "Drawing all day." In other words, he stayed on board the ship, working on drawings, while his younger companions went ashore to hunt birds.

And what of Thomas Lincoln's journal? Given the tale presented in *Ornithological Biography*, surely we would expect him to write something about the exciting chase, the securing of the specimen, Audubon's elation at seeing it was a new species, and the proclamation right there on the spot that this bird would be "Tom's Finch." That would have to be a peak life experience for any young naturalist! But he didn't write anything for June 27, or for several days after. Not until July 4 did he make a casual mention of the bird: "Mr. A. finished a drawing of a new finch which I shot at Esquimaux Islands."

There's another reason to doubt Audubon's story of the sparrow's song leading him to this discovery: the man wasn't good at finding or identifying birds by sound. "Birding by ear" is a skill much prized by modern birders, but one in which he would have scored poorly. Most

---

*For example, the supposed quote from the journal says that Lincoln's Sparrow is "allied to the Swamp Sparrow in general appearance." By the late 1800s, when Coues was assisting Maria with editing, Lincoln's and Swamp Sparrows were regarded as close relatives, but Audubon never suggested that connection in any of his published writings; he thought Lincoln's was related to a completely different set of sparrows.

historians have missed this point. In the five volumes of *Ornithological Biography*, he described the voices of hundreds of bird species; but unless you know these birds yourself, you won't realize how bad those descriptions are. Even in the present story, the comparison to canaries and European larks is not precise. And as I've mentioned, it's odd to claim this sparrow's song "surpasses in vigour" those of others. As a vocalist, Lincoln's is not nearly as vigorous as the Fox Sparrows that would have been singing in those same woods in Labrador.

So what happened? It's impossible to be sure, but my guess is that Thomas Lincoln and the other young men brought specimens of the sparrow back to the ship on June 27. Audubon, who had spent the day on board working on drawings, studied the specimens and realized they might represent a new species. He may have heard the bird's song on a later excursion to shore, or he may have asked his companions to describe what it sounded like. But in writing of the bird for his *Ornithological Biography*, he couldn't resist placing himself at the scene of the discovery and casting himself in the starring role.

Again, that is just my guess, and I could be wrong. In trying to pin down details of Audubon's life, we find ourselves in a dimly lit hall of mirrors. Stories and anecdotes surround us, many of them contradictory, while verifiable facts are as elusive as the sparrows of Labrador.

Fortunately for me, I'm not here to write a biography of Audubon. Many have been published already, and while I admire biographers and historians, I don't aspire to be one of them. I really don't care whether he was on hand for this discovery, tuning in to a new and unfamiliar song, or just heard about it afterward. It was his expedition; the party of young explorers wouldn't have been anywhere near that wild northern coast if he hadn't organized the trip. He was already responsible for the find, regardless of how the details played out. If he still felt the need to magnify his own role by lying about it in print, that's a sad note on his character, but it doesn't concern me.

No, the discovery of Lincoln's Sparrow intrigues me for a completely different reason. Most historians and biographers who have written about Audubon's Labrador trip have mentioned this find. But as far as I know, no one has pointed out the most curious aspect of it: Lincoln's Sparrow is not, in any way, a specialty of that region. It was not a rare prize waiting to be discovered by the bold explorer who would trek to that remote wilderness. It's a bird with a wide distribution across most of the North American continent.

True, it's not found everywhere all the time. In summer it's strictly a denizen of northern latitudes and upper elevations. But at one time it must have been known to Indigenous peoples across a vast stretch of the regions we now call Alaska and Canada, and in the mountains now known as the Sierra Nevada, the Rockies, the Adirondacks. Whether or not these people had a specific name for it, they would have recognized its rippling, trilling song from streamside willows, and would have known that the singer was a stripy, buffy little bird that would depart in early fall.

And when these sparrows left their western and northern breeding grounds, they would have moved south on a broad front all across the region now called the Lower 48 states. They would have spent the winter throughout what are now the southern states, and well south into Mexico and Central America. And they still do. They are less numerous in the East than in the West, but with a strategic effort during migration seasons, it should be possible to find Lincoln's Sparrows in any county in the eastern states.

John James Audubon might not have seen Lincoln's Sparrows before he traveled to the wild coast of Labrador, but they had probably seen him. They may have peered out from the woodland understory as he strode around his father's farm in eastern Pennsylvania in spring. They probably flushed from underfoot as he rode his horse across brushy meadows in northern Kentucky in fall. They could have lurked in thickets nearby as he explored the swamps of Louisiana in winter. They could have crossed his path in a dozen other places before 1833; but if they did, he never noticed them.

By the time Audubon or his companions "discovered" examples of this species, he had already spent close to three decades in places where he *might* have found them. The notable thing was not the discovery itself, but that these sparrows had eluded discovery for so long.

And they didn't just elude Audubon. They had escaped the notice of Alexander Wilson, and of Wilson's friends and fans like George Ord and Charles Lucien Bonaparte. They had slipped past Mark Catesby and William Bartram during their explorations of the southeastern colonies in the 1700s. They had evaded John Richardson on the Franklin expeditions west of Hudson Bay in the 1820s. So many dedicated naturalists had trekked across eastern North America, looking for undescribed birds, and it's remarkable that these sparrows managed to remain unnoticed until 1833.

But when Audubon picked up the first specimen of the sparrow he would name for Thomas Lincoln, what he held was not the final piece of the puzzle of eastern North American birdlife. Far from it. On that same trip to Labrador, he left other pieces untouched—species that, at the time, were still, under the definitions of Western science, undiscovered.

In forests along the coast, he heard the lilting, fluting songs of thrushes, and sometimes saw these shy, brown-backed birds running or hopping through the understory. He assumed he knew what kind they were, but he was wrong. In summer, those forests hold two thrush species that were still unnamed at that time. They would not be described to science until years later.

He and his companions also saw small birds called flycatchers perching in thickets and nabbing tiny insects in midair. They may have seen two species that were still undescribed then, but if so, they failed to notice them, and these birds would not receive names for another decade. They might have heard the persistent songs of a type of vireo that was unknown then, but if so, they passed it off as another kind of vireo that they already knew.

Nor were all the birds overlooked on the 1833 Labrador journey small or shy forest birds. The explorers saw terns offshore, including some very large ones: graceful seabirds, swooping over the water, silvery wings flashing in the sun; they even found a pair with a nest on a small island. This was a species already known from Europe, but no one realized then that it also lived on this side of the Atlantic. It would have been a fine addition to *The Birds of America*, but Audubon confused it with another large tern he had seen before, and didn't bother painting it.

But at least this expedition did connect with the Lincoln's Sparrow.

I think about this every year when migrating Lincoln's Sparrows pause in my backyard in Ohio. I might miss them during their brief northward rush in May, but they are reliable visitors in late September and October, when the weeds are taller and the brush is heavier along the back of our lot. Elusive skulkers, they may stay down out of sight until I make short churring sounds, like a songbird's alarm calls. Then they pop up out of the goldenrods and dogwood scrub, one or two at a time, peering in my direction, on high alert. At first glance their striped brown look suggests the Song Sparrows that are common here all year, but they show more colorful contrast on their faces, with buff and gray and reddish brown. Their callnotes differ, too, and they raise their forehead feathers, creating a perky peaked look to the top of the head.

When I first started looking at birds, as a child, I struggled to separate Lincoln's Sparrows from Song Sparrows. Or from Savannah Sparrows or young Swamp Sparrows. To be honest, I struggled with identifying *all* the sparrows. But that was decades ago; I've been lucky enough to spend my life focused on birds and other aspects of nature, mostly in North America, but around the world as well. Now I recognize those sparrows at a glance. But that doesn't mean I'm some kind of super expert. No, it means I'm seeing these creatures, not only through the lens of my own experience, but also with the benefit of thousands of written words and illustrations, the distilled and published experience of generations of dedicated naturalists.

And this is true of all the other birds that were missed, two centuries ago, by Wilson, Audubon, and their contemporaries. I see almost all those species every year, either on their migrations through Ohio or on my own migrations around the eastern United States and Canada. Most are not rare. Some, like Lincoln's Sparrow, tend to be a bit shy, but not exceptionally so. Others are right out in the open, like the Mottled Ducks in southern marshes or the Western Sandpipers, which, despite their name, can be found all winter along the southern Atlantic Coast. Sightings of these birds today aren't considered unusual in any way. When I talk to birders now and tell them how long these species remained undiscovered, they are almost always surprised.

Today, every serious birder on the continent can recognize these birds. We know their distinctive markings and their voices. We know where they should appear, and at what season. We expect to find them, and we do. We benefit from two centuries of accumulated knowledge. We have gained so much. But what have we lost?

In this context I'm not talking about the loss of thousands of square miles of old-growth forest or tall-grass prairie. I'm not talking about the loss of vast herds of bison or vast flocks of Passenger Pigeons, or the other species that have been reduced to mere remnants or driven to extinction. For the moment—forgive me—I am only looking through the absurdly narrow window of the momentary experience of birding. We have gained the ability to know every species we encounter.

But how would it have felt to be an active birder* in these regions two centuries ago? What if I could take my modern zest for birding—for finding and identifying as many species as possible—but erase everything I know, and plant my feet on this land in the early 1800s, with only the published information available at the time? What could I have found?

It was the time of a great gap. Indigenous knowledge of nature in eastern North America must have been rich and deep, at one time, but much of that had been fragmented or swept aside by the dawn of the nineteenth century. Western or European science, trailing along behind the colonists, had barely begun to write its own versions of natural history here. Many of the birds were, in that gap, genuinely if temporarily unknown, waiting to be discovered or rediscovered.

What a time it must have been. Looking back, it's hard to avoid

---

*The terms "birder" and "birding" didn't even exist in their current meanings at that time. As early as 1602, Shakespeare had used "birding" to refer to shooting birds (in *The Merry Wives of Windsor*); but apparently its first use in the sense of birdwatching dates to ornithologist Florence Merriam in the 1890s.

feeling a pang of envy. It's a trade-off, I know, comparing our time to theirs. Today we have extraordinary levels of shared knowledge of birds, and of all aspects of the natural world, far beyond anything dreamed of by those naturalists of old.

But in my own dreams I sometimes find myself back there, two centuries or more into the past, hiking through those grand forests, paddling down those wild rivers. In these visions the United States is still a young country, and I am younger still, seeing everything for the first time. Somehow I'm sure that, around the next bend, a flash of wings will reveal some brand-new avian gem, a bird unknown to anyone but me, and still unnamed. These dreams are fleeting, and they come less often as I grow older, but I treasure them for the sense that anything is possible.

1

The Undescribed World

Wе come into this life as explorers. Every newborn child has an innate drive to take in new information, to discover, to explore. This urge to learn is just as basic as the need to eat and sleep. The wide-eyed look of human infants is often described as reflecting innocence, but it could be more about curiosity, about striving not to miss anything.

Other creatures have the same drive. Watch a litter of fox pups romping outside their den. Even as they pounce and tumble, their senses are all on high alert. Looking in all directions, listening, sniffing the air, touching, tasting, they absorb each detail of information about their surroundings, as if their lives depended on it—as indeed they might.

Human babies may not face all the same dangers that would threaten newborn wild animals. But in young humans, the drive to learn has an added layer of focus because *language* is so central to our life and identity. Even months before they begin speaking, infants may be paying close attention, absorbing the way that certain sounds attach to certain ideas. And once they begin talking, they rapidly pick up the words for objects. Almost invariably, the focus is on nouns before verbs. Nouns first: What's this? What's that? What is *this*? Toddlers seem to have a natural sense that each object has a name, and that those names are worth knowing.

For many people, the voracious appetite for learning names will gradually fade. Sadly, some may even view this diminution as a normal part of growing up. But for those who become fascinated with nature, with the abundance of life outside the bounds of human culture, the excitement goes on. I know because I am one of those lucky people. For us, the wonders of nature never disappoint and they never end, and every time we find something new, we want to know what it is. We remain as children, eyes wide, expecting miracles around every corner.

Beginning early in my own childhood, I focused on the names of living things. When I couldn't be out in the yard looking for snails or worms or flowering weeds, I was poring over picture books about big animals and big trees. Once I started focusing on birds at the age of six, I wanted to find them all, to learn what they were called. Every time I learned something new, it didn't satisfy my curiosity, only heightened it.

I was obsessed with discovery, and I can remember using that word consciously and intentionally. I discovered that those black birds wandering the lawn were of two kinds: the short-tailed ones were starlings, the long-tailed ones grackles. I discovered that robins would stridently attack a seven-year-old boy who tried to climb to their nest. I discovered that the off-key mewing in the hedge wasn't a cat, it was a bird, delightfully called a Gray Catbird.

My parents and my favorite teachers would smile quizzically when I told them of my finds. Look, I discovered a bird called a Chipping Sparrow, and here's a picture of it in this library book. Look, I discovered a Horned Lark on the school grounds, and here's a picture. Look—this one was a challenge for a kid with no binoculars, but I heard those rich notes in the treetop and finally spotted it, deep chestnut and black among the green leaves; see, it's called an Orchard Oriole. No, not a Baltimore Oriole, I've heard of those, but this is different. It's an Orchard Oriole. The book says so. I discovered it.

At some point, an offhand comment from a schoolteacher led to a fundamental change in my outlook. "You didn't discover that. You can't say it's a discovery unless it's new to science."

"New to science." "Unknown to science." What did that even mean? It seemed like a knock against normal childhood curiosity. To be sure, many curious kids decide they want to discover something new, but I don't think it happens until they're introduced to the concept. For me, the idea set me back. Apparently, for me to claim I'd discovered a bird, it would have to be one that wasn't in the books already.

"In the beginner's mind there are many possibilities," wrote Shunryu Suzuki. "In the expert's mind there are few." My beginner's mind went into hyperdrive, inventing legions of possibilities on the shakiest of grounds. That grackle flying over, with a tail of an odd shape? I didn't know anything about birds molting their tail feathers, so I assumed it must be some brand-new, unknown type. That sparrow with a white spot on its wing? It didn't match any picture in any book at the library, so it had to be something undiscovered.

For a while, every day brought novelty. I sketched my supposed new finds and exulted in the sense that I was making scientific discoveries. But then I would see those birds again, and doubts would creep in. It was so hard to be sure these creatures were new.

In my own childish way, unknowingly, I was retracing the struggle of every scientist who ever tried to classify living things. Just look at the diverse abundance of life all around us. If we look closely enough, no two individuals—no two birds, no two animals, no two plants—are *exactly* alike. Each one has subtle differences. How do we classify them into separate types? How different does an individual have to be for us to say it's a distinct kind? And if something really is distinct, how can we be sure no one has noticed it before?

There is a huge leap from "This is new to me" to the claim that "this is new to everyone." The first is driven by the innocent desire to learn. The second opens the door to ego and competition and even conflict. It might not be so pure and innocent, but without it, this book would have no story to tell.

What does it mean to say that a particular bird is "known to science"? As a boy I had only the vaguest idea. My lack of a clear definition didn't trouble me. But to proceed with any of the topics in this book, we should consider the question: Whose science are we talking about, and why?

As a teenager reading about biology and ecology, I assumed that real science meant facts and theories and concepts that were written down, shared, and refined over time. Later I began to realize that oral traditions of science are also valid. In the past, Indigenous cultures all over the world certainly had valuable knowledge of the plants and animals in their surroundings. Many still do. Even where they have no written language, highly detailed information can be passed down orally, each generation confirming and building upon the knowledge of their forebears.

From the undoubtedly vast (and largely lost) trove of Indigenous knowledge around the globe, a few fragments have been recognized. In the dry country of the American West lives a small nightbird, the Common Poorwill, named for the sound of its mellow, mournful whistles in the dark. The traditional Hopi name for it, *Hölchoko*, means "the sleeping one." In the lore of the Akimel O'odham and Tohono O'odham, this bird had the magical ability to induce sleep. Just quaint, primitive stories? No: in the late 1940s, modern scientists stumbled across the fact that the poorwill hibernates in winter, making it the first bird known to do so. Another example involves a songbird, the boldly black and orange Hooded Pitohui, of foothill rainforest in New Guinea. As long ago as the late 1800s, an Australian explorer remarked on the curious fact that it was the only local bird native hunters would not eat. An odd superstition, perhaps? No: in 1990, western scientists discovered that this pitohui is endowed with potent poisons in its feathers, skin, and flesh, a trait previously unknown in any bird.

Beyond such insights into the traits of certain creatures, many Native peoples have shown a remarkable ability to classify and name the whole range of plants and animals in their surroundings. It's hard for "modern" science to analyze such Indigenous classification systems, because contact between western cultures and native cultures usually has an immediate, negative impact on the latter. Details of accumulated knowledge often begin to fade before outsiders even think about cataloging them.

Nonetheless, some ethno-ornithologists have gotten snapshots of these traditional classifications—by finding relatively intact native groups and approaching them with respect. Aboriginal people on an island off northern Australia had distinct names for seventy-five kinds of birds. (By contrast, I'm sure the average citizen in the United States today can't recognize and name seventy-five of their local bird species.) The Tlingit people of southeastern Alaska used generic terms for various groups of small birds that visit the region only seasonally, like fast-flying swallows or treetop warblers. But they had good knowledge of, and names for, permanent residents such as chickadees and jays; and for groups like grouse, owls, and ducks, the Tlingit named the species separately. In highland forests of eastern New Guinea, people of the Fore-language group used a remarkably sophisticated system of classifying animals of all kinds. They had names for practically every species of bird in the region and could recognize them at a distance—even small, drab songbirds that visiting ornithologists struggled to identify. Furthermore, when the Fore were presented with unfamiliar birds from outside their region, they were able to place them in context: they correctly discerned which ones were related to species they already knew.

Clearly all these cultures had a robust knowledge of birdlife, genuinely scientific in its own way, long before any Europeans set foot in their lands. If any type of bird is at all conspicuous, we can be sure that all the Native peoples in its range knew it well and had their own names for it.

Consider a big, black bird that is widespread in the northern hemisphere. I'll call it the Common Raven—because I have to call it something, after all, and that's the official English name given to it currently by a committee of the American Ornithological Society.

It's hard to miss: an impressive creature the size of a large hawk, glossy black all over, living boldly out in the open. Ravens tend to mate for life, and it's common to see a pair high overhead in purposeful, direct flight, one a few yards in front of the other, as they patrol their territory. They may engage in aerial acrobatics, with chases, dives, and barrel rolls, apparently just for fun. Often they give voice to a rich, ringing, guttural croak that may carry half a mile. Members of a pair will communicate with each other, and with other ravens, with a wide variety of harsh or musical notes that probably convey many shades of meaning. Intensely aware and innately curious, they quickly come to examine anything new that shows up in their territory.

Ravens are thought to be among the most intelligent of all birds, at least by the clumsy measures we humans use to judge other life-forms. Certainly they are adaptable. Their diet includes practically anything they can find or catch or scavenge. They steal eggs from the nests of other large birds, and they eat many large insects and small animals, bludgeoning rats and lizards with their massive, pointed beaks. They pick up nuts and grains from the ground, and pluck fruits from fig trees and cacti. They crack open mollusk shells on rocky shorelines and grab scorpions in the desert. They follow packs of wolves or other large predators to feed on the remains of their kills. And although they remain wary, they enter the edges of human settlements to scavenge anything we leave unconsumed.

Their adaptable nature has allowed ravens to inhabit a broad swath of the northern hemisphere, from the edges of the Arctic Ocean in Canada, Greenland, Scandinavia, and Siberia south to highlands of Central America, deserts of North Africa, savannas of northwestern India, and slopes of the Himalayas in Nepal. Although they're seldom seen in large groups, they are almost omnipresent over a vast area of the globe as scattered pairs or singles. Anyone who spends a lot of time outdoors in their range will see ravens, and see them as individuals. And if you get close to a raven you may realize it is looking at you, too, as an individual, sizing you up, with a stare that seems disturbingly close to human awareness.

This imposing bird has a place in the worldviews of many Indigenous peoples across the northern hemisphere. For some cultures, especially in northwestern North America and northeastern Asia, the raven is tied up in their creation stories, or identified as the bringer of light, or connected to human ancestors. At the same time, it's often characterized as a clever trickster or a scoundrel. And every language group within its range has a name for it.

Within North America, names for the raven have been varied, and some of these have been recorded and transcribed by western ethnographers. Among the Lenape or Delaware people, this bird was *winkeòhk-wèt*. For the Shoshoni, it was *to-gwo'-ri-ka*. For the Cherokee, *Kâ'länû*. For the Tlingit, *ye'il*. For the Potawatomie, *kagakshi*. For the Cree, *kachgagoo*. And so on through hundreds of different languages on this continent. In some northern regions, where the raven is especially common and where it figures most prominently in traditional legends, the local tongue might include more than half a dozen titles for this one bird.

Half a millennium ago, before colonial expansion swept away so many Native peoples and their languages, the raven must have had thousands of names. Even today there are dozens in active use, including Corvo Imperiale in Italian, Kolkrabe in German, Quzgun in Azerbaijani, Grand Corbeau in French, and Hrafn in Icelandic.

But in the parlance of modern science, it has only a single name. Every academic ornithologist in the world, regardless of their native language, recognizes this raven as *Corvus corax*.

Why is this name for the raven universally accepted? Strange as it might seem, it's because that name was given to it almost three centuries ago by an eccentric Swedish student of nature who called himself Carolus Linnaeus.

For zoologists, 1758 is year one for modern classification of animals. The raven, *Corvus corax*, was one of a few hundred species of birds that received their official names that year from Linnaeus in the tenth edition of his work *Systema Naturae*. No scientific name applied before 1758 to any bird or other animal is now considered valid—not unless it was formally published again later within the framework that's known around the world as the Linnaean system.

The Linnaean system of classification has been revised in many ways since its introduction in the 1700s, but its current version is the outline used by biologists worldwide. It features a hierarchy of ranks of classification, and a unique two-word name for each known species. To demonstrate, here's a very simple breakdown for the Common Raven:

Kingdom: Animalia (all animals)

Phylum: Chordata (includes all animals with backbones, plus some others)

Class: Aves (birds; some authorities now put birds in the same class as reptiles)

Order: Passeriformes (the perching birds)

Family: Corvidae (the crow family)

Genus: *Corvus* (typical ravens and crows)

Species: *corax* (the Common Raven)

Each category nests within a larger one. The genus *Corvus* includes forty-three other species of crows and ravens in addition to the Common Raven. Besides *Corvus*, the family Corvidae includes about two dozen other genera (the plural of "genus"), encompassing all the jays, magpies, and nutcrackers. The Corvidae make up just one of many families in the large order Passeriformes, which also includes all the families of sparrows, thrushes, swallows, larks, and all the others that fall under the general heading of "songbirds." The aim of the system is to group together, in ever-widening circles, those forms that are most closely related. But for most observers, the focus goes to the species, which we perceive as the basic "kinds" of living beings.

By convention, the genus and species are written in Latin, or in Latinized versions of Greek or other languages. Thus, the Latin *Corvus corax* is a unique identifier for the Common Raven. Use of a binomial (set of two names, genus and species) is an essential part of the Linnaean system.

Priority is another important element. The official scientific name for a species is the *first* one to be applied, under the formal system, to a diagnosable description or specimen of that species. It's not a matter of choosing the most appropriate name, or writing the best description, or even being the person who did the work that led to the discovery. Priority in publication is *all* that counts.

That is a big part of the reason why naturalists and scientists have competed, for more than two and a half centuries, to be the first to discover a new species and describe it to science.

In a full, formal publication, the species designation would include the name of the person who first described it, and often the year of publication, like this: *Corvus corax* Linnaeus 1758. These additional details were especially useful in the past, when communication was much slower, because sometimes the same name would be applied to different species by different people—or even occasionally by the same person. A species name like *pusilla* (meaning "small") might be applied to any smaller representative within some groups of birds, while a scientist with more imagination might call it something else. For compilers of ornithology, trying to untangle a thread of different names that might or might not apply to the same bird, it was essential to know whose description they were following. (Which *Muscicapa pusilla* is this? Oh, it's the one described by Alexander Wilson in 1811, not some other application of the same term. Got it.)

When we look back at the histories of birds' scientific names, there's another common source of confusion: a species is often shifted to a different genus from the one in which it was first described. This was especially true for those named in the earliest years of this system. Linnaeus recognized only a limited number of genera in the birds he described; some of his followers, with a kind of fundamentalist mindset, were reluctant to name any new genus beyond the original Linnaean ones, even as they saw some genera swelling to an unmanageable number of species. This reluctance faded as explorers and travelers brought back specimens of more birds that didn't fit any established categories. Scientists began naming many new genera, sometimes defining them so narrowly that almost every species was in its own genus!

Defining what makes up a genus is mostly a matter of opinion, so designations of many genera have shifted back and forth as we learned more and as attitudes changed. In this long process of figuring out diversity, some birds have been moved from one genus to another more than once. Linnaeus described the Eastern Bluebird of North America (which he had never seen) under the name *Motacilla sialis*. It was later called *Sylvia sialis*, *Saxicola sialis*, and *Ampelis sialis* before winding up with its current name, *Sialia sialis*, sometime after William Swainson established the genus *Sialia* in 1827. In all these lateral moves, even as the genus name changed, the specific name, *sialis*, remained the same, and Linnaeus is still recognized as the original describer.

Most of the genera that Linnaeus proposed are still in use today, although their definitions have become much narrower. The genus *Corvus* still includes the ravens and crows, even as the jays, magpies, rollers, and paradise flycatchers have been moved away to other groups. So the Common Raven, never flitting (as Edgar Allan Poe might say), still is sitting under the permanent marker of "*Corvus corax* Linnaeus 1758," not to be confused with any other creature on Earth or any other application of a similar name within this universal system.

But why is it called the Linnaean system, anyway? Was Linnaeus that much of an innovator, and was scientific classification such a new idea in the 1700s? Not really. Attempts to classify and name living things go back much, much further—for untold ages, of course, in oral traditions among Indigenous peoples all over the world, and even for a couple of millennia in preserved written form in Western civilization.*

In the fourth century BC in Greece, Aristotle wrote up a system that classified hundreds of species of animals. His pupil Theophrastus wrote an even more detailed classification of plants. A few centuries later another Greek, Dioscorides, wrote about hundreds of plant species with an eye to their use in medicine. Botany took the lead over zoology for many centuries thereafter; wild plants were easier to examine than wild animals, of course, and their potential applications in medicine made for a practical incentive. By the 1500s and 1600s in Europe, works classifying thousands of species of plants were appearing. They were written by (among others) the Swiss botanist Caspar Bauhin, the Italian physician and naturalist Pietro Andrea Mattioli, the French botanist Joseph Pitton de Tournefort, and the English parson and naturalist John Ray.

So botany was already a robust science by the time Carl Linnaeus

---

*Ancient writings in China also reveal a detailed level of knowledge, especially about plants, but these early Chinese scholars seem to have put less emphasis on systems of classification.

was born in 1707 in southern Sweden. His father, a well-educated clergyman, was an amateur botanist himself, with an extensive garden. He
began teaching his son the names of plants, along with Latin, geography, and other subjects, at an early age. Legend holds that when Carl
was just an infant, if he began to cry, his parents could calm him by
handing him a flower.

As a student, young Linnaeus had an uneven record. In the equivalent of high school, he did so poorly that his teachers announced he had
no future as a scholar. They said he should apply himself to manual
labor. But he was just focusing his prodigious mental energy on plants
and other living things. Ironically for one who would do so much to
bring order to classifying the natural world, he had a type of genius that
didn't fit well into the orderly sequence of formal education.

But he made it through school and wound up at the university at
Uppsala, north of Stockholm, studying botany and medicine, subjects
still closely linked at the time. His academic progress had its highs and
lows. At first, after scraping together enough money to attend lectures,
he often went hungry, and he stuffed paper in his shoes where the soles
had worn through. But his quirky brilliance couldn't escape notice. An
elderly professor was impressed enough to offer young Carl a free room
and meals in his house and access to the professor's library of scientific books. There were regrettable gaps in the faculty at Uppsala at the
time; but as a result of that (and of the young man's exceptional knowledge), Linnaeus was invited to present lectures while he was still just a
second-year student. His lectures proved popular. On an extracurricular
whim, he wrote a paper about reproduction in plants; it was so thought-
provoking that copies circulated among students and professors at the
university, who attempted to get it published. And throughout this time
he continued to build up his own personal collection of thousands of
plant specimens, insects, shells, and other natural objects. He was getting a superb education, if not a normal one.

Linnaeus was based in Uppsala for almost seven years. One summer he made a three-thousand-mile journey north through Swedish
Lapland—unusual for him; he showed little desire to be an explorer in

the literal sense—and then began writing a treatise on the plants of that northern region, although it wouldn't be published until years later. He continued to attract the support of influential persons. Eventually he was spending more time teaching classes, for money, than taking them. While at Uppsala he took few exams and never received a formal degree from the university. But he was constantly studying and researching and writing. When he left in the spring of 1735, before his twenty-eighth birthday, to go collect a medical degree in Holland, he carried with him more than a dozen scientific manuscripts in various stages of completion.

And one of those manuscripts would be published soon. After settling in Leiden, Holland, that summer, Linnaeus met local scholars and scientists. Two of those men were so impressed with his *Systema Naturae* that they put up the money to have it printed.

Looking at it today, it's odd to think this work could have shaken the entire world of biology. But it did. It had only eleven large pages of content: six pages of densely packed tables and five pages of instructions and definitions, all written in Latin. But within that limited space it made the audacious attempt to list, classify, and organize all of nature, with separate tables for the animal kingdom, the plant kingdom, and the mineral kingdom.

Why did a publication like this have such a profound impact? Was the classification of nature a topic of such burning interest? Yes, it was. Across Europe at the time, homes of the affluent often displayed collections of natural objects—shells, pressed plants, stones, pinned butterflies, stuffed birds, and other things, not only from local surroundings but also from exotic sources. Such a collection was dubbed a "cabinet of curiosities," although it might occupy an entire room, not just the piece of furniture we would call a cabinet today. Among the nobility and the wealthy, it was a point of pride to have diverse and rare items. Albert Seba, a famed apothecary in Amsterdam, had amassed a remarkable collection through travel and trade. It was so admired that, in 1717, Peter the Great bought it and shipped it off to St. Petersburg. But by the time Linnaeus visited Amsterdam in 1735, Seba had built up a new collection that was even more impressive than before.

So people of wealth and influence collected objects from nature, and many wanted to label and organize their collections according to the latest authorities. And although several systems of classification had been proposed, none of those systems enjoyed universal acceptance. Thus, when the young, brash Swede challenged all the existing classification schemes with a new one of his own, it was sure to attract attention.

Any system for classifying life was being stretched at that time by new species coming to light. In Europe, the global center of science, anyone studying birds in earlier eras could have focused on two or three hundred local species at the most. But by the 1700s, random specimens brought back by travelers forced the recognition of more exotic birdlife: The bird-of-paradise. The toucan. The parrot. No one would have guessed there were 42 species of birds-of-paradise, 36 species of toucans, and more than 350 species of parrots. It was almost impossible for the Eurocentric community of science to accept just how diverse life could be elsewhere.

Linnaeus, extrapolating from the climate and environment of Sweden, once estimated that the total number of plant species in the world might top out at about ten thousand. Like others at the time, he had no concept of the dazzling diversity of life in the tropics. He could not have guessed that the South American nation of Colombia, about one-ninth the size of Europe, would yield close to thirty thousand plants, including more than four thousand orchid species. He would have been stunned to hear that our current tally of plant species worldwide is far above three hundred thousand, with new ones still being described. The variety of birds, beetles, mollusks, and many other groups undoubtedly would have shocked him.

Today we know that Europe has a relatively impoverished flora and fauna. Europe has fewer bird species, fewer butterfly species, fewer members of most groups, than any other continent except Antarctica. Perhaps that modest level of variety was a boon to early taxonomists. If a young Linnaeus had gotten his start in the upper Amazon Basin, where a few acres can hold more life-forms than all of Europe, he might have died of exhaustion before completing what would have been a gargantuan first edition of his *Systema Naturae*.

While European scientists in the 1700s might have vastly underestimated the world's diversity of life, they were about to be deluged with it
anyway. During the mid- to late 1700s, specimens of plants and animals
from all over the world would pour into Europe, by-products of a sad
era of colonialism and exploitation. Anyone attempting to compile and
publish works based on these specimens would have to either follow
or invent some system for classifying and naming them. In hindsight
we take it for granted that the Linnaean system won out, but there was
nothing inevitable about it.

Indeed, Linnaeus's work would have been superseded quickly if he
had stopped with the original *Systema Naturae* of 1735. But that was
just the beginning of his astonishing outpouring of published works,
large and small, during the next four decades: Accounts of the plant life
of various regions, such as his Lapland study. Analyses of the holdings
of famed botanical gardens. A treatise on the animal life of Sweden.
Works on diseases and on the uses of medicines. A major work on the
philosophy and fundamentals of botany, laying out his rules for how to
approach the discipline. And he revised *Systema Naturae* over and over,
with each new edition more thorough than the last. In the tenth edition
in 1758, he adopted what would be the most lasting element of his system—the consistent use of binomials, or two-word scientific names, for
each species.* We hold to this standard today.

In the end, the force of Linnaeus's outsized ego was a big factor in the
success of his system. He never hesitated to promote his own ideas above
those of everyone else. "God created, Linnaeus set in order"—he might

---

*He and other authors had used binomials before, but not consistently. It was accepted
practice to use one word for the genus, and follow it with a word or words that would
separate each species from its relatives. Thus, in the fourth edition of *Systema Naturae* (1744), the Gray Heron was *Ardea cinerea*—with *cinerea* meaning "ash-colored" or
"gray," enough of a description to separate it from the few other herons or heron-like
birds listed. But the one-humped Arabian camel was called *Camelus topho dorsi unico*
to distinguish it from *Camelus tophis dorsi duobus*, the two-humped Bactrian camel. In
the tenth edition in 1758, with the realization that the name didn't have to be a complete
diagnosis, these two were renamed *Camelus dromedarius* and *Camelus bactrianus*, with
their erstwhile four-word names subsumed into the description in the accompanying text.

not have been the first to say it, but he heartily agreed, often suggesting he had been chosen by the Almighty to organize nature. He stated that botanists, as a group, made up "Flora's Army," and designated himself as the general leading that army. At the university in Uppsala, where he became a professor in 1741 and taught for years, he urged his students to go out into the world to find new species—either to describe them under the Linnaean system or to send him the specimens. He referred to those who did so as his "apostles." No false modesty there.

Increasingly in the late 1700s, plant and animal specimens flowed into the centers of science in Europe. Sweden itself was not a colonial power—its earlier attempts at empire had been short-lived—but other countries such as Spain, France, the Netherlands, Britain, and Portugal had ships full of explorers, traders, and colonizers ranging around the globe. With growing awareness that natural novelties would be of interest, more of these travelers began bringing or sending back specimens from distant lands. These didn't always arrive unscathed. Dead birds and other small animals often were preserved in jars of brandy, and bored sailors on long voyages sometimes drank the brandy, leaving the creatures to rot. But enough specimens made it back to Europe to keep Linnaeus and his students occupied with describing them.

The fate of the Linnaean system—the question of whether it would gain lasting influence—was settled, gradually, across Europe during the last few decades of the 1700s. Botanists, recognizing Linnaeus as one of their own, were quick to apply it to the plant world.* But in publications about birds, its use was more uneven.

---

*Ironically, although the outlines of the system survived, its original method for classifying plants was soon abandoned. Linnaeus had divided plant species into groups based on the numbers of the reproductive parts of their flowers: the number of anthers, stamens, and so on. This was popular initially because it was so easy to apply—all you had to do was to open up the flower and count the parts—but it resulted in highly unnatural categories, with unrelated plants lumped together and close relatives separated out into different groups. By 1830 at the latest, this approach had been abandoned in favor of more natural groupings. And although *Systema Naturae* originally included what Linnaeus called "the three kingdoms"—plant, animal, and mineral—scientists soon decided they couldn't classify minerals by the methods that worked for living things.

A Frenchman, Mathurin-Jacques Brisson, gave the system a partial boost with his six-volume work *Ornithologie*, published starting in 1760. Although it appeared only two years after the tenth edition of *Systema Naturae*, it included nearly three times as many birds, with close to 1,500 species and varieties. Brisson was a curator for the natural history holdings of René Antoine Ferchault de Réaumur in Paris, one of the best collections in Europe and one of the richest in bird specimens, so he had access to far more bird material than Linnaeus had seen. Brisson's *Ornithologie* was an expanded catalog of the Réaumur collection—organizing, listing, and describing every bird species represented there, with the addition of some specimens studied in other Paris collections. He gave Latin binomial names to many, but not all of them.

Still, Brisson's *Ornithologie* was admirably accurate and detailed for his era, and he named many new species and genera of birds. As a reflection of its influence, when Linnaeus issued the twelfth edition of his *Systema Naturae* in 1766, he added nearly four hundred bird species that hadn't been in the tenth edition; two-thirds were based on Brisson's work, although he often renamed them. Dozens of Brisson's generic names are still in use today, including *Icterus* (for the American orioles), *Aquila* (for the Golden Eagle and its relatives), and *Accipiter* (for forest-dwelling hawks found almost worldwide).

A British doctor, John Latham, published *A General Synopsis of Birds* in three hefty volumes from 1781 to 1785. His intent, he wrote, was to give "a concise account of all the Birds hitherto known; nothing having been done in this way, as a general work, in the English language, of late years." Latham saluted the work of Brisson and others, and acknowledged the primacy of Linnaeus, but he treated more species than any of them: he had access to museums and private collections at a time when specimens were flowing to England from around the globe. Latham was the first to write a description of the Red-tailed Hawk, now familiar to people all over North America. He described it twice: once as the "American Buzzard," based on a specimen of an adult from the mainland, and once as the "Cream-coloured Buzzard," for a specimen of a young bird sent from Jamaica.

Two species of terns from Mathurin-Jacques Brisson's *Ornithologie*, vol. 1, 1760. Illustration engraved by François Nicolas Martinet. Many of the birds discussed and illustrated in Brisson's work were later formally named by Linnaeus.

But Latham isn't credited as the describer of the Red-tailed Hawk. Why? Because he didn't give it a scientific name, just English names. He had not grasped how important those Latin binomials would be, and how unyielding the rules of priority. So when a German scientist, Johann Friedrich Gmelin, produced a thirteenth edition of *Systema Naturae* in the late 1780s (a decade after the death of Linnaeus), he incorporated most of the new birds described by Latham, and gave them official scientific names under the Linnaean system. Look up the Red-tailed Hawk today and you'll see it's officially *Buteo jamaicensis*, described by J. F. Gmelin in 1788.

Gmelin never traveled to the Americas and never saw a living Red-tailed Hawk. Nor did Latham. Neither Brisson nor Linnaeus had any direct experience with most of the birds they named. In the late 1700s there was often a disconnect between the discoverers and the describers—between the explorers who went out and found animals and plants, and the compilers who wrote them down. But that would change in the early 1800s, with the rise of explorers who would publish their own discoveries. Much of the change would be driven by events in North America.

And part of the incentive for those Americans would come from another European compiler and describer, one of the most prolific and influential of that age.

Born in 1707, the same year as Linnaeus, Georges-Louis Leclerc would come to have almost equal fame by late in the century, when he would be recognized everywhere simply as Buffon: he had been designated as a count, the Comte de Buffon, by France's King Louis XV.

As a young man he drew notice for his brilliance at mathematics and science. By his mid-twenties he was part of the intellectual community in Paris; in 1739, in his early thirties, he was appointed director of the Jardin du Roi, the king's garden—a position he held for the rest of his life. Buffon played a leading role in building up the Jardin du Roi, transforming it into a major museum and center for research into the natural sciences. His position gave him access to resources almost unparalleled at the time. Between 1749 and his death in 1788,

Buffon published thirty-six large volumes of a work he called *Histoire Naturelle, générale et particulière* (Natural History, general and particular). It proved tremendously popular and was translated from French into several other languages. In later decades of the century, every educated person in Europe had likely read at least parts of it.

The *Histoire Naturelle* was encyclopedic in scope. Nine of its volumes, issued from 1770 to 1783, were devoted to birds, with a level of detail not seen before. Buffon described the form and appearance of each species, as had Brisson and others, but he went much further in describing their behaviors and their place in natural habitats. The latter kind of information was mostly based on accounts by others—there is little to suggest that Buffon spent much time observing birds himself—but he considered this aspect of ornithology to be essential. He even invoked behavior in his approach to classification, arguing that it was impossible to judge the true relationships of birds solely based on their physical appearance.

Strikingly, though, the nine volumes of the *Histoire Naturelle de Oiseaux* did *not* employ Linnaean scientific names. Buffon and Linnaeus were caustic rivals. In the prospectus for his ornithology volumes, Buffon took aim at Linnaeus in writing that he was "scorning to subjugate himself to follow others and not wishing to imitate the puerile pedantry of these nomenclaturists, who give structures from their minds and tables of their petty ideas for the plans of nature, and who make ridiculous associations of beings least made to go together. . . ."

No, there would be no Latin binomials here, and Buffon would not be remembered as the describer of new species under the Linnaean system. But in many ways, Buffon was ahead of his time. In his volumes on geology he suggested that prevailing views of the age of the universe (about six thousand years, based on biblical analysis) were far off the mark, and that the Earth was much older. And almost a century before Darwin published his *On the Origin of Species*, Buffon was writing about processes that sound suspiciously like evolution.

Not that he was a modern evolutionary biologist. He insisted he believed the creation story as outlined in Genesis. But he was willing to

consider that creation might have produced a more limited number of original species, and those could have diversified into the forms we see today—so that horses, donkeys, and zebras, for example, all could be descended from the same original stock. He suggested that species could change over time because of local climate or other conditions relating to where they lived—which is true. In particular, he thought that species could change for the worse. And he managed to present some of his ideas in ways that were so offensive that people would want to prove him wrong.

Although he had never traveled to America, Buffon assumed he knew enough about it. He had concluded that the New World was cooler and more humid, on average, than the Old World. He remarked on the fact that Quebec, at the same latitude as Paris, was covered with snow and ice in winter. (At that time no one fully understood how ocean currents warmed western Europe.) And he regarded the verdant forests of eastern North America as a negative, not a positive: ". . . as the earth is everywhere covered with trees, shrubs, and gross herbage, it never dries. The transpiration of so many vegetables, pressed close together, produce immense quantities of moist and noxious exhalations. In these melancholy regions, Nature remains concealed under her old garments."

So America was cold and damp, Buffon wrote, and less conducive to healthy life. "In America, therefore, animated Nature is weaker, less active, and more circumscribed in the variety of her productions; for we perceive, from the enumeration of the American animals, that the number of species is not only fewer, but that, in general, all the animals are much smaller than those of the Old Continent. No American animal can be compared with the elephant, the rhinoceros, the hippopotamus. . . ." He went on to write that when species were native to both sides of

opposite page: Golden Eagle from Buffon's *Histoire Naturelle des Oiseaux*, vol. 1, 1770. Buffon included thirteen pages of text about this species, in addition to this engraved illustration, but he refused to use scientific names of the Linnaean system.

the Atlantic, individuals in the New World had degenerated from their original form, and that the same would happen to domesticated animals brought from Europe to America.

In Buffon's view, most aspects of nature were degenerate, and simply inferior, in America. The animals were smaller, weaker, less varied, less virile. Most of his readers in Europe weren't surprised by these ideas and didn't have any trouble accepting them.

In America, though, the reaction would be different. The American Revolution had succeeded. The United States had achieved independence from Britain with the signing of the Treaty of Paris in 1783, the same year that Buffon, in Paris, published his final volume on birds. Science in general, and ornithology in particular, would take hold only gradually in the new nation. But over the next few decades, one force driving American naturalists would be a desire to prove Buffon wrong—to show that the nature of this continent was, in fact, magnificent, and well worth exploring.

2

Names and Numbers

His friends were there to shield him from the stares of curious bystanders. The officials were there to make sure he carried out his punishment, but their presence would also help block the view. Scant comfort for a man facing the most humiliating moment that could mark the life of a poet. In the central square of Paisley, Scotland, in February 1793, Alexander Wilson had been sentenced to burn his own poems in public.

It wasn't punishment from extreme critics for writing bad verse. Wilson's poetry showed great promise. One of his longer ballads, published anonymously, had been mistaken for the work of the celebrated Robert Burns. But Wilson had become an activist as well as a poet, angered by the treatment of weavers in local mills. He began writing verses critical of the all-powerful mill owners, and one of them filed charges of criminal libel against him. His troubles increased when he got involved in a scheme to blackmail another mill owner with another critical poem. Jailed four times in two years, the focus of enmity from powerful men, he could see his prospects for a peaceful life in Paisley slipping away. In May 1794, at the age of twenty-seven, Alexander Wilson left Scotland forever to sail to the United States.

It would take him some time to find his footing in the New World. Wilson wouldn't abandon his poetry altogether, but within a decade it

would be eclipsed by his growing interest in birds; and he would go on
to have an indelible impact on American ornithology.

Some aspects of North American birdlife had been well known for millennia. Much of that knowledge was lost after European conquistadors
and colonists arrived; disease and displacement shattered civilizations,
breaking the chain by which Indigenous knowledge had been passed
down and refined through generations. It would take a few centuries
for scientific information in the European style to catch up with parts of
what had been lost.

During the late 1700s, almost all the scientific naming of North
American birds was published in Europe. Linnaeus had started the clock
for the modern system of Latin binomials with the 1758 edition of his
Systema Naturae. Others, including Brisson, Gmelin, and Latham, soon
added to the canon. The French Comte de Buffon rejected the Linnaean
system of naming, but his work expanded the total amount of published
information about birds.

None of these men had ever been to North America. They based
their descriptions on notes, drawings, and sometimes specimens, sent
by those who had journeyed to the new continent. Most of the Spanish and French explorers who visited the area that would become the
United States had little to say about birds, aside from comments about
their abundance or their edible qualities, but the British had taken more
specific note of natural history.

The artist John White took part in the first attempts in the 1580s to
establish an English colony at Roanoke, in what is now North Carolina.
It's now remembered as the "Lost Colony," and White is remembered
mainly for his watercolors of Native Americans and their customs,
which were reproduced and published in England soon after. His illustrations of more than thirty bird species (along with various other
animals) were mostly ignored for years, but gained eventual respect for
their accuracy. The English clergyman John Banister lived in Virginia
from 1679 to 1692, and although he paid scant attention to birds, he
made valuable observations on plants, insects, and snails. The English

writer John Lawson arrived in the Carolina colony in 1700 and spent several years exploring. His book, *A New Voyage to Carolina*, published in London in 1709, included extensive details on natural history. The section on birds listed more than 120 species, most of which we can recognize today from his brief descriptions.

The Royal Society, England's (and the world's) preeminent scientific organization then, had been founded in the 1660s. Its members believed in the advancement of science worldwide, and evinced a sense of special responsibility for cataloging nature in the British colonies in America—not by traveling there themselves, mind you, but by supporting those who did. In their *Transactions* they had published many of Banister's observations from Virginia, and they were interested in Lawson's *A New Voyage to Carolina*, especially after the author announced his intention to produce a more thorough natural history of the region. Unfortunately, Lawson rashly offended some Tuscarora warriors in 1711 and didn't survive the encounter.

It was just the next year, by coincidence, that a young Englishman named Mark Catesby arrived in America. He had a modest inheritance that gave him some freedom to travel, and good connections in Virginia, where his older sister was married to a prominent physician. As a boy, Catesby had met the great naturalist John Ray, and had developed a lasting friendship with Ray's disciple and collaborator Samuel Dale. It was probably Dale who taught him the basics of botany and horticulture. By the time Catesby sailed to Virginia he had an interest in seeing the plants and animals of the New World, and enough background knowledge to make the most of the opportunity.

During seven years in Virginia, with a side trip to Jamaica and other Caribbean islands, he was honing his skills as a naturalist: making careful drawings and notes, learning to preserve specimens, and sending back specimens and living plants to Dale and others at home. When he returned to England in 1719, he found he had a reputation and a network of contacts among men of science, including Fellows of the Royal Society. Before long, they were suggesting that Catesby might pick up on John Lawson's project to write a natural history of Carolina.

So when Catesby sailed back across the Atlantic to Charleston in 1722, he had funding from important patrons, and a mission: to study, write about, and illustrate the plants and animals of America.

It's hard for a modern birder to imagine what it was like. Catesby was not heading into territory where the birdlife was totally unknown; he had seen the earlier illustrations by John White and the annotated list from John Lawson, and he had built up experience during his time in Virginia, even if he had been mostly looking at plants during that visit. But now he was also focused on birds: "There being a greater Variety of the feather'd Kind than of any other Animals (at least to be come at) and excelling in the Beauty of their Colours, besides having oftenest relation to the Plants." Birds were the most visible elements of animal life—visible but elusive, prone to fly away at any moment, and thus requiring sharp attention. Around any bend in the trail, a flash of color or a burst of song might reveal some wondrous bird never noticed, pictured, or described by any Englishman.

Mark Catesby was experiencing the thrill of discovery in ways that would never be possible for the scientists who, later in the 1700s, applied formal scientific names to species while they sat in their museums in Europe. No doubt the latter men felt excitement as well as they perused published accounts for diagnosable new creatures or opened boxes of specimens shipped from afar. But they were not out there feeling the sun and wind as they tracked those creatures through meadows and forests. They were not raising their guns and shooting those specimens, as Catesby was.

In his published works, Catesby rarely mentioned shooting birds. Such mention wasn't necessary; it was understood that that was a part of nature study. He made this admission about the Yellow-breasted Chat: "They are very shy Birds, and hide themselves so obscurely that after many Hours Attempt to shoot one, I was at last necessitated to employ an *Indian*, who did it not without the utmost of his Skill." Most of the time, though, he merely gave the weights of the birds, or fine details of their structure, or the contents of their stomachs, without explaining why he had these creatures in hand. He sometimes indicated how common a bird was by describing how many could be shot in a short time. Curious about the ratio of males to females in the flocks of Bobo-links (which he called Rice-birds), he mentioned opening up "scores" of them to check their internal organs. No reader of his time would have batted an eye.

Readers today are more likely to react. And I can empathize. I'm one of those people who makes the extra effort to catch that pesky wasp or fly or spider in the house and release it outdoors, rather than swatting it. I mourn the death of every bird. When I began reading extensively about the early history of ornithology, it was jarring to see all the casual mentions of killing, even though I realized it was an essential part of research.

Attitudes toward wild birds in the 1700s and early 1800s were dif-ferent from those of today. There was no category of "game birds" because all birds, from robins to eagles, were considered fair game, and regularly eaten. Going out back to shoot a few birds for dinner was no big deal—no more than looping through the drive-through today to pick up an order of fries. So it might have been considered odd, but not cruel or unusual, to shoot birds for science.

For science, or for illustration. Mark Catesby would produce il-lustrations of more than one hundred species of North American birds, mostly quite accurate in detail. A century later, Alexander Wilson, John James Audubon, and others would create pictures of far more bird spe-cies in much greater detail. None of these illustrations would have been possible without the artists having the birds right in front of them, either captive or, usually, dead.*

From May 1722 to January 1725, Catesby explored the region that

---

*It's strange to me that people can look at an Audubon bird portrait, with every feather rendered in exquisite detail, and then be shocked to find out that he shot birds. Tell me how—in an era before binoculars or cameras—he could have painted all those details otherwise. Of course he shot birds. And sometimes all these early ornithologists shot far more birds than necessary, and I don't like it, either; it doesn't help to say that it was merely a reflection of the times. But there are some people today who can shrug off the fact that Audubon bought and sold slaves, and then be outraged that he shot birds, and they leave me mystified.

is now South Carolina, traveling from the coast to the foothills of the Appalachians. Sometimes he stayed with a friend in Charleston or at the homes of plantation owners. Sometimes he hiked for days with Chickasaw or Cherokee hunting parties, for safe passage through the wilderness and to learn from them about plants and animals of the region. He collected specimens and shipped them to his patrons and supporters, made detailed watercolor paintings of his subjects, and took thorough notes. Then he spent about a year on similar pursuits in the Bahamas before sailing home in 1726.

Back in England, Catesby threw himself into preparing his work for publication. *The Natural History of Carolina, Florida, and the Bahama Islands* appeared in ten parts, each containing twenty color plates and accompanying text, between 1731 and 1743 (with an eleventh part published as an "appendix" in 1747). Producing the parts in series, and financing the publication through sales of subscriptions, was a frequent approach for natural history writers during the eighteenth and nineteenth centuries, although some failed to accumulate enough subscribers to proceed. Catesby's work, informative and attractive, was a success. In the first five parts, each color plate featured one or more birds, usually associated with some typical plant—for example, a Baltimore Oriole (he called it the Baltimore Bird) among the foliage of a tulip tree. The facing page would present text for both bird and plant, with considerable information about each.*

Catesby illustrated and wrote about nearly four hundred species of plants and animals, including 109 birds, many of them previously unknown to European science. Despite that, he isn't officially listed as the describer of any species. His work was published before 1758, the starting point for our modern Linnaean system of names. However, more than seventy of the bird species listed by Linnaeus in the tenth or

---

*This facing-page format may have been based on Maria Sibylla Merian's *Metamorphosis Insectorum Surinamensium*, a beautiful work on insects and other natural history in Dutch Guiana (Suriname), South America, published in 1705. Merian, a German naturalist and scientific illustrator, was a notable pioneer in the natural sciences, especially entomology; but most Americans today are unaware of her work and influence.

Carolina Parakeet by Mark Catesby, from *The Natural History of Carolina, Florida, and the Bahama Islands*, vol. 1, 1731.

twelfth editions of his *Systema Naturae* were based directly* on Catesby's work, and many even wound up with similar names. Catesby had
provided Latin names for all his species, but in that era these could be
of any length. His scientific name for the Yellow-bellied Sapsucker was
Picus varius minor ventre luteo. Linnaeus, insisting on binomials (two-
word names, genus and species), shortened that to *Picus varius*. It's now
placed in a different genus (*Sphyrapicus*) but the species name is still
varius and Linnaeus is still credited as the describer.

It seems unfair—and it is. Linnaeus invented the rules of the game
and set himself up to be the winner. But although the official scorekeep-
ing of the Linnaean system reduced Mark Catesby to an asterisk, he
did have a major influence on American ornithologists who followed,
and even on some of the bird names we use today.† In one case, as I'll
describe in chapter 3, he planted a seed of confusion about thrushes that
would grow into a tangled thicket of error for almost a century and a
half. Such are the possible effects of being among the first on the ground
in a new field.

One of Catesby's major supporters in London was Peter Collinson,
a prosperous merchant and serious gardener, who was eager to obtain
examples of plants from the New World. Collinson played another key
role in North American natural history through his support of John
Bartram, a self-taught botanist in Philadelphia, beginning in the 1730s.

---

*Directly, or indirectly. The historian Rick Wright has pointed out that Linnaeus may not
have owned a full copy of Catesby's work. Instead, he apparently got his Catesby information secondhand, through the writings of George Edwards, another English naturalist.
Edwards published seven volumes on birds between 1743 and 1764, incorporating many
of the birds originally discussed by Catesby, and Linnaeus relied on the Edwards volumes
as his source for these North American birds.

†As a migratory bird, the Summer Tanager is present in eastern North America only in the
warmer months. The same is true for scores of other migrant species, but no other bird
has the word "Summer" in its official English name. The reason goes back to Catesby.
He depicted two birds that were red all over, the males of species known today as Northern Cardinal and Summer Tanager. The cardinal was a familiar year-round resident, and
Catesby simply called it the Red Bird. To distinguish the migratory tanager, he called it
the Summer Red-Bird. Through all the changes in classification since, the modifier "Summer" has stayed with it.

Bartram already had been experimenting with native plants in his private botanical garden on the Schuylkill River outside Philadelphia. His contact with Collinson allowed him to convert his hobby to a business. He gathered plant specimens, cuttings, and seeds, shipping them off to London for Collinson to distribute to others, and in return he received financial support, reference books, and correspondence with many of the leading scientists of Europe.

We might call John Bartram the first professional botanist in North America. And although he didn't pay as much attention to birds, his third son, William, developed a broad interest in nature, and he would have a major impact on ornithology.

As a teenager in the 1750s, William Bartram displayed a talent for drawing plants and birds, encouraged by his father's overseas colleagues. Peter Collinson sent him good drawing paper. George Edwards, a leading ornithologist in England, sent him two volumes of his *Natural History of Birds*. For young William, it may have been the perfect combination of encouragement and challenge: If Dad could find plants locally that were unknown to the scientists of Europe, shouldn't there be potential for some novel birds, too? He prowled the woods between the family gardens and farm and the banks of the Schuylkill, senses on high alert, primed for discovery, just like any avid teenage birder today.

He found several birds that didn't match any in the few reference books available. At the age of seventeen, after an especially productive spring and summer of 1756, he sent specimens and detailed notes to Edwards for fourteen species of birds. Almost all of them turned out to be unknown to Western science at that point. Edwards published accounts of them in one of his next books, part 2 of his *Gleanings of Natural History*, and graciously gave the young man full credit for each. For the bird we now call the Golden-winged Warbler: "The above-described bird I received from my friend Mr. William Bartram; who says, that in the month of April they appear in Pensilvania, where they are only passengers to the northward. . . . They are observed to feed on insects." About the Blue-gray Gnatcatcher: "These birds, with their nests, I received from my obliging friend Mr. William Bartram; who says, that they arrive in Pensilvania in March from the southward, and in April begin to build their nests. . . . They continue with them all the summer, and disappear at the approach of winter." Clearly Bartram had taken the time to observe these species and learn their habits.

This volume of *Gleanings* was published in 1760, when Bartram had just turned twenty-one. It must have been a heady experience to be acknowledged in this work of international merit. But he didn't pursue a career in natural history right away. He bounced between Pennsylvania and North Carolina, joined his father on a trip into northern Florida in 1765 to 1766, and failed at a few business ventures. His break came in the 1770s when John Fothergill, another English plant collector, financed his expedition south in search of new plants and other aspects of nature. From 1773 to 1776, William Bartram journeyed through the Carolinas, Georgia, and Florida, taking notes on everything he saw—including the birds, some of which were unknown to Western science at the time.

In 1777 he returned to Philadelphia. The American Revolution had dampened support from British collectors, so William settled in to help manage the family farm and Bartram's Garden. He wrote a book about his explorations; the title was fifty-four words long, so it's usually just called *The Travels of William Bartram*. When it was finally published in 1791 it was an immediate success, hailed for its scientific details and memorable writing. Along with descriptions of landscapes, plants, alligators, weather, and Native American culture, the book contained enough information about birds to secure Bartram's place among the leading American ornithologists of the 1790s.

But he wasn't the only one, and not the one with the widest fame. That distinction would go to Thomas Jefferson.

Yes, the primary author of the Declaration of Independence, later to be the third president of the United States, was an ornithologist. Jefferson had a voracious curiosity about practically everything. His keen interest in natural history may have been partly a response to the French Comte de Buffon's theory that living things in America were smaller, weaker, less varied versions of their ideal forms in the Old World. The claim piqued Jefferson's patriotic pride. He took extreme measures to refute it, going so far as to have the skin of a large cougar and a gigantic stuffed moose sent across the Atlantic to Buffon in Paris. In his book *Notes on the State of Virginia*, published in the 1780s, the longest chapter argues against Buffon's claims, with page after page of comparisons to try to demonstrate that North American nature was in no way inferior.

Jefferson's book also included one of the first regional bird lists published in the United States, a table of 125 bird species known for the state of Virginia, cross-referenced to their Linnaean scientific names and to other sources. Compiling such a list might seem like a slim qualification, but ornithologist and historian Matthew Halley has turned up unpublished manuscripts proving that Jefferson was seriously engaged in bird study. He even wrote up technical details on two birds he believed to be unknown to science. One of them really was—so if he had published his account, he would be credited as the describer of the species we now know as the Palm Warbler.

During the 1790s, Jefferson spent much of his time in Philadelphia, then the nation's capital. He was frequently in contact with Charles Willson Peale. Another genius and polymath, Peale was an artist (he painted one of the most famous portraits* of Jefferson, in 1791) and a scientist, the founder of the first major natural history museum in the Americas. If he had succeeded in publishing some of his early findings, Peale would be remembered as a major force in American ornithology, rather than as a footnote (albeit an important and underrated one) in the stories of others.

As a booster of his city and his young nation, Peale felt that a great museum in Philadelphia would help the United States to claim its place among the more civilized countries, so he labored to develop one. His museum held displays on other topics, but a major theme was natural

---

*One of his sons, Rembrandt Peale, painted two of the other best-known Jefferson portraits, in 1800 and 1805.

history, especially birds.* Building up the bird collection was a family project, with Peale's daughter Sophonisba and several of his sons helping to shoot bird specimens and prepare them for display. By the early 1800s, C. W. Peale wrote that the museum contained 760 bird species (or forms that he believed to be species), arranged in 140 display cases. He had begun with local and American birds and then had traded with European naturalists to add many foreign species. The result was a remarkable survey of the world's avifauna, with a focus on the mid-Atlantic region of the United States.

For years, Peale had planned to publish a catalog or book based on his collection. It would have been a work of major significance. Some of the most important ornithological works in Europe in the 1700s had been of this sort: Brisson's *Ornithologie*, based on the Réaumur collection; the bird volumes in Buffon's *Histoire Naturelle*, based on collections at the Jardin du Roi in Paris; John Latham's *A General Synopsis of Birds*, based on various collections in England. Peale's published work might have been of equal stature. Beginning in 1794, he collaborated with the French naturalist A. M. F. J. Palisot de Beauvois to prepare such a catalog, meaning to publish it in parts, financing it by subscription. But after a first number—fifty-six pages long, treating general principles and a few mammals—appeared in 1796, the project stalled. Frustrated by the subscription business, Peale kept seeking another source of funding.

In the meantime, Beauvois and Peale had organized the bird specimens into roughly Linnaean categories, assigned four-digit numbers to each species, and cross-referenced English, French, and Latin names for all those that were known under the Linnaean system. Their draft list (which historians have been unable to locate) could have been the basis for a valuable publication, and we might be citing Peale and Beauvois

---

*Like Jefferson, Peale may have been driven partly by a desire to disprove Buffon's theory about the "degenerate" state of nature in the New World. James Madison had recommended Buffon's work to Peale earlier as a source of information. Peale acknowledged that Buffon's volumes on natural history were helpful in identifying specimens, but added that "I have been obliged to censure his hasty errors on the subjects of this Country."

today among the founding documents of American ornithology. But Peale gave up on getting it printed. In 1803, he arranged for his daughter Sophonisba—then seventeen years old, and already skilled at collecting and preparing specimens—to put the data to practical use. Sophonisba painted the "Peale number" for each species, along with its name in three languages, onto the frames for each display case in the museum's gallery of birds.

That long room in Peale's Museum, with its 140 carefully arranged and labeled display cases, was like an American Ornithology in physical form. It would be a few years before something along those lines would appear in pages of an actual book, but it was on its way. A rebellious Scottish poet, newly transplanted to the United States, would see to that.

William Bartram, Thomas Jefferson, and Charles Willson Peale were all born in America. Alexander Wilson was not. But after arriving in the United States in 1794, he would become a promoter of everything in his adopted nation—especially its birdlife.

Wilson had always had some interest in nature. In Scotland he had known the common birds and had often gone hunting on the moors. The first letter he wrote to his parents from America at the end of July 1794 held this telling comment: "As we passed through the woods on our way to Philadelphia, I did not observe one bird such as those in Scotland, but all much richer in colour. We saw great numbers of squirrels, snakes about a yard long, and some red birds, several of which I shot for curiosity."

His curiosity about the birds remained in the background for a few years as he bounced around the Philadelphia region, working a variety of jobs before becoming a teacher at the Milestown School. Five years of teaching there brought him some stability and the respect of his neighbors, and in 1801, he was asked to speak at an event celebrating the inauguration of Thomas Jefferson as president. Wilson's speech was so well received that many newspapers printed it. Everything was going well—but then a few months later he fled Milestown and went into hiding.

What was the trouble? Historians aren't sure; Wilson's distraught letters to friends at the time reveal much anxiety and few clues. It may have involved an affair with a married woman, which might or might not have flowered only in his hapless imagination. Whatever the reason, it led to a turning point in Wilson's life. Early in 1802 he would take another teaching position, this time at the Union School at Gray's Ferry, just southwest of Philadelphia. The move would put him almost next door to Bartram's Garden.

William Bartram was then sixty-three years old, well respected for his accomplishments, and well connected to Charles Willson Peale and others in the thriving Philadelphia scientific community. Alexander Wilson was thirty-five and still socially awkward—that would never change—and still seeking an outlet for his intellect and ambition. As the grand old man of American natural history, Bartram could overlook the awkwardness and encourage the interest in nature, and he did.

Before long, Wilson was knocking on his neighbor's door to ask questions about plants and birds, and to get pointers to improve his drawings. The presence of the older man's niece, Nancy Bartram, may have been part of the incentive for these visits, but the growing intensity of Wilson's focus on birds came to be reason enough. In June 1803 he wrote to a friend: "I have had many pursuits since I left Scotland, Mathematics, the German Language, Music, Drawing, &c., and I am now about to make a collection of all our finest birds."

Once he had decided on this course, he seems to have gone into high gear. He prowled the woods where a teenage William Bartram had collected specimens of birds new to science half a century earlier, and he peppered the now-senior Bartram with questions. He kept various birds in captivity to observe them, including some captured and brought to him by his students. He worked tirelessly to improve his drawing skills, often sitting up at night and drawing by candlelight. Eventually he visited Peale's Museum downtown, where the galleries of specimens, and detailed labels painted by Sophonisba Peale, already presented "a collection of all our finest birds." And as Wilson gathered his notes and drawings, his dream of producing a book on ornithology came into focus.

Publishing a major book with colored illustrations was an expensive challenge, but like Catesby and others before him, Wilson thought he could issue a series of parts and fund the work through subscriptions. In a stroke of good fortune, in 1806 he left his teaching position and took a job editing an encyclopedia to be produced by a major publishing firm. When he described his idea for his great work on birds, the company's owner reacted with enthusiasm and suggested they could probably arrange to print it. So Wilson moved into Philadelphia, settled into a day job writing and editing material for the encyclopedia, and worked on the prospectus and first volume of what would become *American Ornithology*.

Among ornithologists and serious birders today, most are at least vaguely aware that a man named Alexander Wilson once authored a pioneering work on North American birds. Hardly any of them have read any part of it, and Wilson has receded into a gray, two-dimensional figure in the background for the birding community. But *American Ornithology* was a remarkable document. The first volume, published in September 1808, contained nine hand-colored plates and 158 pages of text, depicting and describing thirty-four species of birds. In accuracy and information content it rivaled anything published in Europe up to that time, and as further volumes were published, they set a solid foundation for bird study in the United States.

Wilson's first volume in 1808 was a shocking demonstration of how quickly he had learned the subject. Just five years earlier, he'd been sending drawings to William Bartram and asking: "If from the rough draughts here given you can discover what Birds they are, please to give me their names." And a year later: "I send for your amusement a few attempts at some of our indigenous birds. . . . Be pleased to mark the names of each with a pencil as except 3 or 4, I do not know any of them." But by the time he was preparing volume one of *Ornithology*, he was writing about every species with the confidence of personal experience. In almost every species account, he contradicted and corrected errors made by previous authors, including the leading naturalists of

Europe: John Latham, Thomas Pennant, George Edwards, the Comte de Buffon, even the great Linnaeus. The antiauthoritarian streak that had landed Wilson in trouble in Scotland now served him well in science, as he fearlessly challenged any statement he perceived to be false.

He reserved some of his harshest criticisms for Buffon. Like Thomas Jefferson (whom he idolized) and C. W. Peale, Wilson was offended by the Frenchman's claim that animals in the New World were degenerate versions of those in Europe, and he took every opportunity to contradict him. In his account of the Northern Flicker, a large and colorful woodpecker, he didn't hold back. After courteously correcting Linnaeus and others, who had imagined that the flicker was a type of cuckoo, he unloaded on Buffon. "The abject and degraded character which the count de Buffon, with equal eloquence and absurdity, has drawn of the whole tribe of Woodpeckers, belongs not to the elegant and sprightly bird now before us." He went on to quote, and ridicule, Buffon's statements about how a woodpecker must "lead a mean and gloomy life," "constrained to drag out an insipid existence," while "the narrow circumference of a tree circumscribes his dull round of life." He concluded: "It is truly ridiculous and astonishing. . . . Buffon had too often a favorite theory to prop up that led him insensibly astray; and so, forsooth, the whole family of Woodpeckers must look sad, sour, and be miserable, to satisfy the caprice of a whimsical philosopher who takes it into his head that they are, and ought to be so."

Under the American Redstart, Wilson again decried "This eternal reference of every animal of the new world to that of the old." He caustically suggested that in Buffon's view of life, even the grasshopper-like katydids that made rasping noises in American trees at night could have been originally those famed songbirds of Europe, the nightingales, "degenerated by the inferiority of the food and climate of this upstart continent." And later, writing of the Canada Jay: "Were I to adopt the theoretical reasoning of a celebrated French naturalist, I might pronounce this bird to be, a debased descendant from the common Blue Jay of the United States, degenerated by the influence of the bleak and chilling regions of Canada." Buffon had been dead for twenty years at that point; but for a new patriot like Wilson, the sense of wounded American pride was still very much alive.

Such harsh and sarcastic barbs were rare in *American Ornithology*, although they showed up more often in Wilson's letters to friends while traveling.* Most of the content focused on solid information about each bird species, based primarily on his own observations, specimens he had examined, and notes from others whom he trusted.

Wilson was a superb writer—he had worked as a poet, teacher, and editor—and much of his text sparkled with original language as he described the behavior of his subjects. He wrote of a mixed flock of small birds in winter "proceeding regularly from tree to tree thro the woods like a corps of pioneers . . . the rapid motions of their bodies, thrown like so many tumblers and rope dancers into numberless positions, together with the peculiar chatter of each, are altogether very amusing; conveying the idea of hungry diligence, bustle and activity." Or about the Eastern Screech-Owl: "On contemplating the grave and antiquated figure of this *night wanderer*, so destitute of every thing like gracefulness of shape, I can scarcely refrain from smiling at the conceit, of the ludicrous appearance this bird must have made, had nature bestowed on it the powers of song, and given it the faculty of warbling out sprightly airs while robed in such a solemn exterior." He included original short poems for some species (or long ones for some of his favorites, such as the Eastern Bluebird and Eastern Kingbird). Although he focused the text on facts, it hardly made for dry reading.

And his illustrations were accurate and competent. They faithfully conveyed the structure and markings of each bird. Multiple species

---

*For example, in New England: "Lawyers swarm in every town, like locusts. Almost every door has the word Office painted over it, which, like the web of a spider, points out the place where the spoiler lurks for his prey." In Boston: "Wherever you walk, you hear the most hideous howling, as if some miserable wretch were expiring on the wheel at every corner; this, however, is nothing but the draymen shouting to their horses." In Georgia: "The innkeepers in the Southern States are like the vultures that hover about their cities, and treat their guests as the others do their carrion: are as glad to see them, and pick them as bare." Between these sour notes, though, he often expressed admiration for people he met or beautiful places he visited.

Oriolus Spurius. Orchard Oriole. *1. Female. 2. and 3. Males of the second and third years.*
4. Male in complete plumage. a. *Egg of the* Orchard Oriole. b. *Egg of the* Baltimore Oriole.

Drawn from Nature by A. Wilson. 4 *Engraved by Ilerson.*

usually were grouped on each plate, to keep the number of color plates down for the sake of economy. To make all the birds fit on the page, he sometimes figured them in odd positions, but not absurdly so. Extraneous backgrounds were kept to a minimum. These were utilitarian pictures such as we might find in a modern field guide, not intended as works of art.

Were there errors? Of course—inevitably, given the fragmentary state of information at the time. (This was especially true in later volumes, when Wilson was dealing with birds he didn't know as well.) Any modern birder can find mistakes in these pages. We know now that the Eastern Screech-Owl has two color forms, with feathers either red-brown or gray, and owlets of both colors may hatch out in the same brood. Naturalists previously had classified these as two different species. Wilson repeated the error and compounded it by claiming the reddish birds lived near Philadelphia year-round, while the gray ones were scarce winter visitors from the north. (The species is nonmigratory, and the gray owls are now more common than the red ones near Philadelphia, although their status in the past could have differed.) But overall the work compiled accurate information and corrected a plethora of errors from earlier publications.

For Wilson, the completion of this first entry in 1808 was a triumph—and a challenge. His employers at the publishing company had covered the cost of printing volume one, but there would be no volume two unless he could sign up at least two hundred subscribers to keep the series going. He must become not only an ornithologist and writer and illustrator, but a traveling salesman, too.

So he would make multiple trips through the eastern states: North

opposite page: Orchard Orioles by Alexander Wilson from his *American Ornithology*, vol. 1, 1808. To save space and cost, Wilson usually illustrated several species on each color plate. But because previous writers had been so confused about Orchard Orioles, he made a point of illustrating four different plumages of this species.

through New England. South through Maryland, Virginia, and the Carolinas to Georgia. West across the Appalachians to Pittsburgh, then Kentucky and Tennessee, then south to Mississippi and New Orleans. Everywhere he sought new species to include in his work, but his overriding goal, for the sake of keeping his publication afloat, had to be the search for more subscribers. Wilson was not the most extroverted man, and it must have taken a major level of resolve to keep knocking on the doors of prominent citizens, strangers all, to show them an example of his first volume, knowing he would face rejection from most. But he kept at it, and soon garnered more than enough subscribers to ensure the series would continue.

Passing through Washington, D.C., in December 1808, Wilson knocked on the door of the White House (it was just called the President's House then) and asked to see the president. No, he didn't have an appointment, he said, but Thomas Jefferson would recognize his name. He had exchanged letters with Jefferson, thanks to connections made by William Bartram, and the president was already an early subscriber to *American Ornithology*. Within a few minutes, Wilson was ushered in to meet Jefferson. The poet who had been jailed like a criminal in Scotland a few years earlier spent the afternoon in lively conversation about birds with the president of the United States.

It's curious to note Wilson's seemingly muted reaction when he discovered new species. He did discover, describe, and name some birds that had been previously unknown to Western science—and quite a few more that he thought were new, but had been described already by others or were just different plumages of known birds. But in his writing, whether in *American Ornithology* or in his letters, he rarely betrayed any hint of excitement about these finds.

Consider his discovery of the Fish Crow.* This species is widespread along the southeastern coasts of the United States, and far up many of

---

*The naturalist John Abbot, working in Georgia, may have noticed the Fish Crow independently, and he sent a specimen, but it arrived after Wilson had already drawn the species and was about to publish his account of it.

the major rivers. It's a little smaller than the widespread American Crow, and has a few subtle structural differences, but even experienced birders today can seldom identify it with certainty without hearing its different voice. Wilson noticed this bird first along the coast of Georgia, listening to its callnotes and observing its aquatic tendencies. He encountered it again along the lower Mississippi River. Then he realized it also occurred closer to home, around Cape May, New Jersey. Finally he heard those diagnostic calls and saw small flocks of these crows along the lower Delaware and Schuylkill Rivers, and even flying past Bartram's Garden. Only then was he willing to give the species a formal description, in his volume five; he called it Fish Crow, *Corvus ossifragus*, the same name it bears today. But his text was couched in quiet, reserved terms: "I can find no description of this bird by any former writer. . . . Having myself seen and examined it in so many and remotely situated parts of the country, and found it in all these places alike, I have no hesitation in pronouncing it to be a new and hitherto undescribed species."

No stylistic flourishes, no drama. Wilson could write lyrically about the birds themselves, but not about his own discoveries. In personal style, he was the polar opposite of a flamboyant self-promoter. The quality of his work would speak for itself.

There are moments in history when some small event, almost imperceptible at the time, alters the future in large ways. In the history of bird study, one such moment was in February 1802, when the struggling Alexander Wilson moved in next door to William Bartram, the one man in America most qualified to be his mentor. Another such moment occurred in March 1810 when Wilson, on another journey to seek subscribers and bird specimens, walked into a store in Louisville, Kentucky.

Wilson probably knew already that the young shopkeeper might be a prospect for a subscription to *American Ornithology*. In Pittsburgh a few weeks earlier he had met Benjamin Bakewell, a prosperous local businessman; Bakewell almost certainly mentioned that his niece, Lucy, was married to a Frenchman who loved to draw birds. So it was more than a coincidence that he entered the store that John James Audubon and his partner, Ferdinand Rozier, had opened less than two years before.

Once inside, though, he found more—and less—than what he had expected. We can't be sure what happened during that first meeting; Wilson's surviving notes amount to just a few words, and Audubon, as we know now, tended to embellish every tale. But as he described the encounter years later, Audubon was struck by his visitor's appearance—"His long, rather hooked nose, the keenness of his eyes, and his prominent cheekbones, stamped his countenance with a peculiar character"—and even more struck by the text and illustrations in the two volumes of *American Ornithology* that Wilson opened on the counter.

For a bird-crazed young man on the frontier, eager to learn but lacking any kind of reference works, Wilson's books must have seemed like a miracle. Audubon claimed later that he had picked up his pen and was ready to sign for a subscription, when his partner, Rozier, commented in French: "My dear Audubon, what induces you to subscribe to this work? Your drawings are certainly far better; and again, you must know as much of the habits of American birds as this gentleman." The first part of this claim might have been true at that point, but the latter part was not, at least not yet. Regardless, Audubon paused, and put down his pen. He would not be subscribing after all.

Wilson may have caught the gist of Rozier's comment, or he might have remembered Benjamin Bakewell mentioning the young man's artistic bent. Whatever the reason, he asked to see some drawings. Audubon pulled out his portfolio, which, he later claimed, was already filled with more than two hundred portraits of birds.* The two men went through them one by one. Wilson made a laconic note in his journal: "Examined Mr. A's drawings in crayons—very good. Saw two new birds he had, both *Motacillae*." As Audubon described Wilson's reaction, "His surprise appeared great" that anyone besides himself might be working on such a collection.

---

*This was probably an exaggeration, but if not, the collection must have contained many duplicates. Audubon certainly was not familiar with two hundred species of birds by 1810.

And then, Audubon wrote, "he asked me if it was my intention to publish, and when I answered in the negative, his surprise seemed to increase. And, truly, such was not my intention. . . . I had not the least idea of presenting the fruits of my labours to the world."

We don't know how much of this narrative, if any of it, reflects the actual conversation between the two men. And we don't know when Audubon first considered publishing his work.* But I believe it was this encounter that started him thinking along those lines, and if so, it planted the seed for one of the most remarkable publishing ventures of the nineteenth century. It showed Audubon that it was possible, even desirable, for a person in America to publish a work with illustrations and text about birds, to release it in parts, and to finance it by selling subscriptions to the whole series.

It would be another ten years before Audubon would begin seriously gathering the material for such a work, in 1820. The first handful of illustrations would not be issued until 1827. Ultimately the publication would appear in four huge volumes of color plates and five volumes of text between 1827 and 1839. Numerous other editions would follow, and from then on, right up to the present day, the works would seldom be out of print. Audubon's fame quickly, and permanently, surpassed Wilson's. Today most birders, and even many members of the general public, have a sense of who John James Audubon is. Quiz those same people about Alexander Wilson, and not one in a hundred will recognize the name.

Of the two men, Wilson was a much better scientist and a better writer. But he could not compete with his rival's illustrations. In the public eye, every other consideration was swept away by the visual impact of Audubon's work.

Today Audubon is regarded primarily as an artist; and there's irony in that, as that wasn't his main goal. He felt that Wilson had an immense

---

*At one point Audubon claimed he hadn't thought of publishing until he met Charles Bonaparte in 1824. We know that isn't true, because he had mentioned the idea repeatedly in his journals and correspondence before that.

advantage with his earlier start, so he was simply trying to outdo him in every way he could. Wilson's illustrations had been adequate for their purpose, which was to present the appearance of each species. Audubon would go further. He would paint his portraits on huge sheets of paper so that even the largest birds could be shown at life size. He would place his subjects in animated, dramatic poses, in the act of living, not at rest. (Some early critics complained that his birds were unnecessarily flamboyant, detracting from their scientific value.) Departing from the "bird-on-dead-stick" approach of many earlier illustrators, he would place his birds on carefully rendered native plant species, often in full flower, as Mark Catesby had done, and sometimes include other animals as well. When possible, he would include dramatic backgrounds, or find other ways to make the compositions memorable. Some of Wilson's plates also showed birds in action, or among foliage, or against scenic backgrounds, but on average they were plainer and simpler.

And, significantly, Audubon would strive to paint *more different species* than Wilson had.

It's worthwhile to linger on this last point, as it demonstrates that creating fine art was not his chief goal. If he had been motivated primarily by artistic passion, his approach would have been different. For a worthy comparison, consider the example of Lars Jonsson, regarded by many as the greatest bird painter living today. Lars is a birder as well as an artist, and he has traveled the world and painted many different species. Early in his career, he painted every European species for a field guide. But now, over and over, he returns to some of his favorite subjects, producing gorgeous watercolors or oils of birds like eiders and terns that he sees near his home in Sweden. There's little to suggest Audubon did anything like that after his earliest days of practicing. Once he'd launched his great work, he was ever on the watch for new and different species to depict. Toward the end of his project he would sometimes cram six or more unrelated birds into the same drawing—composition be damned, and placing them on that generic dead stick after all—just to fit in as many species as possible.

In his correspondence and sometimes in his published text, Audubon could not resist comparing himself to Wilson in a starkly enumerative way. How many new species had he named? How many different birds had he illustrated? Even though he would produce some genuine works of art with lasting value, the driving motivation was about numbers.

On that fateful day in Louisville in 1810, all these developments were far in the future. Audubon's drawings were already quite good, but not alarmingly so, nothing like the brilliance he would achieve later. The two men went hunting together, and Audubon later claimed that Wilson "obtained birds which he had never before seen." He noted the older man's melancholy air and his rather cool and distant demeanor, but he was left with the impression that their encounter, based on their shared interest, had been cordial enough.

Wilson seems to have seen it differently. In a caustic paragraph in his journal, he dismissed Louisville, where he had "neither received one act of civility from those to whom I was recommended, one subscriber, nor one new bird. . . . Science or literature has not one friend in this place."

Wilson's mood must have improved during the next month, as he journeyed east to Lexington and then southwest to Nashville, gaining new subscribers at every stop. He discovered three new species of the small, sprightly songbirds known as warblers, giving them English names commemorating the region where he'd found them: Kentucky Warbler, Nashville Warbler, and Tennessee Warbler. (He had no way of knowing that the last two were merely spring migrants on their way to the spruce bogs of Canada, so he noted that they seemed rare, unlike the Kentucky Warblers that were singing everywhere in the woods.) Continuing overland to Natchez, Mississippi, he sold more subscriptions and discovered a beautiful new bird of prey, the Mississippi Kite, catching insects in midair as it sailed gracefully over the treetops. Then it was on downriver to New Orleans and a journey by ship through the Gulf of Mexico, around the southern tip of Florida, then back up the East Coast and home by late summer.

Over the next three years, Wilson's output was superhuman. Before leaving on his western trip, he had published only the first and second volumes of *American Ornithology*, so he didn't make much progress on the third volume until he returned to Philadelphia in August 1810. Between that time and August 1813, in between trips to various points in Pennsylvania and New Jersey, he completed the material for volumes three, four, five, six, and seven, almost all of volume eight, and some work for volume nine. This work entailed compiling his notes on each species and writing the text, providing descriptions and names for those that were new to science, and making reference to previously published accounts for those that were not. It involved preparing illustrations for every species, arranging for engraving of the copper plates for printing these illustrations, then overseeing the hand-coloring of hundreds of printed copies of each one.

But this phenomenal burst of productivity had a sad undertone of desperation. Cash flow became an increasing problem, because the preparing and publishing of the volumes outpaced the money coming in from subscribers. At one point Wilson journeyed north through New England to sell more subscriptions; tensions were building with the outbreak of the War of 1812, and in Haverhill, New Hampshire, he was arrested as a possible spy. Even though he was soon released, the arrest probably awakened grim memories of troubles with the law back in Scotland. And there were other obstacles. When colorists quit and could not be replaced, Wilson began hand-coloring the printed plates himself, adding vast numbers of hours to his workload.

During the same period, a successful Philadelphia businessman named George Ord took an interest in Wilson's work, but not a financial interest, not at first. Instead, even though he was a novice at ornithology, he wanted to get involved, going out and shooting specimens that weren't necessarily helpful to the project. The attention flattered Wilson, but in some ways, Ord put him under even more pressure.

And through it all there was an internal pressure, the drive to discover more species, the urge to learn everything possible about the bird-life of the new continent. There was so much to know. Wilson wanted to take another trip south, where he was sure he would find still more undescribed species, but there was no time. He was still finding what seemed to be new species of warblers—or were they flycatchers?—even on the outskirts of Philadelphia. On repeated trips to the shoreline of New Jersey he was beginning to sort out the most confusing of the sandpipers and plovers, coming to grips with problems that had stymied the best ornithologists of Europe. He was on the verge of understanding so much more. He just needed more time.

But he was out of time. In July 1813 he wrote to a friend: "I am, myself, far from being in good health. Intense application to the study has hurt me much." In a word, he had been working himself to death. He continued writing text for his unfinished volumes, but on August 19 he shifted his attention to writing out his will, and by the morning of August 23, 1813, he was gone, dead at the age of forty-seven.

Consumed by his unfinished work, Wilson made one final Hail Mary attempt to get it completed: he named his new follower, George Ord, as coexecutor of his estate. If the man was so interested in being involved, well, let him prove it. Ord stepped up to the challenge. He finished preparing volume eight of *American Ornithology* for printing and then compiled the text for volume nine, and both were published in 1814. Ord went on to become a competent ornithologist and a leader of the local scientific community, serving as an officer of the Academy of Natural Sciences of Philadelphia for many years. He would prepare a new edition of *American Ornithology* in the 1820s and would do more than any other single person to keep Alexander Wilson's reputation alive.

Of course, the dying Wilson had no way of knowing this future. In his fevered dreams, as his mind wandered, he might even have wondered whether his work would be upstaged by that shallow French lad he had met in Louisville. Not that it would have seemed likely at the time. Young Audubon was still dabbling in art and ornithology, but he had moved farther downriver in Kentucky, and he would spend the next several years failing to forge a success as a businessman.

Interlude:
Channeling the
Illustrator

When the Dream Came

Anyone who draws or paints birds will be compared, eventually, to John James Audubon. Most of us don't like it. But it's unavoidable.

Audubon is, by far, the most famous bird painter in history. No one else comes close. His acclaim was pretty much guaranteed by the time his *Birds of America*—four huge volumes with 435 dramatic color plates, showing hundreds of birds at life size—was completed in 1838. Several other bird painters arguably have been better, but none had a chance of eclipsing the global preeminence that one man has held for almost two centuries.

In my own origins as a watcher and painter of birds, Audubon played a negligible role. I came into the field in a most haphazard way, fueled by backyard fascination and a random handful of library books. Then a relative gave me a stack of old *Audubon* magazines, but it was just a word to me, and I didn't think about it being the name of a person. The first artist to capture my imagination was Roger Tory Peterson, who had developed and illustrated a revolutionary field guide to birds back in the 1930s and who was still going strong when I was a child three decades later. I read his columns and articles (in, ironically, those old *Audubon* magazines), and I spent hours trying to copy the illustrations from his field guides. It was only when I saw Peterson referred to as "the twentieth-century Audubon" that I started to take that other name seriously.

Student artists often copy the works of masters to absorb lessons in technique. I was never tempted to copy Audubon pieces. After dabbling in various approaches as a teen, my first serious illustrations were intended to show differences between species to help birders identify them. For the first book I wrote and illustrated, the *Peterson Field Guide to Advanced Birding*, I did pen-and-ink drawings, with some coaching from Roger Peterson himself. For a series of magazine articles on bird identification during the 1980s and 1990s, I did paintings in gouache, or opaque watercolor. These were done with only as much detail as a person would see in the field, through binoculars. I kept effects of light and shadow to a minimum because it was important to show the actual colors of the feathers.

Later I produced my own series of field guides, illustrating the books with digitally edited photographs, not with paintings. But I missed the creative process of wielding a brush, so I took up oil paintings of birds. Freed from the need to illustrate technical points, I started experimenting with directional light, with plumage details minimized in favor of three-dimensional shadows.

This approach took me even further away from the feather-by-feather detail and local color emphasized by early nineteenth-century bird illustrators. I probably never would have tacked back in that direction had I not become fixated on a specific question about the history of that era.

It happened almost by accident. In an example of how life sometimes completes a circle, I became a field editor for the National Audubon Society (NAS), working on their magazine—the same magazine that had helped inform my world decades earlier—and on material for

their website. NAS is devoted to bird conservation, not to celebrating Audubon as a person, but one of the perks on their website is a complete gallery of all 435 color plates from his *Birds of America*. At some point I went through the entire online gallery to review the associated text for accuracy. In the process I began to notice, and then to focus on, the birds that were *not* included. Despite the breadth of the collection, many avian species in North America had eluded Audubon's brush.

Some omissions were easy to understand. The Prairie Falcon is widespread in the western half of the continent, and undoubtedly had been well known to Indigenous peoples for millennia. But it always occurs in low numbers, with solitary individuals flying fast across open plains. Early European-American explorers might have seen it, but if so, they didn't recognize it as something different, and it wasn't described to science until 1850. Audubon never had a chance with that one, or with many other western and southwestern species. But what about widespread eastern birds such as the Philadelphia Vireo, Gray-cheeked Thrush, or Caspian Tern? How had every European-American naturalist managed to miss all these birds before the mid-1800s?

These were absorbing questions. And they led me to a more random question: If Audubon had connected with these species, what would his illustrations of them have looked like?

It was just an idle thought at first. But for months it lingered at the back of my mind, periodically popping to the fore. I had never tried to imagine someone else's undone artwork, or even considered such a thing. Now my curiosity was awakened. What would John James do?

I started analyzing. Okay, so Audubon never painted a Snail Kite, but he did other kinds of hawks. Here are two Broad-winged Hawks perched among the foliage of a hickory branch, one with a wing outstretched to show more detail. Here are two Red-tailed Hawks sparring in midair, one with a hapless rabbit clutched in its talons. Here is

opposite page: Same bird, different artists: two views of the Snowy Egret, to demonstrate alternate styles. Above by Kenn Kaufman, below by John James Audubon.

a young Red-shouldered Hawk that has just pounced on a bullfrog in a muddy marsh. I began spending more and more time studying those color plates, looking for common elements that defined their style.

Some points were obvious. All his birds are painted at life size, meaning some large species have to be in odd, contorted poses, even on paper measuring more than two feet by three feet. All his birds are viewed at eye level. The vast majority are shown against a backdrop of white, except for white birds, which are usually set off against blue or gray skies. Everything in the foreground—birds, leaves, flowers, insects, seashells—is depicted in exquisite fine detail. The more I studied, the more I understood why Audubon referred to his bird portraits as drawings, not paintings; every one of his works had been drawn in extreme detail before any color was added. The postures and behaviors shown for the birds might stretch disbelief at times, but every marking on every feather is a faithful copy of reality.

So I had spent time studying the style, analyzing the compositions, imagining how John James would have depicted those birds he never saw. But I hadn't put any imagined illustrations down on paper. It took a global health crisis to shake me out of my inertia.

In March 2020 the United States awakened to the threat of Covid-19, with overwhelmed hospitals, mounting death tolls, massive uncertainty, legions of closings and cancellations, and abrupt changes of plans for millions of people. For me, for a start, it shut down what would have been a busy spring and summer of travel. Rattled by the news, casting about for distractions, I seized on my hypothetical musings about nineteenth-century drawings that had never been done.

What are you waiting for? I chided myself. *Are you just going to think about this forever without actually creating anything?* I took my first halting steps toward producing my own pseudo-Audubons. Stuck at home in Ohio, dodging a pandemic, I tried to channel the process of the artist's own first steps, more than two centuries earlier.

Young John James Audubon (who had been Jean-Jacques until he boarded the ship in France) arrived in the United States in August 1803 and was struck down by the yellow fever epidemic of that summer. Two

Quaker ladies nursed him back to health and helped him improve his rudimentary English—he would sprinkle his speech with "thee" and "thou" for the rest of his life—and then he went on to his father's property, Mill Grove, in the Valley Forge area west of Philadelphia.

His father—a French sea captain, businessman, slave trader, and entrepreneur—had sold an estate in Haiti several years earlier and used the proceeds to buy Mill Grove, a 284-acre tract with woods and farm fields, a sawmill, a flour mill, and potential for mining. He sent his son to America to prevent him being drafted into Napoleon's army, and probably also to put him to work helping Mill Grove's tenant manager. The latter goal was doomed to disappoint, however, because the young man showed little interest in running the farm, the mills, or the mines.

John James was probably no more selfish and self-absorbed than the average eighteen-year-old boy. But he was accustomed to privilege, accustomed to pursuing his own interests and having servants to take care of details. In Pennsylvania he busied himself with riding, hunting, fishing, playing the violin, dancing, attending every kind of social event, and courting his neighbor's beautiful daughter, Lucy. And he spent countless hours observing the local birds and attempting to draw them.

He had been obsessed with birds as a boy in France and had already practiced drawing them. But now he became more critical of his results, more determined to portray his subjects with a higher degree of accuracy.

People who haven't done much drawing may think some innate talent allows artists to look at an object once and then reproduce it in lines. But memory can take you only so far. Every bird illustrator I know has needed some model to work from, whether sketching from life or photos or from a dead specimen of the bird, to get the details right.

Sketching birds directly from life can be challenging—they seldom hold still, and they may fly away at any moment—but it can be the best way to capture their authentic shapes and postures. Some of the most respected bird illustrators today, like David Sibley and Killian Mullarney, have spent countless hours in the field, watching through a spotting scope and sketching what they observed. Without a good telescope, it would be much more difficult. Audubon had no optical aids in the early 1800s, but he tried drawing from life anyway.

Perkiomen Creek flowed past Mill Grove, and in the bluff above the bank was a shallow cave that he began using as a retreat. A pair of Eastern Phoebes used the cave also, building a nest just inside the entrance. These gentle gray-and-white songbirds came to accept his presence as he sat watching their behavior, and one day it occurred to him that they would make ideal subjects:

> A thought struck my mind like a flash of light, that nothing after all could ever answer my enthusiastic desires to represent nature, than to attempt to copy her in her own way, alive and moving! Then, on I went with forming hundreds of outlines of my favorites, the pewees [his name for the phoebes]—how good or bad I cannot tell, but I fancied I had mounted a step on the high mount before me. I continued for months together in simply outlining birds as I observed them either alighted or on wing but could finish none of my sketches.*

He could finish none of his sketches. It just wasn't possible to capture enough detail on living, moving subjects. He went back to shooting birds—not the phoebes, though; he had too much emotional attachment to them—and working from the freshly killed specimens.

He tried tying them up by one foot and letting them hang, wings fully spread, while he recorded every feather. The resulting images didn't resemble the living bird, and Audubon rued that "in this manner I made some pretty fair signboards for poulterers!" He tried attaching strings to various parts of a specimen and suspending it like a puppet, with only fair results. He tried making a model bird, a sort of avian mannequin,

---

*Considering this early attempt, it's odd that his phoebe painting used in *The Birds of America* wasn't done until two decades later, in the mid-1820s—and that it does a relatively poor job of conveying the shape and usual postures of the species. Sketching the phoebes may have been good practice, but any perceptions gained didn't carry over into the final illustration.

out of wood, cork, and wire; it was so bad that a friend looked at it and laughed out loud, so he smashed the model and threw it away.

John James went on obsessing day and night over this challenge. One morning, long before daylight, a new idea jolted him awake. Even when he wrote about it years later, his excitement was palpable in the rush of words. "I leaped out of bed fully persuaded that I had obtained my object.—I ordered a horse to be saddled and without answering to any of the various questions put to me, mounted and moved off at a hard Gallop toward the then little Village of Noristown distant about Five Miles.—on arriving there not a door was open—nay It was not yet day light. . . ." He went to take a bath in the nearby river. Then he "returned to the Town and entered the first oppened Shop—Enquired for Wire of different sizes, bought some, Leaped on my Steed and was at Mill Grove again in a very Short time.—the wife of my Tenant I really believe thought that I was mad, as on offering me Breakfast, I told her I wanted my Gun. . . ."

Who could blame her for thinking him mad? But he was possessed by an idea, not by demons. Striding down to Perkiomen Creek, he shot the first bird he saw, a Belted Kingfisher, and brought it back to the house. "I sent for the Miller and made him bring me a piece of soft board—when he returned he found me filing into Sharp points pieces of my Wire. . . . I pierced the body of the Fishing bird and fixed it on the board—another Wire passed above the upper Mandible was made to hold the head in a pretty fair attitude. . . . The last Wire proved a delightful elevator to the bird's tail and at Last there Stood before me the real Mankin of a Kings Fisher!"

He had hit on a method that he would use, with minor refinements, for the rest of his career, including for most of the subjects in his *Birds of America*. A freshly killed bird, still soft and pliable, could be placed against an upright board, held in a precise position with a series of wires and pins. A square grid drawn on the board was helpful for confirming the proportions of the bird's outline in the drawing. Since Audubon was depicting his subjects at life size, he could use an artist's compass or dividers to measure details on the specimen—the width of a wing feather, the length of a toe—and transfer measurements to the paper. The technique made it possible to create exact and accurate drawings.

I had gleaned all this from half a dozen biographies and from Audubon's own essay, "My Style of Drawing Birds." But knowing his methods didn't put me any closer to duplicating them. Even if it had been legal in 2020 for me to shoot birds to use as art models—and it certainly was not—I wouldn't have considered it. In trying to duplicate Audubon's results, I would need a different process for getting shapes and details correct in the basic drawings.

I began my experiments with a focus on two birds: Caspian Tern and Gray-cheeked Thrush. I chose the tern after considering my possibilities. The thrush, on the other hand, chose me.

The Caspian Tern is a graceful, long-winged flier, silver-gray and white with a hefty crimson beak, and it's the largest of the terns, about the size of an average gull. It's also a widespread bird, found on many oceanic islands and on parts of every continent except Antarctica. When the Prussian scientist Peter Simon Pallas described it to science in 1770, he named it for the Caspian Sea in Eurasia, where he had encountered it for the first time. For me it was the perfect subject during a period of lockdown in Ohio, because I could slip out and study Caspian Terns from May to October on certain Lake Erie beaches within ten miles of my house.

Remarkably, this bird—big, conspicuous, readily available—was one Audubon overlooked, although he certainly saw it in Labrador and probably elsewhere. He and Wilson and all their contemporaries managed to confuse it with the Royal Tern, common on southeastern beaches, which is almost as large and has a thick beak of orange, not red. To tangle the story further, they lumped both Caspian and Royal Terns under "Cayenne Tern," a name that had also been applied to a different bird from South America.

During the 1840s, William Gambel figured out that the Royal Tern was distinct. And in May 1850, George Lawrence stood up at a meeting of the Lyceum of Natural History of New York to announce that the erstwhile "Cayenne Terns" on our Atlantic Coast were two kinds: not only the Royal Tern discussed by Gambel, but also the Caspian Tern, by then well known from Europe. Other naturalists soon confirmed that he was correct. But Audubon never knew or drew the Caspian Tern. I was free to reimagine what a portrait of this bird, done in his style, would have looked like.

I would have to start with a detailed and accurate drawing, and it would have to be life-size. That put limits on the posture of the bird (or birds) in the drawing. Audubon had painted several of the smaller tern species in flight, but the Caspian has a wingspan of about four feet from one wingtip to the other; even with the extra-large watercolor paper I was using, there was no way I could fit a flying individual into the confines of a page. I would have to depict the bird standing on the ground, as Audubon had done in his portrait of the Royal ("Cayenne") Tern.

Sketching from life is one of the most satisfying things I ever do, at least on days when it's going well. I place the spotting scope on a sturdy tripod so I can use it hands-free. Finding some bird that sticks around, I stand watching it through the scope, holding a hard-backed sketchbook in my left hand and a pencil in my right. I watch until I can feel myself shifting into a visual zone, then I start drawing—looking back and forth from the scope eyepiece to the sketchbook. If the bird is active I'll just do outlines, trying to capture shapes and postures. If it sits still, I'll get into more detail. If my eye-to-hand conduit is working smoothly, converting shapes and patterns into lines on paper becomes a subconscious thing. It's meditation with a visual, avian focus.

When Caspian Terns aren't sweeping through the sky or plunging headfirst into water to catch fish, they spend a lot of time standing on open beaches. They may turn their heads, droop their wings, preen their feathers a bit, but mostly they're still. So I could look back and forth from scope to sketches, refining my drawings and adding detail, until the tern moved to a different position and I had to start a new outline.

In those early days of the Covid-19 pandemic, as government officials scrambled to figure out responses, some wildlife areas and state parks were closed to the public. But I knew one nearby Lake Erie beach that was under no such restriction, and I went there in early May and

Caspian Terns sketched directly from life by the author.

filled pages in my sketchbook with impressions of the terns. Audubon never could have done this—not for lack of skill, certainly, but for the lack of good optics. Occasionally when traveling by ship he could borrow the captain's spyglass to scope out, dimly, the denizens of a distant sandbar. But no telescope available in the early 1800s was good enough for observing ornithological details. So I had the advantage. After a couple of days of attempts, I felt I was making good progress. But then that beach closed also, and I lost my source of sketchable Caspian Terns.

A few days later, while I was still debating what to do next, a surprising avian visitor showed up outside my door. If I were superstitious, I would have taken it as a sign. My wife, Kimberly—also stuck at home—came to tell me she had glimpsed a thrush at the back of the yard, and it looked like a Gray-cheeked.

In forested patches along the Lake Erie shoreline, just a few miles north of our house, five species of brown thrushes can be expected to pause during their spring migration in May. But farm fields surround our place, and the trees in our small yard don't tend to entice woodland birds like thrushes to stop and visit. Sometimes we'll see a Hermit Thrush or a Swainson's Thrush in the brushy back edge of the lot, but the Gray-cheeked Thrush is more of a forest-interior creature, more likely to seek out deep cover. Kimberly was right, though. A Gray-cheeked Thrush had chosen our yard as a stopover habitat, and it stayed for two full days.

Sketching it became my main goal during that time. Thrushes don't stand still like terns, so observing it took more effort. This one moved all around the yard, coming out in the open more often than Gray-cheeks usually do. After losing track of it temporarily, I would see it lurking in a flower garden or under a hedge: moving along with bounding hops or short delicate steps, pausing with neck upstretched as it looked around, alert, wary, wide-eyed. I realized I could observe the thrush at leisure without scaring it away if I stayed inside the house and watched through the windows.

So I began filling up pages in my sketchbook. Mostly I was drawing rough and simple outlines, indications of a momentary pose. Whenever I had a good study of the structure of the wing, or the pattern of its head or chest, I would try to get a few more details down. But I was reminded of young John James and his attempts to draw his beloved phoebes from life: *I could finish none of my sketches.*

Likewise, I could finish none of mine. These sketches from life might be useful in creating compositions, but they couldn't document the feather-by-feather detail I would need to channel Audubon's results. Some additional step would be necessary.

And even as I struggled to get my drawings of this bird right, to capture its slender grace and the subtle expression of its face, a thought distracted me. I just could not get over how strange it was that Audubon had missed the Gray-cheeked Thrush completely during the years he had spent to the south of here, along this bird's migratory route, in Kentucky.

A Gray-cheeked Thrush sketched directly from life by the author.

3

A Thicket of Thrushes

By the time I was out of my teens I had visited forty-eight of the fifty U.S. states. It had happened as a side effect of my travels as I hitchhiked all around North America—including two trips up the long gravel highway to Alaska and back—in single-minded pursuit of all the birds I could find. Several years later, stopping over on a flight to Australia, I notched Hawaii as number forty-nine. Finally, as my fortieth birthday approached, I entered my fiftieth and last state: Kentucky.

How had I missed Kentucky before that? In my early hitchhiking travels, for covering distance, I almost always took the interstate highways: those bold veins and arteries of travel, dreamed into life by Eisenhower in the 1950s, that stretch across every corner of the Lower 48. Thumbing for rides on the interstates was illegal, but there were enough long-haul travelers, enough drivers who might pick me up, to make it worth the risk of arrest. So I followed not just any interstate, but the ones that seemed most direct. Crossing through the eastern states I'd be on I-10 along the Gulf Coast, I-40 through Tennessee, I-70 through Indiana and Ohio. Going north or south I'd follow I-5 up the West Coast, I-35 through the central states, I-95 along the Atlantic Seaboard. Parts of five interstates did cut across Kentucky, but they didn't seem direct enough for this impatient kid. I had nothing against Kentucky. It just didn't lie on the main routes.

In earlier times, Kentucky most definitely lay on the main routes. During the 1700s, in a series of dubious treaties and purchases, the Iroquois, Cherokee, and others had ceded most of the region to Britain. After the Revolutionary War, the United States claimed all of it. Settlers poured into the region in the 1780s, following the wilderness road that Daniel Boone had established through the Cumberland Gap, and following tales of a bountiful, fertile place of opportunity. Land speculators bought tracts there and then wrote glowing accounts of this region, to pique interest and pump up the value of their investments. One such speculator, John Filson, wrote a whole book about Kentucky and included a florid, romanticized biography of Daniel Boone; pirated translations and copies of the book sold well in Europe and America, turning the backwoodsman into a celebrity.* At the same time, Kentucky's status as a glorious land of plenty was internationally accepted as fact. It was admitted to the United States as the fifteenth state in 1792.

The Ohio River, which forms most of the state's sinuous northern border, was even more important as a route of travel. Stretching west-southwest almost a thousand miles from Pittsburgh, Pennsylvania, to the Mississippi River, it was the interstate highway of its day, the main artery for commerce and travel west of the Appalachians. When Thomas Jefferson wrote in 1781 that "the Ohio is the most beautiful river on earth," he had never seen it himself. The comment may not have reflected any judgment on its visual appeal, but rather his sense that the river was beautifully suited for transportation and trade. It would become even more so in the early 1800s, once steamboats made it possible to travel upriver as easily as downriver.

The lure of Kentucky was irresistible to the young John James Audubon and his bride, Lucy. Married at her father's estate in Pennsylvania in April 1808, they set out for the West, traveling to Pittsburgh and then

*Many tall tales later added to the legend of Daniel Boone. Two came from Audubon, who wrote of the man's remarkable skill with a rifle and amazing powers of memory when they hunted together in the forests of Kentucky. But at the time these encounters supposedly took place, Boone was almost eighty years old and living in Missouri.

taking a flatboat (which Lucy considered "an exceedingly tedious and primitive mode of travelling") down the Ohio River to Louisville. After a couple of years there (and after his 1810 encounter with Alexander Wilson), they moved 125 miles downriver to Henderson, Kentucky, farther west of Cincinnati and across the river from the Indiana Territory. Henderson was then a small town, and more to the artist's liking than Louisville, surrounded by wilder country. He opened a general store, but business was slow at first. To put food on the table, he often went hunting in the forests and fields, or fishing in the river—giving him a perfect excuse to be outdoors, observing nature. In his leisure time he continued drawing birds and taking notes on their habits.

The years in Henderson furnished much of the foundation for Audubon's knowledge of North American birds, giving him a baseline for comparison when he started traveling more widely after 1820. The strong seasonal occurrence of various avian groups is easiest to learn by staying in one place, watching them come and go, and in Henderson he had time to do that.

He observed great flights of ducks arriving in the fall to spend the winter on the Ohio River, followed by Peregrine Falcons that came from the north to hunt them. He watched as various songbirds arrived from the south after a long winter, and sensed that some were only pausing on their way north. He noted the nesting habits of the many birds that stayed through the summer. He determined that some flocks were passing through on their way between summer and winter homes: golden-plovers on the fields of northern Kentucky in March; terns and sandpipers on the Ohio River in September. And he saw that certain birds, like the confiding little Downy Woodpeckers, were faithful and constant residents, never migrating away.

The Kentucky years would end with economic ruin by 1819, but for a time, Audubon's young family prospered there. In some ways, this period represented the closest thing to a normal, stable life that his family ever had. Much later, he would write: "The pleasure I felt at Henderson and under the roof of that log cabin can never be effaced from my heart until after death."

The affection that Audubon felt for Henderson has been reciprocated, many times over, in the modern era. When I drive into the city today—arriving by interstate highway after all, after taking I-69 south through Indiana—signs for the Audubon Chrysler dealership greet me on the outskirts. Driving around town, I see signs for a pawnshop, printing shop, dental practice, metals supplier, and various other businesses with names honoring Audubon. In a park along the river downtown is a statue of the artist, and sculptures representing many of his most famous or dramatic paintings line the city streets. More than two centuries after he moved away, his memory is still alive here.

Nowhere is it more alive than in the John James Audubon State Park, a wooded, slightly hilly tract on the north side of town. The park hosts an outstanding museum, with displays that not only commemorate Audubon's time in Henderson, but also present an overview of his entire life and his work, putting it all in context of the era in which he lived. I have spent many hours in that museum. But when I visit the park, most of my time will be outdoors. Trails wind through the gentle hills and ravines, through a beautiful example of eastern hardwood forest, with maple, beech, oak, sweet gum, tulip tree, and so many more, a rich and varied habitat. Some of the trees are huge, and it's not hard to imagine they might be more than two hundred years old. And some of the nonmigratory, permanent resident birds, from big Pileated Woodpeckers to little White-breasted Nuthatches, could be direct descendants from those that ranged through these same woods in Audubon's day.

If I'm here on a morning in early May, however, my focus will be on the birds that do migrate, especially those songbirds that are now arriving from the tropics.

No naturalist of the early 1800s had any concept of the magnitude of these migrations. They were starting to get a sense of the seasons and directions of movement, but they could not have grasped the numbers of birds moving, nor the distances they were traveling. Even today, with the benefit of advanced technology and vast networks of observers, we are still working out the details of this astounding phenomenon.

The number of songbirds and other small land birds migrating north and south across the eastern United States every spring and fall runs into the billions. It's a movement that mostly goes unseen, as the majority of these birds migrate at night. At the peak of the season, on an evening when skies are clear and winds are from a favorable direction, vast numbers of migrants take off just after dusk and fly through the night—navigating by the stars, by the Earth's magnetic field, and by other clues. At dawn they descend, scattering over the landscape, seeking out woods or meadows or marshes where they can rest and feed for a day or several days.

On a big night in the spring or fall, a million birds may migrate over Henderson. Several thousand may land in the area at dawn. But as they spread out through every available scrap of habitat, they will go unnoticed except by the birders out looking for them.

In early May, with the passage nearing its peak, most of the arriving migrants will be those that travel the farthest. The short-distance migrants will have moved earlier in the spring: birds like native sparrows and juncos, able to subsist on seeds in cold weather, are just leaving winter homes in the central and southern states to travel to the northern states or Canada. Now comes the varied multitude of insect-eating birds, traveling from deep in the tropics—Mexico, the Caribbean, Central America, South America—to summer homes that may be in the far north. A Swainson's Thrush that pauses in Henderson in May could be in the middle of a remarkable journey, having spent the winter east of the Andes in Peru, and headed to somewhere in central Alaska.

We know all that now. Two centuries of detailed observations and focused research have brought us this clarity. When we go out birding, each one of us gets only fragmentary glimpses of the whole picture, but we can fit our own sightings into the framework of accumulated knowledge and feel that we have a good sense of what's going on.

What would it have been like, though, to step into the boots of Audubon and walk out into the forest around Henderson on a May morning in 1811? No binoculars, no reference books—not even those two volumes by Wilson that you passed up at Louisville. No clue as to the expected timing of migration, beyond the idea that it's spring now, and some birds should be moving north. The woods seem alive with birds this morning, but how could they be different from those that were here yesterday? When they flit from thicket to thicket, or from one treetop to the next, are they migrating, or just going about their daily routines?

As much as I'd like to do so, I can't put myself in this mental mode for long. After decades of birding, my mind automatically fills in the blanks when I pretend to ask myself about such matters. Fortunately, spring migration is such a miraculous thing that no matter how many facts I learn about it, my sense of wonder remains undiminished.

So I'm out here at the edge of John James Audubon State Park in the dim half-light before dawn, and I can hear Swainson's Thrushes overhead. Nocturnal migrants often make short callnotes as they fly, for no obvious reason, and on the night of a big movement, an alert listener might hear many such notes showering down from the dark sky. Most sparrows and warblers make simple lisps and chips, but the thrush notes are more distinctive. Swainson's Thrush has a beautiful flight call, soft and liquid, like a muted bell, or like the sound of a drop of water falling into a forest pool. The birds are flying lower as the sky grows lighter, and I can hear the thrushes more clearly, along with the notes of other species. The migrants will now be able to see the wide Ohio River ahead, so many will choose to drop into the trees near at hand.

Birding at dawn is often best on the edge of the forest, where sunlight will strike the treetops first. But I'm thinking about thrushes now, and they're likely to be low in the shadowy forest interior; so as soon as it's light enough, I start hiking. Before long, I see a thrush hopping along the trail's edge.

It's larger than a sparrow, smaller than a robin, with a slim body and pointed wingtips. If this bird is one of the migrants that just arrived, it was flying all night, but it still looks filled with energy. The thrush takes a few springy hops and then flies, with quick, snappy wingbeats, a little farther down the trail. Through my binoculars, I can see that the bird is a study in browns. Olive-brown back and wings. Scattered brown spots on the pale gray chest. A wash of rich tawny buff at the sides of the neck. A bold ring of the same buffy color around each eye, like a pair of spectacles, confirms my first guess: a Swainson's Thrush.

That was a fairly safe guess. Five species of brown-backed thrushes migrate through Henderson, but Swainson's is usually the most numerous one in May—as it seems to be today. I can hear the voices of other individuals in distant thickets, doing a softer, lower version of that musical flight call that came from the sky at dawn. Walking the trails for the next hour, I see another half-dozen Swainson's Thrushes, and hear callnotes of a few more. A couple of times, I even hear one singing. It's a lovely song starting with a clear note, then a slight pause, then an uneven series of notes climbing to a higher pitch. Even though these birds are still at least five hundred miles from the nearest point in their breeding range, some of them are already tuning up—hesitantly, as if practicing, saving their best performances for the forests of the far north.

After seeing Swainson's Thrushes along the trails, I'm not surprised to spot another, perched at a distance in a dense tangle. Something about it doesn't look quite right, though. I have to maneuver to get a good view, but before the bird flits away deeper into the shadows I've seen enough detail. Same size and shape as a Swainson's, or perhaps a touch more slender. A plainer and paler face, lacking the well-defined ring around the eye. Colder gray-brown on the side of the neck, without buff tones. It's a different species, a Gray-cheeked Thrush.

Although the Gray-cheek is less numerous than the Swainson's Thrush, it's not rare. In its migrations it occurs everywhere in the eastern United States where the Swainson's does, but on average it migrates farther: its winter range is entirely in South America, with none lingering through the season in Mexico or Central America, and its summer

opposite page: Swainson's Thrushes on pokeweed (*Phytolacca*), by Kenn Kaufman. Of all the bird species overlooked by Audubon, Alexander Wilson, and their contemporaries, the Swainson's Thrush is the most surprising. It's a common migrant throughout eastern North America. The early naturalists undoubtedly saw it, but long-lasting confusion over the small brown thrushes kept them from realizing that it was something different and unnamed.

breeding range extends farther north in Arctic regions of Canada, out into stunted trees at the edge of the tundra.

There are places in the boreal forest where both species can be heard singing at once, the ethereal whistles of the Swainson's Thrush climbing the scale, the thinner notes of the Gray-cheek descending instead. Out near Nome in far-western Alaska, beyond the last of the forests where Swainson's would thrive, Gray-cheeked Thrushes sing from scrubby thickets of willows and alders along streams through the barrens. Beyond that, some Gray-cheeks cross the Bering Strait to Siberia, an epic final stage of travel for a bird that weighs barely more than an ounce and that may have spent the winter in Brazil.

In migration through the eastern states, Gray-cheeked Thrushes have essentially the same seasonal timing as Swainson's Thrushes, and they pause in the same forested habitats. But birders see them less often. They seem more secretive, staying farther back in the undergrowth. On a big migration day when many Swainson's are passing through, a Gray-cheek glimpsed deep in a thicket is easy to pass off as its more common cousin. So this species often escapes notice by being overlooked. It is even missed by birders actively watching for it.

The list of birders and ornithologists who have overlooked the Gray-cheeked Thrush is a long one. John James Audubon's name is on that list. When I finish my hike today I'm going to stop again at the park's museum; in the reproductions of his art, I know I won't see any depictions of the Gray-cheeked Thrush. He never painted it, at least not knowingly, and never was aware of its existence.

Here is the strange thing, though. Unlike some modern birders, Audubon didn't miss the Gray-cheek by passing it off as the Swainson's Thrush—because he never connected with that bird, either. Nor did his predecessor and rival, Alexander Wilson. Nor did any naturalist pursuing birds in eastern North America in the early 1800s. Both of these thrush species were described in the 1840s, with Swainson's first noted on the Pacific Coast and the Gray-cheek discovered on its wintering grounds in South America. No one recognized these birds as part of the eastern avifauna until even later.

That these two common thrushes managed to evade detection by scientists for such a long time makes for one of the more bizarre and tangled tales in the history of ornithology.

To understand how it happened, it helps to begin with what we know now about the five brown-backed thrush species that are common migrants through Kentucky, through Pennsylvania, and throughout the eastern half of the United States.

Most recognizable is the Wood Thrush. A little larger than the others, it's also more boldly marked, with round black spots on the chest and a bright reddish-brown back. It nests all over the eastern states, south to the Gulf Coast, so it's a familiar summer bird for many. (This morning in the state park at Henderson I've seen a few Wood Thrushes; outnumbered by the Swainson's, they are much more vocal, singing short, rich, mellow phrases over and over. These are probably local males, announcing their claims to their summer territories.) It spends the winter mostly in Mexico and Central America.

Distinctive in range and timing is the Hermit Thrush. It's smaller, like the Swainson's and Gray-cheeked Thrushes, and like them it spends the summer mostly in the far north. Unlike them, it's a short-distance migrant. It can be found in winter all across the southern and central United States, and it migrates earlier in spring and later in fall than the other brown thrushes. Here at Henderson, a few Hermit Thrushes stay through the winter, and the spring migration of the species peaks in April, mostly before the others arrive. Seen in good light—not always easy in the forest shadows—it can be told from the others because its dull olive-brown back contrasts with its more reddish-brown tail.

The third and fourth species are the Swainson's Thrush and Gray-cheeked Thrush, which I've already described. Fifth is the Veery—which, despite its different-sounding name, is a close relative of the others and similar to them, just very lightly marked on the chest and somewhat more reddish-brown on the back. Veeries spend the winter deep in South America, but they don't get as far north in summer as

the preceding three species, concentrating in southern Canada and the northern edge of the Lower 48 states.

All five of these brown-backed thrushes have beautiful songs, heard mainly on their breeding grounds, with clear whistles, airy trills, and flute-like notes. With practice, a birder can identify each species. But a careless or superficial description of the song of one might apply to any of them.

Likewise, while the Wood Thrush has a distinctive appearance, the other four—Hermit, Swainson's, Gray-cheeked, and Veery—are so subtle and so similar that it would be possible to look at them and decide they were all the same species. In a sense, that was exactly what happened in the early days of American bird study.

Mark Catesby, pursuing birds in the 1720s in the region that's now South Carolina, was quite discerning in figuring out many that he found. But he was confused by thrushes, without realizing that he was, and his confusion would echo through ornithology for a century and a half.

After Catesby's return to England, the first volume of his *Natural History of Carolina, Florida, and the Bahama Islands* was published in 1731. In it he included the account of a bird he called the "Little Thrush," or *Turdus minimus*. He described it in a few lines:

In Shape and Colour it agrees with the Description of the European *Mavis*, or *Song-Thrush*, differing only in Bigness; this weighing no more than one Ounce and a quarter. It never sings, having only a single Note, like the Winter-Note of our *Mavis*. It abides all the Year in *Carolina*. They are seldom seen, being but few, and those abiding only in dark Recesses of the thickest Woods and Swamps. Their Food is the Berries of Holly, Haws, &c.

opposite page: Hermit Thrushes by John James Audubon. This portrait clearly was based on specimens of the real Hermit Thrush, but Audubon's written text about the species was filled with details that would have applied better to other kinds of brown thrushes.

A hand-colored illustration of a nondescript, thrush-shaped bird, mostly brown with random spots, partly hidden among holly leaves, accompanied the text.

Catesby and his readers in England would have been familiar with the Song Thrush, a bird almost the size of our American Robin, brown on the back and with numerous dark spots on the chest. A similar but smaller bird ("differing only in Bigness") in America could have been any of the brown thrushes. But Catesby's description, brief though it is, doesn't apply perfectly to any of those species. None of those species "abides all the Year in Carolina." The Wood Thrush occurs in the forests of the Carolinas in summer, the Hermit Thrush is fairly common there in winter, and the others all pass through in spring and fall migrations. So from the outset, Catesby's "Little Thrush" was at best a composite.

Catesby's work was published before 1758, when Linnaeus launched modern zoological classification, so none of his bird names are considered "official." His descriptions were still good enough to serve as the basis for later publications by others. In 1760, British scientist George Edwards included an account of the "Little Thrush" in the second volume of his *Gleanings of Natural History*. But Edwards had more than just Catesby's publication to go on—he had a physical specimen of the bird. It had been sent to him by his eager young correspondent in Philadelphia, William Bartram.

Edwards was sure the specimen sent by Bartram represented the same bird described by Catesby, so his account added to the composite nature of this "species." He quoted Bartram that these birds arrived in the Philadelphia area in April and stayed all summer, and quoted

opposite page: "The Little Thrush" by Mark Catesby, from *The Natural History of Carolina, Florida, and the Bahama Islands*, vol. 1, 1731. At least five species of small brown-backed thrushes migrate through the region covered by that volume, but Catesby assumed he was seeing just one. His description presented a mash-up of several of them, while his illustration wasn't a good match for any. For more than a century thereafter, ornithologists struggled to reconcile Catesby's "Little Thrush" with the multiple thrushes they encountered.

T. 31

Turdus minimus ___
The little Thrush.

Agrifolium Carolinense, &c.
The Dahoon Holly.

Catesby's comment that they were present in the Carolinas all year. None of the brown thrushes stay all year in the Carolinas. The Hermit Thrush is the one that remains there in winter, but that species isn't around Philadelphia in the summer.

In addition to text, Edwards included an illustration done directly from Bartram's specimen. More detailed than the earlier one by Catesby, it still wasn't diagnostic for any one of the thrushes. In overall color it looked closest to the Veery, but its chest pattern and face pattern were more suggestive of the Gray-cheeked Thrush. Still, nothing about the text or illustration suggested that more than one species might be involved. Edwards declined to give scientific names to the birds he described, and the "Little Thrush" didn't receive its official designation as a species until almost thirty years later.

When German scientist J. F. Gmelin produced a thirteenth edition of *Systema Naturae* in the late 1780s, intended as a continuation of Linnaeus's work, he described 290 new bird species. These included the "Little Thrush," which he gave the formal name of *Turdus minor*. (*Turdus* was the original genus for all the thrushes, and our American Robin and similar species around the world are still in that genus.) As a basis for this description, Gmelin didn't just have to rely on the publications by Catesby and Edwards. He also consulted *Arctic Zoology* by Thomas Pennant, which included notes on a small thrush collected in Newfoundland or Labrador in 1766. Like Pennant, Gmelin assumed this was yet another example of the "Little Thrush" mentioned first by Catesby. Gmelin compiled all the notes from previous authors and added that the 1766 bird had "eyelids encircled with white"—a detail that would apply best to the Swainson's Thrush or Hermit Thrush, but again was far from diagnostic. So the composite "Little Thrush" continued to take on more elements from multiple species.

Fortunately, Gmelin did also describe and name the Wood Thrush, recognizing that it differed from the others. So when Alexander Wilson started looking at these birds a little over a decade later, in the early 1800s, he began with the assumption that eastern North America had more than one species of brown thrush.

Not everyone shared this view. William Bartram—who had written about the Wood Thrush in 1791—was not convinced it was different from the "Little Thrush." He finally agreed after Wilson asked him to examine the illustration of the latter in Edwards's publication, based on a specimen collected fifty years earlier by Bartram himself!

Wilson wrote about the Wood Thrush in the first volume of his *American Ornithology*, published in 1808. He knew the bird well. He gave an accurate account of its nest and its habits in the woods around Philadelphia in the summer. Drawing on his background as a poet, Wilson described the Wood Thrush's song this way: "He pipes his few but clear and musical notes in a kind of ecstasy; the prelude, or symphony to which, strongly resembles the double-tongueing of a German flute, and sometimes the tinkling of a small bell; the whole song consists of five or six parts, the last note of each of which is in such a tone as to leave the conclusion evidently suspended; the finale is finely managed, and with such charming effect as to soothe and tranquilize the mind, and to seem sweeter and mellower at each successive repetition."

Wilson also argued that the Wood Thrush had to be a different bird from the "Little Thrush" of Catesby and Edwards. He knew that bird, he said, and not only was it smaller, it could be found in the Carolinas in winter, unlike the Wood Thrush. Furthermore, Wilson asserted, the "Little Thrush" was no songster: it "utters, at rare times a single cry, similar to that of a chicken which has lost its mother." He claimed, decisively, that "if Mr. Catesby found his bird mute during spring and summer, it was not the Wood Thrush."

Wilson did not present an account of the smaller thrush until four years later. In volume five of *American Ornithology*, he wrote of a bird he called the Hermit Thrush. It's the same bird we know as the Hermit Thrush today, with the diagnostic detail of having the "tail coverts and tail inclining to a reddish fox color," unlike the "deep olive brown" of the remainder of the upperparts. Bizarrely, though, he claimed this bird was the "Little Thrush" of Catesby and Edwards, even though no such contrast between back and tail had been mentioned or illustrated by either of them. His Hermit Thrush account preceded one for a bird that he called the Tawny Thrush, which he claimed was brand-new, even though it was a much better match for the description and illustration of the "Little Thrush" given by Edwards. But at the time, no one was in a position to question him.

Wilson's classification of the thrushes was well entrenched by the latter part of Audubon's years at Henderson, before he started traveling the continent in the 1820s. Although Audubon never hesitated to contradict Wilson when he could, his usual position was to stick to the precedent of *American Ornithology*, which was, after all, the accepted standard at the time. It's not surprising that he continued with the assumption that he was seeing three kinds of brown-backed thrushes.

In most cases, Audubon's bird portraits were based on actual specimens. By studying his paintings, we can usually identify his birds, even if he himself was confused about what they were. His painting of the Wood Thrush (plate 73 in *The Birds of America*) was accurate, and his text account for it in *Ornithological Biography* made it clear that he knew the bird—not surprisingly, since it's common in the summer around Henderson. He called it "my greatest favourite among the feathered tribes of our woods" and he wrote movingly of how his spirits were lifted by this bird's beautiful song. On the other hand, he also claimed that it was numerous in Louisiana in the winter. That isn't true today and almost certainly wasn't then: only a few stragglers remain north of Mexico after November. He probably saw Hermit Thrushes, which are common in winter in the southern states, and mistook some of them for Wood Thrushes.

It was all downhill from there. Audubon's painting of the Hermit Thrush—or at least his first one, on plate 58 of *The Birds of America*—was detailed and accurate. But his text account of it in *Ornithological Biography* was mystifyingly off. He began by writing that it was "another constant resident in the Southern States, more especially those of Mississippi and Louisiana, where it abounds during the winter months, and is found in considerable numbers during spring and summer." It's true that Hermit Thrushes abound in the southern states in winter. But they depart before the end of April and don't stay through summer.

(None of the brown thrushes occur in the Gulf Coast states in the summer, except the Wood Thrush, which Audubon knew was a different bird.)

He also wrote about their nests as if he had found several, and claimed the birds raised two broods per year in Louisiana. But Hermit Thrushes have never been found breeding anywhere near Louisiana, and his descriptions of the nest sites, nests, and eggs were far from accurate. Unless he made up all these details—which is possible, given his history—Audubon must have found nests of other species and assumed them to be those of Hermit Thrushes. And regarding its voice, all he had to say was that "its song is sometimes agreeable," an odd comment about a bird celebrated today as one of our finest singers.

The third brown-backed thrush Audubon drew was one he called the Tawny Thrush, although in his text he also referred to it as the Wilson's Thrush. Modern ornithologists have almost universally assumed that this bird corresponds to the Veery. However, as Matthew Halley has pointed out, the reproductions in *The Birds of America* and the artist's original watercolor all showed a cold grayish-brown bird, duller than any eastern population of the Veery and closer to the overall coloration of the Gray-cheeked Thrush.

Audubon's text account for the Tawny Thrush in *Ornithological Biography* could apply equally well—or equally poorly—to any of the eastern thrushes. He included a loose, general description of overall behavior and nesting habits. Of the bird's migration, he stated that it "is never seen or heard in Louisiana during spring," but the Veery is a common spring migrant through Louisiana, and so are the Swainson's, Gray-cheeked, and Hermit Thrushes. His description of its song was more complimentary than his brief comments about the Hermit Thrush, but so vague that it could have applied to any bird in this group.

Oddly, toward the end of his big project, Audubon painted the Hermit Thrush again, on one of the last color plates of *The Birds of America*. He called it Little Tawny Thrush on the plate, but by the time he was preparing text for *Ornithological Biography*, he had decided this bird was a new species; he named it the Dwarf Thrush, *Turdus nanus*.

It was based on small specimens collected in the Pacific Northwest and sent to him by John Townsend, but Audubon insisted he had also found examples of this new bird along the Atlantic Seaboard. Today the name *nanus* survives as the designation of a small subspecies of the Hermit Thrush, breeding in southeastern Alaska and coastal British Columbia.

That was as far as Audubon got in untangling the thrushes. Nowhere in his works—not even in the revised, more compact edition he released in the 1840s—was there any delineation of the abundant Swainson's Thrush or the common Gray-cheeked Thrush; they were still obscured behind the generalized concept of a Tawny/Wilson's Thrush.

No one else at the time had any better success with these birds. Thomas Nuttall published *A Manual of the Ornithology of the United States and of Canada* in the early 1830s and included the same three species: Wood Thrush, "Little or Hermit Thrush," and "Wilson's Thrush, or Veery." Nuttall had spent time watching the third species in eastern Massachusetts, and he was among the first to use the name "Veery" in print. He described its nesting behavior accurately, and gave one good description of its song, although his mention of other vocal variations suggests he may have been hearing other thrushes as well. Nuttall was mainly interested in plants, and his notes on the Veery were among his more original bird observations. For the other two, he cribbed his information from Wilson and Audubon, including their errors about seasonal occurrence.

A more notable publication—and one that could have had more potential for getting it right—was a work on birds of Arctic Canada: *Fauna Boreali-Americana; or the Zoology of the Northern Parts of British America*, volume 2, by Swainson and Richardson, published in 1831. The British doctor John Richardson had served as surgeon and

opposite page: Veery by John James Audubon. The illustration clearly shows one of the small brown thrushes, and it has been assumed to represent the Veery. But as Matthew Halley has pointed out, both the published plate and the original watercolor show a bird that seems much too grayish for that species, so it's possible that Audubon was working from a specimen of a different thrush.

naturalist on the first two expeditions of John Franklin, 1819 to 1822 and again in 1825 to 1827, to the vast region stretching northwest from the Hudson Bay to the coast of the Arctic Ocean, and he had brought back a wealth of information on birdlife. He and British ornithologist William Swainson had also compiled information and bird specimens sent back by men associated with the fur-trading Hudson's Bay Company, and then Swainson had arranged the classification of all the species, putting them in context of what was already published.

These two authors were careful in their approach, and Richardson had traveled through the breeding ranges of some of the relevant species, but they still failed to clarify the thrush situation. They decried "the great confusion in which the nomenclature of the small North American Thrushes has long remained," and added, correctly, that "as to the 'Little Thrush' of Catesby, it appears totally impossible to identify it with any one species." But their treatment wasn't much better. They didn't mention the Wood Thrush, which doesn't get as far north as Arctic Canada. Their account of the Hermit Thrush was brief and partly accurate. But they also discussed two more species, the Little Tawny Thrush and Wilson's Thrush, both of which could fit the Veery or perhaps something else. Then they added an extraneous note about a bird called the Silent Thrush, which Swainson had described based on a specimen from Mexico.

Meanwhile, the two brown thrushes most numerous in northern Canada—Swainson's and Gray-cheeked—were still not formally described. It's ironic that one of them ultimately was named for William Swainson, who didn't do anything to help sort them out.

The true status of the thrushes that migrate through eastern North America would be worked out only gradually. The Swainson's Thrush would be described in 1840 by Thomas Nuttall, under the name of Western Thrush, based on a specimen and sightings from the Pacific Coast (although, as Matthew Halley has pointed out, the original specimen was probably of a Hermit Thrush). The Gray-cheeked Thrush would be described in 1848 by the French scientist Frédéric de Lafresnaye, based on a specimen shot on the wintering grounds in South America.* Then in 1858, Spencer Baird described the Gray-cheeked Thrush again, as Alice's Thrush, from migrants taken in Illinois and along the upper Missouri River. It would be years before scientists realized that Lafresnaye's description and name had priority.

Having these birds described and named wasn't enough to clear up the confusion. As late as 1872, ornithologist Elliott Coues was treating the Gray-cheeked Thrush (under the name Alice's Thrush) as a variety of Swainson's Thrush, breeding farther north. Gradually, though, scientists worked out the details, and the classification and names seemed to stabilize.

Are they stable today? No. Consider the status of Bicknell's Thrush. First noticed in 1881 in the Catskill Mountains of New York, Bicknell's was described in 1882 as just a subspecies of the Gray-cheeked Thrush. By the 1940s its overall range was understood: breeding locally from the mountains of New England and upstate New York north into the Maritime Provinces and Quebec, and wintering in the Caribbean, mainly in the Dominican Republic. But it was so similar to other Gray-cheeked Thrushes that most birders ignored it. Not until 1995—when, on the basis of detailed studies, it was elevated to the status of a full species—did birders really start trying to identify Bicknell's Thrush.

We're still trying. During spring and fall migration, when both Bicknell's and Gray-cheeked Thrushes pass through the Atlantic coastal plain, we struggle to find an example of Bicknell's that looks acceptably distinctive. In spring the great hope is to find one that's singing, since some details of the song are diagnostic. But most birders finally add this enigmatic bird to their life lists by making a pilgrimage to the mountains of upstate New York or New England in the summer, pinning it down on its breeding grounds.

---

*Adding to the confusion, Lafresnaye called his bird *Turdus minimus*, the same name Mark Catesby had used, unofficially, for his unidentifiable "Little Thrush" 117 years earlier.

Some scientists have suggested that Bicknell's isn't a distinct species, and should be combined with the Gray-cheek again. And it's possible that Swainson's Thrush will be split into two species, separating the more reddish-brown-backed birds of the Pacific Coast from the more olive-brown-backed birds farther east. None of these changes would have much impact in Henderson, Kentucky; Bicknell's Thrush essentially never shows up that far west, and only the eastern, olive-backed form of Swainson's Thrush passes through. But for North America as a whole, the instability of the thrushes reflects how the age of discovery never really ends.

For John James Audubon, tending his store and his young family in Henderson in the second decade of the 1800s, all of that was far off in a distant and unimaginable future. As a spare-time, amateur bird student then, he had no reason to question the prevailing classification of the thrushes—even if evidence to the contrary flitted through his local woods every spring and fall.

Most people, most of the time, go with the current of their times—like a flatboat floating down the Ohio River, or like migratory thrushes riding on warm southerly breezes on a night in May. Even strong-willed, talented, flamboyant individuals often take the easy road without thinking about it. Audubon was comfortable enough where he was and might have stayed there indefinitely.

But he would be swept up by the economic currents of the era, and that would change everything. A couple of bad investments would turn disastrous as a widespread and growing financial crisis gripped the country, culminating in the Panic of 1819. Crushed and bankrupt, in his mid-thirties, Audubon found himself starting over with nothing. From that dark time, he would emerge with a mission. Studying and drawing birds would no longer be a mere hobby. Instead, birds would become his life's work, the central fact of his identity.

opposite page: Gray-cheeked Thrush with red columbine (Aquilegia), by Kenn Kaufman. Like the Swainson's Thrush, this bird is a common migrant through eastern North America that managed to escape detection for decades. Its status is still uncertain; there is ongoing debate whether the Gray-cheeked Thrush is really a distinct species from the almost-identical Bicknell's Thrush.

Interlude:
Channeling the
Illustrator

The Feather Problem

Feathers are astonishing. Made of keratinous material similar to that of human hairs or fingernails, the typical feather has a central shaft with a flat surface, called the vane, on either side. The vane is like a piece of stiff paper, and it looks solid but isn't. It's made up of long, thin barbs, each lined with tiny barbules and even tinier hooks that interlock to hold the surface together. The vane can be easily pulled apart and, thanks to those tiny hooks, even more easily zipped together again. Incredibly lightweight, the longest wing and tail feathers are still strong enough to help lift a huge bird like a pelican or an eagle into the air.

Most birds are almost completely covered with feathers, but there's nothing random about their arrangement. On almost all birds, the feathers grow out of precisely arranged tracts, spreading out to cover areas of bare skin between the tracts. The arrangement is even more precise on the wings, tail, and back of a bird. An American Robin has nineteen long flight feathers in each wing and twelve tail feathers, with the bases of all those feathers protected by neatly arranged rows of covert feathers. Each of those feathers has an exact shape. That shape may vary by age or sex (on many songbirds, the outer wing feathers are more pointed on young birds than on adults), but that variation is predictable. The markings and colors on each feather are predictable as well, and together they make up the total color pattern of the bird.

This complex precision of feathering seems beautiful and miraculous, and it is. And it has a particular impact on bird illustrators: it's really hard to fake it. Drawing anything takes skill, but if you draw a dog or cat, you can brush in a general sense of fur and no one will count the hairs. If you draw a bird and get the number or shape or position of the larger feathers wrong, practiced eyes will notice. To reproduce the appearance of each species, especially in a detailed, life-size drawing in the Audubon style, takes the highest quality of reference materials.

Audubon achieved this detail by working from freshly killed birds, pinned up in lifelike poses, where he could check and measure everything. Later in his project he often had to work from stiff, stuffed skins, using his experience to imagine poses for them, while getting feather details from the specimens. In the past, I had visited museum collections to check on feather patterns for illustrations, but it wasn't practical for this project. For fine detail, I would have to rely almost entirely on photographs.

Fortunately, things like autofocus, image stabilization, high-resolution digital cameras, and super-telephoto lenses have revolutionized bird photography in recent decades. I'm not a serious photographer, but I've accumulated thousands of bird pictures of hundreds of species, some of which are sharp enough to show much of the feather detail I need. Even more fortunately, I'm blessed with other sources as well. Although I don't have supreme photographic skills, some of my friends do, and they let me use some of their images for reference.

Yes, Audubon had the advantage of having the freshly killed bird right in front of him, where every feather could be examined much more directly than in a photograph. But he had to work fast, because those freshly killed specimens wouldn't stay fresh for long. Especially not in hot weather. Illustrators today may have to look more closely to figure out the feather patterns in photos, but we don't have to worry about how they will smell if we go back to them for reference a week or a month later.

4

Hidden Identities

When I jumped in the back seat of the car, my assumption was that the long-haired teenager riding in front with the driver must be her grandson. He wasn't, though. He was a hitchhiker like me, and she had picked him up just a few miles earlier.

The kid said his name was Chase, and he looked about my age—which was seventeen, although on that trip I'd been telling people I was nineteen. He had left his home in Georgia a few days earlier, after a violent falling-out with his dad, and he was on the road to get away. As for me, I was heading west from a couple of weeks in southern Florida. "Just hanging out," I lied. "Wild scene in Miami, you know." I'd actually been exploring Florida for the abundance of colorful birds there, avoiding cities like Miami. But I wasn't about to share that point with strangers.

The driver was doing most of the talking, though. Slim and gray-haired, with wrinkles of kindness on her face, she was talking about Jesus. Her eyes locked on mine in the rearview mirror, then fixed on Chase, then glanced at the road ahead, in an endless cycle, while she gestured with one hand for emphasis. Chase and I, clearly both suburban boys raised to be polite, nodded and mumbled agreement with everything she said.

We were moving west through the panhandle, the strip of land that stretches out along the Gulf from Florida's northwest flank. If you travel that way today you can glide along Interstate 10, separated from the passing landscape; but back then, in the early 1970s, large sections of I-10 remained unfinished, and the two-lane U.S. 90 cut through the heart of the countryside, deeply embedded in the local culture. I had been uneasily noting that it was a world away from the cosmopolitan fringes of southern Florida cities. The beat-up pickup trucks, the guns, the Confederate flags told me that this was a different Florida, and that I was out of place.

That feeling of being out of place increased after the kindly Jesus lady dropped us off at the edge of a town. She was turning off the highway, going to her sister's house back in the boondocks somewhere, and she wanted to leave us in a place where we would be sure of getting another ride.

This wasn't necessarily going to do the trick. On a bench in front of a shabby gas station, Chase and I discussed our next move. If we tried thumbing for rides along the main drag here in town, almost all the traffic would be local, including local police. If we walked west along the highway out of town, we'd be venturing into unknown territory. Either approach carried risks. But it was starting to look like staying here would be risky, too.

A black Ford Fairlane cruising by slowed to a crawl, and the four young men riding in it stared at us. There was nothing friendly in their gaze. They continued down the road, but a few minutes later they came back the other way, still staring. Then three guys in a blue El Camino treated us to the same dead-eyed, unwelcoming look. We noticed that the Fairlane and the El Camino had pulled into a parking lot just down the street, and the young men seemed to be talking about something. Possibly about us.

Maybe, I thought, we'll be meeting Jesus sooner than I'd expected.

Only a few vehicles had stopped at the gas station while we'd been sitting there—all locals, judging by the way they chatted with the kid working the pumps. But when the Cadillac pulled in, we sensed that it wasn't from around here.

The fading silvery-green Cadillac would have been a luxury car a dozen years earlier. Now it looked like it had gone through tough times. So did the two guys who stepped out of the car, spoke briefly to the station attendant, and stood looking around with disdain.

They were an odd pair. One man, with muscles bulging under a torn T-shirt, had a dark complexion, high cheekbones, and long black hair; I guessed he was at least part Native American. The other guy was shorter and thinner with a narrow face, a sandy crew cut, and sunken eyes that looked suspicious and mean. When he spoke, in a voice as thin as his face, his accent sounded vaguely British. Both of them exuded a feral edginess.

Chase stood up. "I'm gonna ask them for a ride."

"What?" I said. "You sure?" But Chase was already walking toward them. Awkwardly, I followed a few paces behind.

The big guy spun around when Chase spoke to him, as if poised to throw a punch, but then he relaxed and studied us with obvious amusement. "You boys just passing through?" Not exactly a genius deduction, since we were standing there uncomfortably with backpacks. "Where you going?"

"West," I said. "New Orleans," said Chase.

"Put up ten bucks for gas," the big guy said, "and we can take you as far as New Orleans."

I was near the end of my trip and almost broke, but eager to be out of that town. Chase and I each handed the guy five dollars, grabbed our packs, and scrambled into the back seat of the Cadillac.

It was one of the most unsettling rides I ever had during several years of hitchhiking. The two guys asked our names but never shared theirs. Mentally I had tagged the thin one as Ratface and his muscular partner as Hawkeye, although of course I didn't say those names out loud. Ratface drove. Hawkeye sprawled in the passenger seat; a couple of times he took a handgun out of the glove compartment and cleaned it absentmindedly.

We answered politely when spoken to, but most of the time the two guys ignored us, talking between themselves. A few times they seemed to be discussing robberies they'd committed, and then they would break off and look back at us, while I stared out the window and tried to pretend I hadn't heard a thing. Once they got into an argument that escalated until they were shouting and cursing at each other, and they jumped out as if they would fight right there on the road shoulder. ("Oh, man, don't move," Chase breathed.) But after they squared off, Ratface seemed to remember that Hawkeye was twice his size; he apologized, they got back in the car, and we continued west.

It wouldn't have surprised me at all if Ratface and Hawkeye had stopped on a quiet stretch of roadside to kill us for our meager possessions. But they didn't. Near midnight, we rolled right into the pulsing heart of central New Orleans.

For about four years in my late teens I was traveling much of the time, thumbing rides around North America, sleeping out on the ground, living on the cheap. In those years I always tried to avoid the cities. After all, I was traveling to see as many birds as I could. Cities offered few birds but many unknown dangers, and I was more comfortable in wilder zones.

But New Orleans was different. I wanted to see New Orleans. Not because of Mardi Gras or Bourbon Street or the French Quarter—I'd barely even heard of them. I wanted to see New Orleans because it had played a complex role in the history of bird study.

In the early 1800s, New Orleans was by far the most important metropolis in the South. The city had been founded by the French in 1718, ruled by Spain in the late 1700s, then returned to France before being sold to the United States as part of the Louisiana Purchase in 1803. Andrew Jackson's defeat of British forces in the Battle of New Orleans in 1815 had captured the public imagination, sparking the beginning of Jackson's improbable, and unfortunate, rise to political power. So New Orleans was famous. It was the Paris of the South, with more than half the population still speaking French in the 1820s, but with strong Spanish, English, and Afro-Caribbean influences as well, a rich gumbo of cultures.

New Orleans was also an essential waypoint for travel in the early 1800s. If a person west of the Appalachians wanted to go to the eastern states or transport goods there, they could make the slow trip eastward, overland, on terrible roads. Or they could take the longer but much easier option of traveling by boat down the Ohio River and the Mississippi to New Orleans, then by ship through the Gulf of Mexico, around the peninsula of Florida, then north along the East Coast or across the Atlantic. So important was this route that Thomas Jefferson, at the beginning of his presidency in 1801, began negotiating to buy New Orleans or at least codify permanent access for Americans. He was as surprised as anyone when Napoleon countered with an offer to purchase the entire Louisiana Territory—a vast area stretching from the Gulf to present-day Montana, nearly doubling the size of the young United States.

So New Orleans was firmly under U.S. jurisdiction and firmly established as a key stop for travelers. Alexander Wilson, on his one major westward trip, spent the spring of 1810 traveling down the Ohio River as far as Louisville, Kentucky, and then went overland through Tennessee and present-day Mississippi before arriving in New Orleans in June. He spent eighteen days there—mostly seeking subscribers for his *American Ornithology*—before boarding a ship for the long way home to the Atlantic Coast. Other naturalists, including Thomas Nuttall, spent time in New Orleans.

But no one embraced the city so fervently as John James Audubon. Consider this remarkable passage from the brief autobiography he wrote for his sons, Victor and John, around 1835:

> It seems that my father had large properties in Santo Domingo, and was in the habit of visiting frequently that portion of our Southern States called, and known by the name of, Louisiana. . . . During one of those excursions he married a lady of Spanish extraction, whom I have been led to understand was as beautiful as she was wealthy. . . . My mother, soon after my birth, accompanied my father to the estate of Aux Cayes, on the island of Santo Domingo, and she was one

of the victims during the ever-to-be-lamented period of the negro insurrection on that island. . . . My father, through the intervention of some faithful servants, escaped from Aux Cayes with a good portion of his plate and money, and with me and these humble friends reached New Orleans in safety. From this place he took me to France.

It's a dramatic story. And like many of Audubon's stories, it's mostly a fabrication, woven around a few loose strands of fact.

His father, Captain Jean Audubon, did have landholdings in Santo Domingo in the Caribbean, including an estate at Aux Cayes. And there was an uprising. It was a revolution in which enslaved Blacks defeated their French masters and Napoleon's forces—shocking the world, establishing the independent nation of Haiti, and hastening the demise of slavery throughout the western hemisphere. But it couldn't have led to the demise of young Audubon's beautiful, fictional Spanish mother, because the revolt didn't start until 1791. By that time the boy was six years old and living in France, having been taken there from Aux Cayes in 1788 or 1789.

Birth records from the late 1700s are often sketchy, especially for mariners' illegitimate children born overseas. But biographer Francis Hobart Herrick tracked down old documents, including a doctor's itemized invoice brought home to France by Captain Audubon, suggesting that the boy was born at or near Aux Cayes on April 26, 1785. The boy's mother, according to multiple lines of evidence, was a twenty-seven-year-old French chambermaid named Jeanne Rabin, who died within a few months.

This version is not quite proven as fact. As ever with Audubon, there is space for some doubt, or the possibility of other interpretations. But it's based on the best evidence available, and it's almost universally accepted by historians today.

Herrick's biography wasn't published until 1917. Throughout the late 1800s and into the 1900s, with no obstacles to wild speculation, many people embraced the idea of Audubon's origins in Louisiana. Some claimed more than one specific house as his precise birthplace. The most popular myth regarded the Marigny mansion at Fontainebleau on the north side of Lake Pontchartrain, just north of New Orleans. Herrick also laid that idea to rest with detailed research, showing that the timing would have been impossible.

So, as much as we might like the story, we can't say that Audubon was born in Louisiana. But it would be fair to say he was reborn there, in a sense, when he arrived in New Orleans in early January 1821.

He had just come through the lowest point of his life. His young family had lost everything after prospering for most of a decade in Kentucky. Superficial biographies of Audubon may suggest he failed at business because he was always off chasing birds; but for a few years in Henderson, while his drawing and bird study were relegated to his spare time, he succeeded as a storekeeper. He had made a couple of bad investments, but he might have recovered from those—if not for the economic downturn that swept the country, culminating in widespread financial crisis in 1818 to 1819. Bankrupt, forced to sell everything, jailed for debt, Audubon had to start over with nothing.

Nothing, that is, except the knowledge and artistic ability he had been gradually building up for years, and an idea that had languished at the back of his mind ever since meeting Alexander Wilson in 1810. Publishing a great work on birds had been no more than an idle daydream for Audubon, an idea for a nebulous future, while he focused on the day-to-day of supporting his family. But with nothing left to lose, he could throw aside caution and pursue his grandiose dream at last.

With nowhere to go but up, he set off downriver—down the Ohio, down the Mississippi, heading for New Orleans in October 1820. He took along a teenage assistant, Joseph Mason, who had been his student for art lessons in Cincinnati that year; Mason showed uncommon promise at botanical illustration, and the plan was that he would paint the plants in Audubon's bird portraits.

These two couldn't afford passage on a steamboat or a private keelboat, so they made the trek on a flatboat carrying goods downriver. Even the marginal cost of that passage was beyond their means, so Audubon paid their way by hunting wild game to feed the others on board. Those other passengers were rough characters, cut from the same cloth as my erstwhile travel companions Ratface and Hawkeye.

It was a slow and uncomfortable trip, but Audubon's spirits seemed to be on the rebound. He was drawing birds now, whenever possible in the crowded conditions of the flatboat, and taking notes on birds observed every day: ". . . killed a Common Crow Corvus Americanus Which I drew; Many Robins in the woods and thousands of Snow Buntings Emberiza Nivalis—several Rose Breasted Gros Beaks—We killed 2 Pheasants, 15 Partridges—1 Teal, 1 T.T. Godwit—1 Small Grebe all of these I have Seen precisely alike in all parts—and one Bared Owl this is undoutedly the Most plentifull of his Genus—I felt poorly all day and Drawing in a Boat Were a Man cannot stand erect gave me a Violent headache." There's a self-conscious feel to his notes, including the unnecessary inclusion of scientific names, the numbers of individuals of each species, and the comments on their status, reflecting a sense that he was now gathering data for a formal publication. Flat broke on a flatboat, far from his family and unknown to the world, he had a focus and a mission to drive him forward through every adversity.

It took almost three months to reach New Orleans, but Audubon was watching birds the whole way. In the past, when it was just a hobby, he could have shrugged off any he didn't recognize; but now he had an incentive to identify everything, and an eager expectation of discovery—surely in this region there must be birds that Alexander Wilson had overlooked. His anticipation continued to build after he arrived in early January 1821. Birds were everywhere. He could seek them along the banks of the wide Mississippi or in the marshes and woods north of the city, or he could go to the market and examine hundreds of birds brought in daily by local gunners. Frequently he did a kind of crude census at the market, noting what birds were for sale and in what numbers: "Vast Many Green Wing'd & blue winged Teals—hundreds of Snipes, pures, Solitary Snipes—Green back'd Swallows—but robbins have disappeared." Sometimes he bought specimens there to use as models for his drawings, although more often he made comments like "Remarked in the Markets many Purple Gallinules: but all so Mangled that I could not see one fit to draw." Or: "Saw in Market—2 White Herons—one New Species of Snipe, but could not Draw any of them, being partly pluck'd."

As much as he might have wanted to spend all his time now draw- ing birds, reality demanded that he make some money. Reluctantly he turned away from the riverfront and began walking the streets, looking for people who could afford to pay to have their portraits drawn.

During my first visit to New Orleans as a teenager, as much as I might have wanted to focus on birds, I didn't see many. I wound up hanging out with Chase and three other teens, all visiting from elsewhere. In retrospect I think all of us were lying about something: our ages, our names, our backgrounds, or all three. Kids on the road, trying out new identities, trying to figure out where we were going next. I saw a few gulls flying over the city, but I didn't know where to look for anything historical relating to Audubon.

Fortunately, that wasn't my last chance. Decades later I was back in the city with my friend David Muth, a birder and historian with a deep knowledge of New Orleans. David showed me the stretches of the north shore of the Mississippi where Audubon would have walked to the east, watching migrant swallows and other birds over the river. He showed me the route of the old portage from the Mississippi up to the edge of Lake Pontchartrain, a route used even before the city was established; Audubon probably walked that way multiple times, includ- ing the March day when he witnessed a flight of thousands of American Golden-Plovers.

We visited the open-air market, still located where the portage meets the river. "When I was a kid," David told me, "it still had a bit of the old flavor. With a little imagination, one could conjure up the place where the rafts and barges were off-loaded and the products sold streetside in the stench and bustle of the 1820s." The stench may be gone, but the place is still bustling—now with tourists, mostly here to buy souvenirs.

Conjuring up the past is easy in the lower French Quarter. Along many of the narrow streets, the close-packed houses and other buildings come up to the edge of the sidewalks, their stucco walls broken by wooden doors and tall wood-shuttered windows. This was the original neighborhood of New Orleans, and David tells me that concerted efforts to preserve its historic character go back at least to the 1920s. Many of the street names and street numbers are unchanged from two centuries ago. Audubon and Joseph Mason rented a room at 706 Barracks Street in January 1821, and when we stopped by that address, we saw a plaque on the outside wall commemorating that history.

From these humble lodgings, the artist would walk to the pricier parts of town. He had made enough contacts that he was now getting commissions to draw portraits for $25 each—a lot of cash in the 1820s—and a few opportunities to teach drawing lessons. So he could afford to cover basic expenses, send some money back to Lucy and the boys waiting in Cincinnati, and take some full days to devote to drawing birds.

Audubon had spent time in New York and Philadelphia, so he was no stranger to cities, but he'd never been in a stranger city than New Orleans. It had such a rich mix of cultures and languages, and such a range of economic strata, from great wealth to abject poverty. In his current state he was closer to the latter extreme and self-conscious about his status and his threadbare clothes. That undoubtedly added to his unease during his most unusual encounter in the city.

He'd been walking up one of the main thoroughfares, lugging his portfolio, when a beautiful young woman approached and asked him, in French, if he was the artist sent by the French Academy to draw the birds of America. Audubon replied that he drew them for his own pleasure, and she persisted: "You are he that draws likenesses in black chalk so remarkably strong." At his affirmative answer, she continued, "Then call in 30 minutes at 26 Rue Amour and walk upstairs. I will wait for you. Do not follow me now."

Audubon was unnerved, but did as instructed. Upstairs in the woman's private chambers they sat and talked. He was agitated—trembling like a leaf, he recalled later—and she tried to calm him: "I will not hurt you," she teased. But his agitation increased as she explained what she wanted. Audubon must swear to keep her place of residence, and her name if he should happen to learn it, secret. She would provide high-quality paper and fine colored chalks. She wanted not just a portrait of her face, but of her full figure—in the nude. Draw me like one of your French girls. At this he was so shaken that she told him to go out for a walk to compose himself and then come back in an hour to get started.

For a week and a half he returned almost every day to work on the portrait. He never got over being intimidated—especially not after the "Fair Incognito," as he called her, came over and sat next to him to critique and correct some aspects of his drawing. Eventually he was finished, though, and she paid him with a beautiful, high-quality gun, as a memento and something useful for his work. Perhaps the strangest aspect of the whole episode was that, although Audubon mentioned it only obliquely in his journal, he described the encounter in great detail in a letter to his wife. By that time, evidently, he had recovered from the experience enough for his brash audacity to return.

The young woman's identity will probably remain hidden forever. Some historians have suggested she was a mistress of one of the richest men of the city, perhaps one of the same men for whom Audubon drew a simple $25 portrait. Be that as it may, his interactions with the affluent would soon bring him advantages of an avian kind.

The wealthy and powerful Pirrie family had been visiting New Orleans from their plantation, Oakley, a hundred miles upriver near St. Francisville. Lucretia Pirrie, the matriarch of the family, was impressed by Audubon's talents, and made him a remarkable offer: $60 a month, and room and board for himself and Joseph Mason, in return for tutoring their daughter, Eliza, in art, music, and other topics. And after a few hours of tutoring each day, he would be free to range through the woods and bayous around Oakley, bringing back bird specimens to draw.

So in June 1821, the artist and his young assistant relocated upriver, to begin what would be a productive three and a half months of progress.

The Oakley House is preserved as a state historic site,* well worth exploring today. For visitors who expect a white-columned mansion and a *Gone with the Wind* vibe, the first reaction may be surprise at the relatively spare, elegant simplicity of the house. For naturalists, the first reaction may be to notice that the forests here are not like those around New Orleans. The area near St. Francisville is ecologically different from the rest of Louisiana, a hilly region with many plants and animals rare elsewhere in the state and some of the richest biodiversity in the entire southeastern coastal plain. Audubon had arrived here by sheer coincidence, but he recognized his luck, as he wrote in his journal. "The Aspect of the Country entirely New to us . . . the Rich Magnolia covered with its Odoriferous Blossoms, the Holly, the Beech, the Tall Yellow Poplar, the Hilly ground, even the Red Clay I Looked at with amasement—such entire Change in so Short a time, appears, often supernatural, and surrounded Once More by thousands of Warblers & thrushes, I enjoy'd Nature."

Warblers and thrushes wouldn't have been there by the actual thousands at that season, but there were certainly more kinds of breeding birds near the Oakley plantation than around Audubon's New Orleans quarters, and he was eager to explore and learn.

I can picture him setting out, filled with anticipation, his eyes shining like his shiny new gun, from the simple ground-floor room he shared with other hired workers. The forest was undoubtedly farther from the main house than it is today—this was a large working plantation, after all—so Audubon had to walk some distance to get to rich upland forests

---

*It's ironic that this was designated as a historic site merely because Audubon spent a few months there; he was hardly the only interesting person associated with the place. This immediate area was not originally considered part of the Louisiana Purchase, and it continued under Spanish rule until the United States claimed it in 1810. Lucretia Pirrie's first husband, Ruffin Gray, represented the Spanish Crown as the local alcalde: something like a combination of mayor, sheriff, and tax collector. When he died, Lucretia successfully petitioned to retain ownership of the plantation—an unusual position for a woman in that era—and then she married the next alcalde, James Pirrie, but retained most of the control of the estate. Their daughter, Eliza, Audubon's student, turned out to be just as headstrong as Lucretia. The lives of the Pirrie women would make a worthy topic for a biographer.

or low-lying cypress swamps. Once he reached those shaded realms, the possibilities seemed boundless. Few Western naturalists had visited this region. Wilson had passed through in 1810 and had discovered the Mississippi Kite upriver at Natchez. But Audubon was sure Wilson had missed some birds, too, and he intended to find them.

Less than two weeks after arriving at Oakley, he had his first candidate. On a hot, humid afternoon, he and Joseph Mason were hunting turkeys in woods a few miles from the house when a small yellow bird appeared: "I saw it innocently approaching us until within a few yards, anxiously looking, as if trying to discover our intentions; but as we stood motionless, it once came so near that I could easily have reached it with my gun barrel. It moved nimbly among the twigs of the low bushes, making now and then short dashes at flies." Concluding that it was an undescribed species, he named it the Louisiana Fly-catcher at first. (Later, in his formal publication, he called it Selby's Fly-catcher to honor the English naturalist and artist Prideaux John Selby.) Then in early August, along the edge of a cypress swamp, Audubon shot at two small birds that were fighting, wounded one, and realized when he picked it up that it appeared to be something new. He called this one the Cypress Swamp Fly catcher at first, later amended to Bonaparte's Fly-catcher after the ornithologist Charles Lucien Bonaparte.*

Neither of these birds was actually new to science. And neither one was a flycatcher. The latter one, from the cypress swamp in August, was a Canada Warbler—a scarce migrant through the area. Although it had been described to science in 1766, Audubon had probably never seen it before. But the other one was a young individual of a species he already knew fairly well, the Hooded Warbler. He did a painting of a Hooded Warbler that summer at Oakley, but he didn't seem to notice that his "Louisiana Fly-catcher/Selby's Fly-catcher" was the same bird, with slightly less distinct markings on the head.

*These birds were both included in the earliest numbers of Audubon's *Birds of America* and *Ornithological Biography*, when he was trying hard to curry favor with influential people on both sides of the Atlantic; an easy way to compliment someone was to name a species for them.

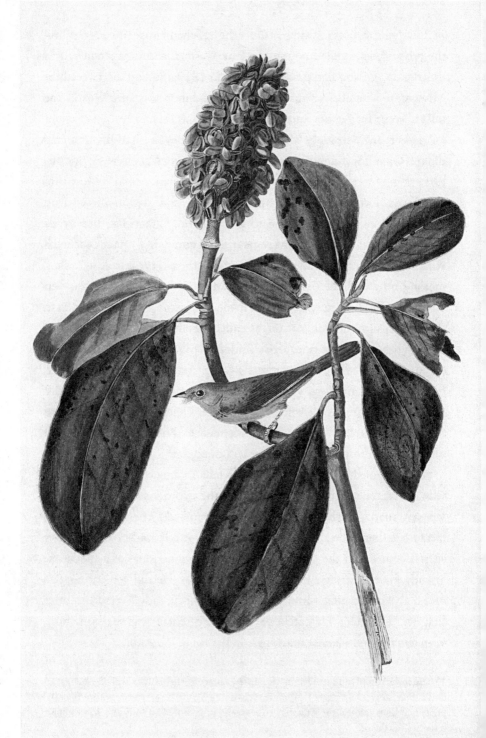

Any modern birder who reads Audubon's notes on birds at the Oakley plantation (those he saw, and those whose absence he remarked) is likely to be mystified at how he classified them. He saw Red-eyed Vireos there, but called them "Red Eyed Fly Catchers," and gave them the scientific name of a warbler. He referred to the Ruby-crowned Kinglet as the "Ruby Crowned Wren," and also gave it the scientific name of a warbler. He classified the Ovenbird (a warbler), Northern Mockingbird, and Gray Catbird as thrushes. He noted the Eastern Kingbird, a type of flycatcher, and gave it the scientific name of a shrike. Looking back, we're tempted to ask: How could he hope to classify these birds with any precision when he couldn't even place any of them in the right family?

How indeed? The flycatcher family, the warbler family, the wren family, and so on—today we recognize all these as groups that are clearly different. Modern birders, even beginners, learn to divide up birds into families. Field guides and reference books are arranged that way, and it seems logical and helpful to recognize these natural groups. So we're taught early on that bluebirds and American Robins, despite their different colors, belong to the thrush family. Purple Martins are larger than their relatives, but they're still confirmed members of the swallow family. Flickers are bigger and browner than most woodpeckers, with flashy wing colors, while sapsuckers have weird feeding habits reflected in their name; but they all have the chisel-shaped beaks, strong tree-gripping feet, and pointed tail feathers that mark them as belonging to the woodpecker family.

After a while it becomes second nature to think of birds in this way. Families are the easiest category to grasp, much more so than other

opposite page: "Bonaparte's Flycatcher" by John James Audubon. When Audubon encountered this bird in 1821 in Louisiana, he thought it was a species of flycatcher new to science, and he later decided to name it in honor of the French scientist Charles Bonaparte. The bird was actually a young Canada Warbler, and others eventually pointed this out, but Audubon never wavered in his first conviction that this bird was something new and different.

levels in the taxonomic hierarchy, like order or genus. Without looking it up, we may have trouble remembering that hummingbirds and
nighthawks are classified in the same order, but it's easy to think of
the hummingbird family as a distinctive group. It may seem odd that
big-beaked pelicans and long-legged herons are in one order, while two
other groups of long-legged birds, storks and cranes, are placed in two
different orders; but treating the pelicans as a distinct family is easy to
understand.

At the same time, most birders don't pay much attention to the
genus of each bird, aside from a few highly distinctive genera. The generic names of many North American sparrows have changed within
the last couple of decades (the Seaside Sparrow moved from the genus
Ammodramus to *Ammospiza*—big deal, right?), but only obsessives like
me have kept up with all the changes. For most birders it's good enough
to remember that they all belong to the American sparrow family.

It's logical to ask why Audubon didn't employ this basic grouping
to organize the birds he found. But there's a good answer, and it's a
surprising one: the category of "family" was not yet in general use for
classification at that time. This category was not included in the original
Linnaean system at all. In the tenth edition of *Systema Naturae*, Linnaeus
divided the class Aves (birds) into six orders, each containing from four
to seventeen genera. There was no intermediate stage between order
and genus. So his order Picae included all the parrots, toucans, cuckoos,
woodpeckers, kingfishers, hummingbirds, crows, birds-of-paradise, and
so on, each represented by a single genus. The system almost worked
at the time, when so little was known of the world's birdlife. His single
genus of hummingbirds, *Trochilus*, listed eighteen species. Today, more
than 360 hummingbird species are recognized, divided among more
than one hundred genera. If they were tossed in among all those crows
and cuckoos and kingfishers (which now add up to hundreds of species
and dozens of genera), chaos would reign.

The category of the family makes rich diversity manageable. It's one
of the most useful elements of what we now call the Linnaean system,
and ironically, Linnaeus never used it. Nor was it used by naturalists

pursuing birds at the beginning of the nineteenth century. Alexander Wilson, preparing his *American Ornithology* for publication in 1808, adopted a classification scheme that had been published by John Latham in England earlier, basically following the Linnaean model. Audubon, traveling the frontier in the early 1820s, carried William Turton's English translation of Linnaeus's *Systema Naturae*. Both men wanted to measure up to accepted scientific practice, and that meant trying to fit each new bird into an established genus within a few large, loosely defined orders. They would not have considered placing the bird into a family, because the system didn't include that category.

Their lack of this basic group wasn't such an obstacle as it might seem. With the limited knowledge of total diversity at the time, the genus could serve in the same capacity as the family does today. This new bird, does it appear to be a woodpecker? Pop it in the genus *Picus*. Does it seem like a warbler? Slip it into the genus *Sylvia*. Does it strike you more as a flycatcher? Make it a member of the genus *Muscicapa*. Can't decide? Flip a coin. In practical terms, with a new or potentially new species, naturalists just needed a pigeonhole in which to place it.

Consider the birds known as flycatchers. Europe has a few species of small songbirds that usually forage by perching in a semi-open spot, flying out to catch insects in midair, then returning to their perch. The French ornithologist Brisson set up a new genus for them, *Muscicapa*—based on the Latin for "to catch a fly"—in 1760, and Linnaeus included it in the twelfth edition of *Systema Naturae* in 1766. Today, more than a dozen species in Africa, Asia, and Europe are still included in the genus *Muscicapa*. But it included far more species than that in the late 1700s and early 1800s, when it was used as a catchall for small fly-catching birds from all over the world.

In the first six volumes of *American Ornithology* between 1808 and 1812, Alexander Wilson recognized fifteen birds from eastern North America as flycatchers and placed them in the genus *Muscicapa*. One, the "Small-headed Flycatcher," can't be reconciled with any bird known today, although its illustration suggests a warbler. Of the remaining fourteen, four are now classified in the American warbler family, one is in the gnatcatcher family, and four are in the vireo family. Five are now classified as flycatchers, but that statement is misleading because the American flycatcher family is entirely separate from the flycatcher family of the Old World. They may share a few habits, but they are unrelated. In Wilson's day, though, that distinction was unknown; and under the standards of the time, it was unimportant, too.

This basic point is easy to overlook: What does it mean to say two individual humans are related, or two species are related? In both cases, it means they share a common ancestor. You may look like a certain movie star, or like the king of France, but that resemblance means nothing unless you can show that you came from the same branch on the family tree. Likewise, two bird species may look similar, but we can't say they're related unless they evolved from the same ancestral stock. A natural classification would faithfully reflect that history. Before Darwin, such considerations hadn't come into play, and groups of species were delineated for convenience. Even after a few naturalists, like Charles Bonaparte, started inserting the category of "family" between the order and the genus, the connections were based mostly on outward appearance or general behaviors.

So in early American ornithology, the tendency was to place every bird into an established group already known from Europe. In some cases, that produced wildly misleading results and names.

Consider what's now known as the American blackbird family, Icteridae. The roughly one hundred species range throughout the western hemisphere, but none live in the Old World, so scientists from Europe had no frame of reference for them.* And they're a varied group. Some are indeed black, like the long-tailed Common Grackles that stalk about on lawns, or the Red-winged Blackbirds that sing from every marsh. Others are more colorful, like the yellow-chested, brown-backed meadowlarks of the prairies, or the orioles, adorned with orange or yellow or chestnut. They vary in habits, too, from the cowbirds that lay their

---

*The Common Blackbird of Europe is a member of the thrush family, related to the American Robin.

eggs in the nests of other birds to the Bobolinks that sing in flight over northern meadows and then migrate to southern South America for the winter. The first European naturalists to encounter these birds had no reason to group them together, and instead allied them with a wide variety of Old World types.

Look at how Mark Catesby treated these birds after seeing them in the southeastern colonies in the early 1700s. Catesby gave each bird a Latin name (often several words long), an English name, and a French name, providing multiple clues as to how he viewed their identities. In his work on natural history he described and illustrated seven species that are now included in the American blackbird family, linking them to six different (and unrelated) groups of Old World birds.

He referred to the Red-winged Blackbird as the "Red-wing'd Starling." It was a logical connection; European Starlings are also black birds that form large flocks outside the breeding season. He included a grackle—seemingly a mashup of the Common Grackle and Boat-tailed Grackle—and called it the "Purple Jack-Daw," making it a relative of the crows. He saw the Eastern Meadowlark walking on the ground, like the familiar larks of Europe, and called it *Alauda magna*, the "Large Lark." He thought the Bobolink was a type of bunting and the Brown-headed Cowbird was a sparrow. For the Baltimore Oriole and Orchard Oriole, by coincidence, he used the genus name *Icterus*, which is what they're called today, but his original names didn't stick. Later authors put them in the genus *Oriolus* for many decades, identifying them with the Old World orioles, an unrelated family. Catesby didn't use the name "oriole" at all, and apparently didn't think of the connection. For what we call the Baltimore Oriole today, his name was the "Baltimore-Bird." And the slightly smaller Orchard Oriole? That was the "Bastard Baltimore."

Almost a century later, when Alexander Wilson launched *American Ornithology* in 1808, he still wasn't using the category of family in his classification, but his English and Latin names for each species showed where he thought their relationships lay. He still treated meadowlarks as actual larks, orioles as Old World orioles, and Red-winged Blackbirds as starlings. He classified both the Bobolink and the Brown-headed Cow-bird as buntings. It's not clear what he thought of the Common Grackle and the Rusty Blackbird; he placed them in the genus *Gracula*, which is used today for a few types of myna birds in southern Asia, but it had wider application at the time.

Remarkably, by just two decades later, the brilliant Charles Lucien Bonaparte had come a long way toward working out what these birds were. In a synopsis printed in 1828, one of the first publications to make extensive use of families as a category, he grouped meadowlarks, American orioles, grackles, cowbirds, Red-winged Blackbirds, and even the anomalous Bobolink into one family. His arrangement wasn't per-fect—he also included crows, jays, and the true (Old World) starlings in this family—but he showed great perception in seeing past the dif-ferences among the varied American blackbirds and focusing on their similarities.

But such abstract ideas were far from the mind of John James Audubon, on the loose in Louisiana in 1821. Years later he would start to show some interest in the higher classification of bird groups; for now, he just wanted to find species that were new to science. Certainly he was seeing members of what would become the blackbird family. There were Orchard Orioles around, no need to call them "Bastard Baltimores" now, in greater numbers than he'd ever seen. There were "Red-wing'd Starlings" in the marshes. "Purple Grakles" were com-mon—again, probably a mash-up of the Common Grackle and Boat-tailed Grackle; the latter had been described as a separate species by the French ornithologist Louis Jean Pierre Vieillot just two years before, but Audubon wouldn't have known that yet. He didn't care about any of these. For the first time in his life he was free to go afield in territory where novel finds seemed likely, and he was determined to make the most of the opportunity.

He thought he made several such discoveries during that first year of exploration. Most turned out not to be new. His "Selby's Flycatcher" and "Bonaparte's Flycatcher," as I've mentioned, proved to be young individuals of known species of warblers. His "Children's Warbler" was

a Yellow Warbler. His "Roscoe's Yellowthroat" was a Common Yellowthroat that piqued his attention because it was acting oddly. The
Louisiana Waterthrush—a bird that kept him guessing for years—was
a bird that had been overlooked by Alexander Wilson, but it wasn't
undescribed; Vieillot had given it a name a dozen years earlier, based on
a specimen from Kentucky. One of Audubon's few genuine discoveries
that year was Bewick's Wren, which he encountered on one of his last
days at the Oakley plantation in October.

So in that first full year of intense focus, few of his supposed discoveries would hold up under later scrutiny. But he didn't know that
at the time; in his mind, he was reveling in new species. All his "false
positives" heaped more fuel on the fires of his ambition, turning up
his motivation to a fever pitch. He wasn't outdoing Wilson as much as
he thought he was, but he was out in the field, alert to all possibilities,
learning more every day, and producing some of the most striking portraits that would appear later in *The Birds of America*.

I've been writing of Audubon's January 1821 arrival in New Orleans
as if it had been his first time in the city. It was not. He had been there
almost two years earlier on a failed attempt to collect on a debt.

He and some partners had invested in a small steamboat—steam
travel was burgeoning on the Ohio and Mississippi Rivers—and then
sold it to a man named Samuel Bowen. Audubon had a promissory
note from Bowen for thousands of dollars, but when the note came due
in 1819, he learned that Bowen had taken the steamboat and headed
to New Orleans. Determined not to bear this loss, he took two of his
enslaved men to row him and set off downriver in an open skiff in pursuit. On reaching New Orleans, however, he found that Bowen had no
money to pay him, and no steamboat, either: he had turned it over to
another creditor, who had taken it north, out of the jurisdiction of local
courts. Unable to collect a dime, Audubon gave up, sold his two slaves,
and booked a ticket on a steamboat back upriver.

Wait. Stop right there.

The episode is mentioned in most Audubon biographies: couldn't get his boat or his money, so he sold his slaves and went home. The words challenge us with their bland matter-of-factness. Oh, good business move there, John James. Sell those portable assets, and on to the next adventure.

But I can't move on. This is too much. No matter how I pretend the Audubons would have been benevolent enslavers (a contradiction in itself), no matter how much John James glossed over reality by referring to enslaved people as "servants," there is no excusing or condoning this history. He enslaved as many as nine individuals at a time during his family's years in Kentucky, and a few during later periods, and never expressed the slightest regret about the practice.

Those men whom he sold off for a few dollars in New Orleans—they were human beings, with just as much intrinsic worth as the man who so cavalierly sold them. We will probably never know their names, nor what happened to them. But no matter how strong and resourceful they were, it's unlikely they ever could have made their way back to Kentucky. Bought and sold, taken away forever from their loved ones and the places they knew. . . . It was monstrous. In that era, such a transaction had an everyday banality, but that doesn't make it any less evil.

That episode was weighing heavily on my mind as I made my way to the New Orleans African American Museum. The NOAAM sits on beautifully landscaped grounds, just a few blocks inland from the heart of the French Quarter. At the time of my visit, some of the buildings were closed for renovation, but I spent a couple of hours in the main museum house and was impressed and moved by what I saw there.

This was no victims' memorial. The horrors of slavery were clearly acknowledged; but the main element of the museum, the theme that ran through every room, was one of pride. It was a celebration of people who had triumphed over impossible adversity and who had risen to have a powerful impact on the United States and on the world. From the earliest decades of the city, when there was already a thriving free Black community, to the twentieth and twenty-first centuries, when Black New Orleanians revolutionized music, art, culture, politics, and more, this place was a monument to pride and power and success.

And in one of the other buildings, among a gallery of prominent Black citizens associated with the city, there was a space devoted to—John James Audubon. Yes, it's true. Black Americans have plenty of reason to decry Audubon, but some would choose to claim him as well.

At issue are misunderstandings or doubts regarding his birth. Professional historians will tell you that no doubts exist—that his mother was a white woman, Jeanne Rabin or Rabine, who traveled from France to work as a chambermaid in Haiti, where she had an affair with Captain Jean Audubon and died after giving birth. The evidence for this is almost overwhelming. Historians may curse me, I suppose, for inserting that "almost" about a piece of the puzzle that they've already snapped into place. But in a lifetime of studying natural history, I've seen many times when accepted "facts" turned out to be wrong, so I prefer to maintain space for doubt about human history as well.

In the 1780s in Haiti (then called Saint-Domingue or Santo Domingo), apparently there were many liaisons between plantation owners and local women. Captain Audubon had two children there, born to two different women. The second was a girl named Muguet, later called Rose. Her mother, by all lines of evidence, was a mixed-race woman named Catherine Bouffard. No one now questions the conclusion that Rose herself, John James Audubon's half sister, was of mixed race, although she passed for white.

A specific use of language has led to more confusion. In the early 1800s, Audubon's parents were navigating the complicated legal system in France, rewriting their wills, trying to ensure that John James and Rose would not be cut out of their inheritance. In documents sent back and forth between the parents in France and the son in America, the young man is frequently referred to as "Jean Rabin, Creole of Santo Domingo." Today, the word "Creole" is understood to mean a person of mixed race, with both Black and European ancestry. Many people have seized on this as evidence that Audubon regarded himself as partly Black. But in France at that time, the word simply referred to a French citizen who had been born outside the country. There was no racial component to it at all.

When I toured the New Orleans African American Museum, I wanted to see the display that included Audubon. But at the time of my visit, that building was among those closed for renovation. Perhaps symbolically, this was another reflection of the man's identity that would remain hidden.

Several times while writing this book I caught myself starting paragraphs with something like "As his forty-eighth birthday approached"—which would have been misleading, because it's doubtful Audubon would have thought in those terms. Today we take for granted his birth date of April 26, 1785, sleuthed out by biographer Francis Herrick. But the artist never alluded to this date in his journals or elsewhere. When Captain Jean Audubon and his wife adopted the captain's two illegitimate children born in Haiti, the boy's birth date was listed as April 22, 1785, only four days off from Herrick's deduction. But Audubon's granddaughter Maria, writing in the late 1800s—years before Herrick's biography was published—suggested he might have been born "anywhere from 1772 to 1783," and for convenience she settled on a date of May 5, 1780. John James himself, in various legal documents in the early 1800s, gave conflicting versions of how many years old he was, and never specified a birthday.

So it's likely he never knew his birthday. That uncertainty, and the questions surrounding his birth, may help explain why Audubon was often vague or contradictory about his background. Of course, much of that vagueness could have been aimed at hiding his illegitimacy. (He lived in a strange time when buying and selling other humans was shrugged off as no big issue, while being born out of wedlock was cause for shame.) Still, in his writings he sometimes hinted that there was something extraordinary about his origins—something so remarkable that he had sworn to keep it as a secret he would take to the grave.

What kind of secret could have carried such weight? The question swirled in my mind on my first visit to New Orleans. I was young and naive, ready to believe almost anything, and I had just read a book that had left me astonished.

It was a slim volume I'd bought for a dime from a used-book shelf and then read over and over, with the intensity of an impressionable seventeen-year-old. Issued by a prominent publisher in New York, it had appeared in the 1930s, timed for the opening of the museum at the John James Audubon State Park in Henderson, Kentucky. Its author, Alice Jaynes Tyler, was the widow of one of Audubon's descendants. The book's title was *I Who Should Command All*, and its central thesis was that the famous bird painter was, in reality, the Lost Dauphin.

The what?

Exactly. When the book first appeared almost a century ago, the average well-read American might have understood a reference to the Lost Dauphin. But world history marches on, with more and more major events crowding into the timeline and vying for collective memory. Today, fewer people outside of France will remember anything about wild rumors from Paris in the 1790s amid the tumult of the French Revolution.

"Dauphin" was the title for the heir to the throne in the French monarchy. Louis XVI and Marie Antoinette, the last king and queen in those fateful decades, had two sons. The younger one, Louis-Charles, became Dauphin when his older brother died. It was June 1789, Louis-Charles was only four years old, and just over a month later, mobs would storm the Bastille. Soon the royal family would be removed from their palace at Versailles and become essentially prisoners at the Tuileries Palace in Paris, and then absolute prisoners in the Tower of the Temple in 1792; the king and queen were both executed the following year.

Even amid the inflamed passions of the time, no one had the stomach for sending the eight-year-old Dauphin to the guillotine. He remained a prisoner in the Tower, out of sight but still the focus of rumors and speculation. Loyalists hatched plots to help the boy escape, or to have him replaced by a stand-in. According to all official accounts, though, he remained imprisoned until June 1795, when he died at the age of ten.

His imprisonment and death provided fertile ground for alternate versions and conspiracy theories to sprout and grow. Had the boy really died, or had he been spirited away? Fascination with the story of the Lost Dauphin persisted, and it flourished about two decades later, after harsh public attitudes toward the French monarchy had softened. During the early 1800s, more than one hundred men came forward to claim the title, each one arguing that he was the genuine Louis-Charles, miraculously saved from the Tower of the Temple.

Surprisingly, given his penchant for drama, John James Audubon was not one of those claimants. At least, not in any piece of writing that has survived. But some of his heirs believed the idea and clung to any supportive hint. His descendants knew he was roughly the right age—the Dauphin had been born March 27, 1785—although they didn't know just how closely the date matched until Herrick's biography pinned his birthday to April 26 of that year. His love of birds apparently dated to childhood; the Dauphin, according to legend, loved birds, and kept some in a cage while he himself was caged in the Tower. The circumstances of Audubon's birth were open to question; the circumstances of the Dauphin's death were open to question.

And the book I was reading even suggested a storyline. The man who had been the Dauphin's chief jailer in the Tower for seven months left in January 1794, and records from the prison became sketchy after that. And it was just a few weeks later that Captain Jean Audubon and his wife, down in the South of France, took out formal adoption papers for the captain's claimed illegitimate children born in Haiti: the boy Jean Jacques and his apparent half sister, Rose. For author Alice Jaynes Tyler, the timing of this adoption seemed more than suspicious: Was that boy the captain's own, or was this the perfect cover for a prince of the same age, smuggled out of Paris?

Much of the book was obscure to me, since I knew nothing of the French Revolution and didn't recognize the names tossed out in its pages: Chaumette, General Charette, Barras, and many more. I was confused by a seemingly irrelevant subplot claiming the boy had been hidden for a time in Selkirk's Settlement in Canada during the late 1790s. (Only much later would I learn that that settlement hadn't been established until after 1810.) But I couldn't help being drawn in by heartrending passages that were said to be direct quotes from letters written by John James to his beloved Lucy.

"I thought of my birth, of my curious life, and of the strange incidents that brought me to what I am now known to be . . . again I reflected on the consequences . . . and concluded to carry my extraordinary secret to the grave. Oh my Lucy! Oh my father! O! How cruelly situated I am!"

"My high birth, though unknown to the world, was always on my lips and I felt a pride unbecoming my situation. . . ."

"When young, I was easily taught to keep silence . . . but now that I have children myself, children that at one word of mine, would rise to eminence, and would be—*Stop thy pen, or forever be damned, Audubon!*"

And then the source of the book's title: "Dressed as a common man, I walk the streets! I bow! I ask permission to do this or that! I follow the publication of a work on natural history that has apparently absorbed my whole knowing life, *I, who should command all!*"

The book's author had never seen the letters themselves. She had been given a notebook into which Maria Audubon, the artist's granddaughter, had written excerpts—fragments that she thought might be relevant to the mystery of the man's identity. Were these actual quotes from real letters? As a teenager, I saw no reason to doubt them. I did not know that Maria Audubon had erased and rewritten history.

It was Maria who had published in the 1890s a volume purporting to be excerpts from her grandfather's journals, but featuring omissions, changes, and even new added passages. It was Maria who had then burned almost all the original journals, putting them forever beyond the reach of historians. All of Audubon's descendants had a vested interest in polishing the man's reputation, but it was Maria who went to the greatest lengths to make it happen.

So these ambiguous lines—never quite claiming royal birth—could have come from Audubon's letters, reflecting his flair for drama, or they could have come from Maria's imagination, reflecting what she thought he *should have* written. In family lore, that he would not lay claim to being the Dauphin was taken as evidence that that's who he was, acting on a noble promise to keep his identity secret.

Was Audubon born into a royal family? Was he of mixed race? Historians say no. They have settled his identity to their satisfaction. At the same time, ornithologists have settled the identities of all those Louisiana birds: they've sorted out the warblers, flycatchers, blackbirds, and all the rest, they know what is related to what. In both cases, I respect their work and I'm almost certain they are correct. But I will hold on to that "almost." A little uncertainty is not bad, and mystery sometimes has the power to enrich our lives as much as settled facts.

5

Feuding in Philadelphia

"This is the hawk that Audubon stole, so he could name it for his friend Harris," Matthew said, holding up the stiff, neatly stuffed skin of a sooty-brown hawk with chestnut shoulders. "At least, all the evidence points to this being the type specimen itself." He scanned the rest of the tray, his eyes intense but bemused behind his glasses. "And this is Alexander Wilson's original specimen of the American Goshawk. The one that was misplaced for more than 170 years. I think you read my papers on these two birds."

We were standing on the fourth floor of the Academy of Natural Sciences, among rows of gleaming white metal cabinets filled with biological vouchers from all over the world. Outside were the tall modern buildings and bustling streets of Center City, Philadelphia. In the tray in front of us were relics of another age. Here was that goshawk, and here was a Broad-winged Hawk that Wilson had taken at Bartram's Garden. Here was the bird that would have been Morton's Hawk, except that Audubon snatched it from the Academy and took it away to describe it as Harris's Hawk instead. Here were two species of flycatchers that Spencer Baird, still a teenager at the time, had discovered west of Philadelphia, helping to launch his career as a leading ornithologist. I felt a wave of awe as I looked at these specimens. These were physical connections to those who had pursued birds two centuries ago.

There are many reasons why Philadelphia is so central in the history of American ornithology. Most of those reasons go back many years. But one reason is recent: the work of a polymath named Matthew R. Halley. Although Halley is now the assistant curator of birds down the road at the Delaware Museum of Nature & Science, he is still a research associate of the Academy of Natural Sciences and a frequent visitor at the historic Wyck House (where he lived for a while), the American Philosophical Society, and other key historical sites in Philadelphia. Since 2010, Halley has been systematically tracking down unpublished letters and manuscripts, piecing together brief mentions in archives and ledgers, and revolutionizing what we know about the origins of modern bird study.

History is a living thing in the Philadelphia region, where many buildings have stood since the eighteenth century and some families can trace back seven generations or more. A stack of letters in a drawer or a box of record books in an attic can be a treasure trove of historical detail, but only for the person who knows enough to interpret it. Matthew Halley has made numerous such discoveries of primary sources that were once unknown or unrecognized. His many published papers, even during the time I've been writing this book, have inspired me to alter my views of history over and over.

But history is just one of Halley's pursuits, and he's also using futuristic techniques in his research on thrushes and other birds. When I visited recently, the two of us toured sites from the fabulous Wyck House, started in 1690, to the shadow of the sixty-story Comcast Technology Center in downtown Philadelphia, completed in 2018. Our hours of intense conversation ranged over the highlights of bird study from a span of more than three centuries.

In the realm of personal history, I have my own Philadelphia connection. It's anchored here at the Academy of Natural Sciences. Through a fluke, I had the opportunity to work in the ornithology department in the mid-1980s. Although it was a temporary position that lasted only a year and a half, it had a profound influence on my trajectory in bird study.

I didn't learn much about history at the time. I was vaguely aware that Philadelphia had sites and artifacts like the Liberty Bell and Independence Hall, but my focus was on working at the Academy in that moment. It was an amazing place to be. Frank Gill, one of the most dynamic ornithologists of the era, was the head of the bird department: a scholar of the first order, but accessible and friendly, too. Every day I got to talk with other leaders in the field. This ornithology department was looking toward the future. Only much later would I realize that the Academy was also a priceless connection to ornithology's deep history. So I would return, coming full circle, to see what I had missed.

When modern birders in the U.S. think about bird study in the early 1800s—if they do at all—they think of Audubon first and last. His flamboyant, outrageous personality and his outsized drawings are enough to suck all the oxygen out of the subject, leaving other ornithologists as footnotes.

Thus, Alexander Wilson may come across as pallid and two-dimensional. We may give a nod to his pioneering publication, but we forget the bold audacity of his work, his keen powers of perception, his poetic sense, and his biting, caustic wit. Charles Lucien Bonaparte is often summarized merely as Napoleon's nephew—and isn't it nice that he liked birds?—without acknowledging his major contributions to science in both Europe and North America. George Ord fares worst of all because he shows up mainly in Audubon biographies, where he enters the stage as the bad guy: the harshest critic. Seldom mentioned is the fact that almost all his criticisms of Audubon were accurate and justified.

Wilson, Bonaparte, Ord, and Audubon: Philadelphia was the place where their stories intersected. Their confluence there was no coincidence.

For most of the 1700s, Philadelphia had been the largest city in the American colonies and then in the fledgling United States, and it had been the new nation's capital for a while in the 1790s. By the early 1800s it had lost both these distinctions, but continued to be a major center for culture and science. As of the 1820s (and for decades thereafter) it was North America's epicenter for nature study.

Philadelphia was the home of the American Philosophical Society, founded by Ben Franklin and others in 1743, when the word "philosophy" embraced all the sciences. It was the home of William Bartram (until his death in 1823) and of Bartram's Garden. It was the home of Charles Willson Peale's museum, which had the largest public displays of bird specimens and other natural objects in the United States.

And in the connection that carries the most meaning for me, Philadelphia was the home of the Academy of Natural Sciences. Founded in 1812 by a small group of friends, by the 1820s the Academy was recognized as the leading institution for natural history studies in the New World. The list of those elected to membership read like a Who's Who of American naturalists, and many top scientists from Europe were corresponding members.

Local businessman George Ord had already made a name for himself by, among other things, completing and publishing the last two volumes of Wilson's *American Ornithology*. He was elected to membership in the Academy of Natural Sciences in 1815, and soon became vice president. In the 1820s he was preparing to reissue all nine of Wilson's volumes, with some significant edits and additions. Given his stature at the Academy and his connection to Wilson, George Ord was certainly one of the most influential ornithologists in the country at that time, and any newcomers would have found it wise to stay on his good side.

Charles Lucien Bonaparte, the prince of Musignano, almost failed this test when he arrived on the scene in Philadelphia.

Charles had been born in Paris in 1803 and raised mostly in Italy, with a few years in England. His father, Lucien Bonaparte, had chosen wisely in deciding when to support and when to oppose his older brother Napoleon. As a result of this strategy, even during Napoleon's tempestuous career of conquest, rule, exile, return, defeat, and exile again, Lucien and his family had managed to avoid most negative consequences and maintain most of their accumulated wealth. Young Charles's childhood was unusual, but not especially dangerous, and he acquired a superb education. Even by the age of twelve, that education, through his own choice, was increasingly focused on natural history. In his teens he read works in multiple languages on plants, insects, and birds, and the latter came to dominate his attention.

So birds were on his mind when he came to the United States in 1823, at the age of twenty. He had just married his cousin Zénaïde—for whom he would later name a genus of doves—and the young couple crossed the Atlantic to live for a time with her father, Charles's uncle, Joseph Bonaparte, who had an estate in New Jersey not far from Philadelphia.

Unlike Wilson and Audubon, who had come to America knowing little about birds, Bonaparte arrived with a solid basis in ornithology. In Europe he'd had access to libraries and museum collections, and had met some of the continent's top experts. It's likely he had already read Wilson's *American Ornithology* and had begun to compare its classification and names to those used in Europe. Such comparisons became a focus for him after he arrived in this country.

In his early months in New Jersey he explored natural history around his uncle's estate, but he and his wife moved into Philadelphia for the winter of 1823–24, where his orbit included the leading scientists of the city. By late February he was elected to membership in the Academy of Natural Sciences. He attended a meeting of the Academy in March and presented the first section of a lengthy paper, "Observations on the Nomenclature of Wilson's Ornithology."

It was the start of what would become a prodigious output. Bonaparte went on to produce four volumes of *American Ornithology; or, the Natural History of Birds Inhabiting the United States, Not Given by Wilson*. It was, as the title suggests, a detailed supplement to Wilson's original work, adding more species. Because Bonaparte himself was no artist, he hired Titian Peale (one of the sons of Charles Willson Peale, and a competent naturalist) and Alexander Rider to draw the illustrations for the new volumes; the engraving would be accomplished by Alexander Lawson, who had done the same for Wilson's work. Bonaparte went on to publish several landmark works comparing the bird species of North America and Europe, based on his unrivaled knowledge of the birdlife of both continents. Between the 1820s and the 1850s, no one did more to advance the science of classifying and naming birds.

At the beginning, though, he got off to a bad start with George Ord. Bonaparte was careful to acknowledge the importance of Alexander Wilson's work, and to say that any problems in the names used in his *Ornithology* resulted from lack of access to large collections and the latest publications. Even so, Ord seemed offended by the idea that he would question Wilson's conclusions. In a letter to Bonaparte, Ord offered a comment supposedly quoted from a visiting English scientist "who cannot see the propriety of a Frenchman's attempting, or presuming, to meddle with the nomenclature of Wilson's Ornithology."

A short time later, the two had a testy exchange about the use of titles. Charles objected when Ord referred to him as "Mr. Bonaparte." Technically at that time he was designated in the family dynasty as a count, not a prince, but the Americans didn't know that, and he wasn't about to abandon royal status and become a mere Mister. Ord relented, but the use of the title still rankled him. Friction between the two men would continue for years.

But any irritation that Ord felt toward Bonaparte that spring would be eclipsed by the splashy arrival of John James Audubon in Philadelphia.

I've often wondered what interactions Audubon and Wilson might have had if Wilson had not died in 1813, at only forty-seven years old. Would Audubon have been influenced to be more careful and scientific in his approach? Would they have collaborated? Would they have become friends?

We'll never know. It might have been hard for Audubon to overcome his jealousy of the older man. Wilson had enjoyed huge advantages because of his location in the Philadelphia area. He'd had access to William Bartram's guidance and his library. He'd had access to Peale's Museum, with its hundreds of labeled specimens. His employer had put up the money to print the first volume of his *Ornithology*. Bartram had put him in touch with Thomas Jefferson and other scholars. Audubon, laboring out on the frontier, struggled for years to overcome his lack of such resources.

The jealousy could have cut both ways. Wilson, by all accounts, was usually alone, and tended to be melancholy. His attempts at romance all seem to have ended badly. When he met Audubon in Louisville in March 1810, the young Frenchman had a beautiful and vivacious wife, a healthy baby boy, and a lively social life with a circle of local friends. And on top of that, he seemed to have a natural talent for drawing birds. It must have seemed unfair.

More than a decade after Wilson's death, echoes of these jealousies surfaced after Audubon returned to Philadelphia in April 1824. He had visited the city many times during his early days at nearby Mill Grove. Later, on an extended trip back east from Kentucky, he had come to call on Alexander Wilson in December 1811 (finding him cordial but cool) and then returned to the city in July 1812 to become officially an American citizen. Now he was back with a different focus: he was carrying his growing collection of bird portraits, and trying to work out how to get them published.

Not long after arriving, he was introduced to Charles Lucien Bonaparte. The prince was short and rather stout, with some of the same handsome features as his uncle Napoleon. Not yet twenty-one, he had spent most of his life in palaces and grand estates. Audubon, almost thirty-nine, was tall and thin, with a backwoods air born of several years in dire poverty out on the frontier. But they hit it off. Bonaparte praised Audubon's bird drawings, and they spent hours in animated discussions of ornithology.

Not everyone shared the prince's enthusiasm for his new friend. Taken to meet Titian Peale, who was just getting started on illustrations for Bonaparte's planned book, Audubon set a sour tone by stating that Peale's bird drawings were not very good: "He represented them as if seated for a portrait, instead of with their own lively animated ways." Then he was introduced to the engraver, Lawson, who took an immediate dislike to Audubon and was harshly critical of his illustrations. "Ornithology requires truth and correct lines," he said; "here are neither!" Lawson also looked at an Audubon drawing of a Great Horned Owl and declared it to be plagiarized from a figure by Wilson—reversed and enlarged, but still the same drawing.

Lawson's reaction may have resulted partly from his own involvement with Wilson's *American Ornithology* and his close association with George Ord. It was Ord who would become Audubon's most persistent critic in the American scientific community. The enmity between the two of them would never end.

Their interaction began mildly enough. Bonaparte brought the artist to a meeting of the Academy of Natural Sciences, where he showed off some of his portfolio of birds, to a general round of approval. At the time, Ord reportedly objected to having detailed illustrations of plants and birds combined in the same paintings. (Mark Catesby had created similar combinations a century earlier, but local hero Alexander Wilson had employed only minimal plant matter and backgrounds in his illustrations, the better to emphasize the birds.) Other than that, Ord seems to have agreed with the other members present that the birds were well drawn. By a few months later, his attitude hardened. In July 1824, Audubon was nominated for a corresponding membership in the Academy. Even though he was sponsored by three prominent members, at the vote a month later his nomination was denied.

The stinging rebuke of that rejection would bother him for years.

The Philadelphia visit had been good for him in many ways. The connection with Charles Bonaparte would have lasting value. He met many of the leading local naturalists, including Reuben Haines III, owner of the Wyck estate; Haines even took him on a carriage ride out to visit Mill Grove, where Audubon had lived after his arrival in America in 1803. Best of all, he met Edward Harris, a prosperous young gentleman farmer and talented naturalist from across the river in Moorestown, New Jersey. Harris endeared himself to the artist by buying some of his drawings and slipping him an extra hundred dollars to help the cash-strapped Audubon continue his work. ("I would have kissed him," Audubon wrote, "but that is not the custom in this icy city.") The two men formed a lasting friendship that would culminate in two great westward treks in later years.

Still, being denied membership in the Academy was a blow to

Audubon's large and fragile ego. No detailed record of the vote survives, but it's safe to assume that George Ord, in his position as vice president of the Academy, played a part in blocking him from membership.

By all contemporary accounts, Ord had a chilly demeanor, generally unfriendly or even rude. This is often taken as an excuse to cast him in a negative light, as if personality were all that mattered. The standard narrative for years has been that he opposed Audubon for purely self-ish reasons, to protect his own investment in Alexander Wilson's legacy against competition from this upstart. Now it appears the story is not so simple. New research by Matthew Halley suggests that Ord had good reason to be incensed at Audubon in that summer of 1824.

At the heart of the story is the Small-headed Flycatcher. It has been responsible for a degree of controversy that seems unwarranted for a dull, featureless bird that probably never existed.

Alexander Wilson described and illustrated *Muscicapa minuta*, the Small-headed Flycatcher, in volume six of *American Ornithology* in 1812. He had shot one in an orchard in April, he wrote, and others in swamps of New Jersey in June. His illustration matches the general appearance of an American warbler, not anything that would be called a flycatcher today. As warblers go, it's decidedly average, olive above and yellowish below, with pale wing bars and white spots in the outer tail feathers. A pale ring around the eye is visible in the illustration, but not mentioned in the text. Aside from Wilson's claim of "head remarkably small," there's nothing notable about it.

It probably would have been shrugged off as unidentifiable and unimportant except that John James Audubon, a quarter century later, illustrated and wrote about what he claimed was the same bird. Furthermore, he claimed that he had discovered it first, and that Wilson had plagiarized it from him.

Everything about the claim is bizarre. Audubon included it on almost the last color plate of *The Birds of America*—number 434 out of 435—and in the last volume of *Ornithological Biography*, published in 1839. In the latter, he wrote of discovering the species in the early spring of 1808* near Louisville, Kentucky, and making a drawing of it, which, by coincidence, was not among the many drawings destroyed a few years later by rats. He continued: "When Alexander Wilson visited me at Louisville, he found in my already large collection of drawings, a figure of the present species, which, being at that time unknown to him, he copied and afterwards published in his great work, but without acknowledging the privilege that had thus been granted to him." In other words, *he stole my bird*. Audubon went on to cast doubt on Wilson's claim to have found the bird in New Jersey: "All my endeavours to trace it in that section of the country have failed. . . . I have never seen it out of Kentucky. . . . In Philadelphia, Baltimore, New York, or farther eastward or southward, in our Atlantic districts, I never saw a single individual, not even in museums, private collections, or for sale in bird-stuffers' shops."

If Audubon had not stated definitively that his bird was the same as Wilson's, it's doubtful anyone else would have come to that conclusion. Their descriptions and illustrations, vague though they are, don't really match. The face pattern as shown in Audubon's original watercolor is somewhat different from what appears in his engraved color plate, and both differ from Wilson's published version, with a more obvious white eye-ring and a more blended change of color on the face. The two illustrators show the wing pattern differently, with Audubon showing exceptionally narrow white wing bars. Their descriptions of foot color differ. Audubon, unlike Wilson, doesn't regard the bird's head as unusually small.

Did these two really illustrate the same bird, and if so, what was it? Several ornithologists have tried to answer the latter question, even writing lengthy papers in scientific journals. I admire the effort, but I

---

*Sometime in early spring 1808, Audubon left Kentucky and returned to Pennsylvania, where he and Lucy were married in early April. The two of them then traveled west to Louisville together, arriving around the beginning of May. It's hard to see how he could have had time to discover and draw this bird. However, in his writings he often contradicted himself about dates, even regarding events that definitely happened, so we can't read too much into this apparent conflict.

think it's a dead end. The few characteristics ascribed to the bird are all common. The bird could be considered a generic confusing warbler, lacking any of the diagnostic field marks that birders hope for.

Given the state of knowledge at that time, Audubon could have given his Kentucky bird a different name, calling it a new species, and no one would have thought anything of it. Attacking Wilson with charges of plagiarism was a conscious choice.

This drab bird was no avian Helen of Troy, and it's hard to imagine it sparking a war, but it did. And apparently the war began early. We had assumed that Audubon's account in *Ornithological Biography* in 1839 was the first time he had leveled the charge of plagiarism; but Matthew Halley has turned up evidence that he made that accusation first in 1824 in Philadelphia, to an audience of Wilson's admirers.

Even for Audubon, that was a brash move. He could not have failed to recognize how the man's memory was revered by the locals. He compounded his recklessness by claiming further details about Wilson's 1810 visit to Louisville—details disproven when George Ord produced Wilson's diary covering that time. As Ord wrote of the incident later, "The members of the Academy would have had no objection to Mr. Audubon provided they had thought him to be an honest man." Caught in a lie, the visitor lost his chance at membership and gained an implacable enemy.

From then on, Ord's intense dislike for Audubon and his work never wavered. Much of his criticism was expressed in letters to the British naturalist Charles Waterton, who shared his perceptions of the artist. In one 1833 letter, he explained that he had refused to write any reviews of Audubon's work, because "I am confident that I would have a swarm of hornets about my ears, were I to proclaim to the world all that I know of this imprudent pretender, and his stupid book. His elephant folio plates, so far from deserving the encomiums which are daily lavished upon them, are so vile, that I wonder how anyone [with] the least taste or knowledge in the fine arts, can endure them."

The words seem unnecessarily harsh. But by that time, Ord had reason to criticize something much bigger than the Small-headed

Flycatcher: Audubon's fabulous, famous, and utterly fictitious "Bird of Washington."

It was among the first to be pictured in *The Birds of America*—plate 11 in the first volume. A huge brown eagle in regal upright pose on a rock, occupying the entire image, it was labeled: "Bird of Washington, *Falco washingtonii.*" Definitely an eagle (the generic name *Falco* was applied to most birds of prey at that time). But what kind?

North America has two widespread species, Golden Eagle and Bald Eagle. Both show striking changes in plumage pattern as they mature. In Wilson's day, those transitions in color still caused major confusion. In his seventh volume in 1813, Wilson illustrated young birds of both species, and mischaracterized both. He depicted a young Golden Eagle under the name "Ring-tail Eagle," remarking that "in its general appearance it has great resemblance to the Golden Eagle." The brown bird next to it was labeled "Sea Eagle," but he was closing in on the truth: "This Eagle inhabits the same countries, frequents the same situations, and lives on the same kind of food as the Bald Eagle, with whom it is often seen in company. . . . I have strong suspicions, notwithstanding ancient and very respectable authorities to the contrary, of its being the same species, only in a different stage of color." Which, as we now know, it was.*

By the 1820s, that confusion was past. Audubon certainly was familiar with the solid-brown young Bald Eagle: he painted it separately for plate 126 in *The Birds of America*, after having portrayed the white-headed adult in plate 31. But he insisted the Bird of Washington was different. It was much larger, he said, giving measurements that would have made it more than 25 percent larger than the Bald Eagle, including a wingspan of more than ten feet. The arrangement of scales on its feet was different from that of other eagles. Most tellingly, this could not have been the younger stage of the Bald Eagle or any other species, he

---

*Charles Willson Peale had figured out the plumage sequence of the Bald Eagle and had described it in a letter to a French naturalist in 1797, but it took time for this knowledge to be widely accepted.

said, because he had observed a pair of adult Birds of Washington feeding their own young in a nest in Kentucky. Conveniently for the story, when he went back to collect the whole family to have evidence for his sighting, the nest had been abandoned.

The text about this supposed new species was included in the first volume of his *Ornithological Biography* in 1831. But three years earlier, during an extended stay in Britain to oversee engraving and printing of his color plates, he wrote a popular version of the same account. "Notes on the Bird of Washington (*Fálco Washingtoniàna*), or Great American Sea Eagle," was published in 1828 in a new nature magazine in England. By that time he had shown his drawing of the bird to gatherings of scientists and scholars, and included it in exhibitions of his work in Liverpool and Edinburgh. The noble, spectacular "Bird of Washington" was a sensation overseas before it ever drew much notice in America.

For people in England, steeped in the romance of James Fenimore Cooper's novels—*The Last of the Mohicans* had just been published—it was easy to imagine the new continent as a wilderness where such marvelous creatures might lurk unrevealed. For naturalists with experience in the United States, it was harder to accept the idea that the largest eagle had been somehow overlooked by everyone before Audubon.

The artist Titian Peale, probably still smarting from Audubon's criticism, was among the first to question the validity of the bird. George Ord was another. Audubon managed to hurt his own case, in a typical instance of overconfidence. During a March 1830 visit to Philadelphia, he and his friend Richard Harlan saw two brown young Bald Eagles that had been captured by humans. One was alive, and Audubon told Harlan that eventually it would mature and show the white head of the adult. The other was safely dead and stuffed, and wouldn't be changing any more, so Audubon impressed his friend by pronouncing it an example of the Bird of Washington.

Unfortunately for him, Harlan went back later to buy the stuffed specimen and proudly present it to the Academy of Natural Sciences, where it was available for study by others. Competent ornithologists recognized it as a young Bald Eagle. But Audubon, cushioned by his

Drawn from Nature by T. R. Peale

GREAT AMERICAN SEA EAGLE.

Falco Washingtonii. &c.

growing reputation and on the move, couldn't be pinned down. For those at a distance, he could casually mention that a specimen in a Philadelphia museum confirmed his bird's existence. For those who had seen the specimen, he could say it was a mistake.

Audubon never wavered on his claim of this new species. In publications in the 1840s he would call it "Washington Sea-Eagle, *Haliaetus Washingtoni*," but the illustration and text would remain the same. His adversaries never relented from questioning it, but they couldn't prove it was fictitious. They might have feared that if they called it a hoax, they would be humiliated by someone bringing in a specimen of a huge brown eagle with odd foot scales. Maybe it was out there after all. In the phrase popular today with those who seek Bigfoot, space aliens, or other nonexistent beings, absence of proof is not proof of absence.

The definitive word on the "Bird of Washington" would not be published until 2020, and once again it was Matthew Halley whose research provided the final missing pieces. Halley detailed not only the fraud but also the likely motivation for it.

In a 1996 study, art historian Linda Dugan Partridge had pointed out for the first time that the Bird of Washington appears to be copied directly from an early nineteenth-century publication: *The Cyclopaedia*, edited by Abraham Rees and issued serially between 1802 and 1820. There were British and American editions (and Alexander Wilson had worked as an editor on the American edition), and it's not clear which Audubon would have seen. But his mystery eagle is clearly based on *The Cyclopaedia*'s illustration of a supposed Golden Eagle. As detailed by

opposite page: The infamous "Bird of Washington." Audubon claimed to have discovered the largest and most magnificent bird of prey in America, a full 25 percent larger than the Bald Eagle. He named it for George Washington and included it among the first color plates for his *Birds of America*. There is no evidence that such a bird ever existed. For more than a century, biographers have tried to explain how Audubon could have made such a mistake. A better explanation is that he simply invented this spectacular, fictional eagle to draw attention to the publication he was launching.

Partridge, Audubon's bird is more skillfully drawn, but shows the same angle of the head, the same wing position, the same (incorrect) number of tail feathers, even the same highlight in the eye. Only the feet are markedly different. But as Halley discovered, the one foot fully visible on Audubon's bird is an exact match for another illustration elsewhere in *The Cyclopaedia*, a diagram of the foot of a generic bird of prey.

But why? What would drive him to copy from a source that might have been known to many, and then present it as a new species? Halley points out that Audubon had originally labeled his painting in a way suggesting it was a young Bald Eagle. He applied the "Bird of Washington" name later, after he was in England, added his fake measurements to the painting, and fabricated a story about its nesting habits and great size. Why such a high-profile and seemingly random deception?

Halley's painstaking analysis of the timing of events offers some clues. Audubon's 1824 visit to Philadelphia, and his rejection by the Academy and by key individuals there, ended his hopes for getting *The Birds of America* engraved and printed in the United States. He had already been considering the possibility of taking the project to Britain or Europe, and after Philadelphia that became his firm plan. He arrived in Britain in July 1826, and by early 1827 he had engaged William Lizars, of Edinburgh, to engrave the copper plates of his birds and oversee the printing and hand-coloring of the plates. Lizars produced the first ten plates, representing the first two sets of five that subscribers had been promised. But delays dogged the work, and it appeared the whole project might come to a halt.

In Audubon's mind, the situation must have seemed dire. Against all odds, after his disappointments in America, he had crossed the ocean and found acceptance, acclaim, and even a path to publication. But now that path was fading. He found another engraver—Robert Havell Jr., in London—who had the skills to carry out the work, if only Audubon could round up enough subscribers to keep the project going. It was time for extreme measures. To start off the third set of plates in a grand way, he set Havell to work on his imaginary great discovery, his wilderness prize, the largest eagle in America, the Bird of Washington.

It was brilliant marketing. By that time, half a century after the American Revolution, many in Britain were fascinated by George Washington, and eager to believe the story of this noble bird named for him. Even respected scientists there were convinced at first. The enthusiastic reception overseas helped to plant the Bird of Washington in America's imagination. By the late 1830s it had been celebrated in popular books and articles, and the ornithologists who doubted the bird's existence were reluctant to say so in public.

The one universal human superpower is that of self-justification. Somehow, no matter what we do, we find some way to justify it to ourselves. It seems Audubon was gifted with this superpower more than most, but even in his long string of fictions, it's hard to see how he rationalized the invention of his Bird of Washington.

A few hints come in his journals from November 1821, when he was traveling by flatboat downriver to New Orleans (one of his few original journals that was not later burned by his granddaughter Maria). On November 15 on the lower Ohio River he wrote, "Saw more than a Dozen of Eagles and one I had a good view of had a White Tail & a Brown head, Again [Yet] I remark'd that the *Brown Eagles In Ohio* Esp. were at Least 1/4 Larger than the White headed ones." Eight days later on the Mississippi he wrote that he was "convinced that the *Bald Eagle* and the *Brown Eagle* are Two Diferent Species." Elsewhere on the same journey he was clear about understanding that the brown birds were just young Bald Eagles. Still, the idea of a larger all-brown eagle may have lingered in his thoughts. Regardless of why he chose to plagiarize the drawings from Rees's *Cyclopaedia*, it could have occurred to him later to use that illustration for the new eagle that, in his mind, *might* exist. And then it was just a few steps further to invent stories of finding a nest and shooting a specimen to make it all seem more plausible.

The "Bird of Washington" caper had been a terrific gamble. Apparently the message Audubon took from the experience was: *I can get away with anything.* Having pulled off a scientific fraud, he would later engage in scientific theft.

He had been admitted to membership in the Academy of Natural Sciences in 1832, eight years after first being nominated, but continued to have prickly relations with that organization. In the fall of 1836, he visited the Academy—which was now developing its own museum—with a specific goal. John Townsend was still traveling in the West, but he had sent back a collection of bird skins that included some species then undescribed to science. Audubon was eager to examine these, and to paint them and describe them if possible, but some Academy members objected. Wrangling ensued, with Thomas Nuttall and others arguing on Audubon's behalf. His friend Edward Harris even offered to pay an exorbitant amount for duplicate specimens. Finally he obtained examples of twelve new species to paint, with the agreement that all would be credited to Townsend as the describer. But as Audubon expressed later in his *Ornithological Biography*: "Seldom, if ever in my life, have I felt more disgusted with the conduct of any opponents of mine, than I was with the unfriendly boasters of their zeal for the advancement of ornithological science, who at the time existed in the fair city of Philadelphia."

Those feelings probably lingered during his brief visit in July 1837. He couldn't discount the Academy altogether—after all, they had even taken out an institutional subscription to *The Birds of America*, with several individuals chipping in to pay for it. But that summer they were behind on payments for the subscription, as so many subscribers perennially were. Before his visit, Audubon had written to Dr. Samuel Morton, then the corresponding secretary for the Academy, to ask if he could collect the money he was owed.

During that same period, Morton had received something else: a shipment of bird skins, accompanied by a manuscript of information about them, from Mississippi. A corresponding member there, J. C. Jenkins, was contributing these specimens to the Academy's growing collection. The prize among them was a hawk that Jenkins believed—correctly—to be undescribed. His intention was that his description should be published in the Academy's journal and the hawk should be named in honor of Dr. Morton himself.

But when the manuscript from Jenkins was read at a meeting of the Academy a few weeks later, listing the other bird specimens, there was no mention of the hawk. Coincidentally, by that time, John James Audubon had passed through Philadelphia on his way to England, where he would soon paint a bird he would call the Louisiana Hawk, *Falco Harrisii*.

It was the same bird—the same hawk from Mississippi that Jenkins had sent to Dr. Morton at the Academy. But Audubon's account of it in *Ornithological Biography* two years later didn't say so. Instead, he wrote: "The specimen from which I made my drawing, was procured by a gentleman residing in Louisiana, who shot it between Bayou Sara and Natchez. . . . I have received no information respecting its habits; nor can I at present give you the name of the donor, however anxious I am to compliment him upon the valuable addition he has made to our Fauna." But Audubon knew the source of the specimen. In an October 1837 letter to his friend, the Reverend John Bachman, he had written: "The Hawk I received from Natchez proves quite new, and it is a superb bird. I have received a letter from Doc*r* Jenkins of Natchez in which he says that it is not a very rare bird, giving me the measurements, color of the eyes etc." The "letter" was probably the manuscript that Jenkins had intended to have published by the Academy.

Did Samuel Morton give the specimen and manuscript to Audubon, perhaps in partial payment for the shortfall in subscription money? Did the artist simply see an opportunity to abscond with this treasure? Either way, J. C. Jenkins was robbed of his opportunity to name the species.

This brazen theft seems to have been overlooked by modern scholars until Matthew Halley put the pieces together. But apparently it was recognized at the time. Halley found an unpublished diary of J. C. Jenkins in which he plainly wrote that "Mr. Audubon obtained my first specimen, and described and named it without my knowledge or consent." And in the Academy archives is a list, dating from 1839, of borrowed specimens that Audubon was supposed to return; it includes "Hawk sent to the Acad. by Dr Jenkins from Mississippi, lent by Dr Morton to Mr Audubon—*Buteo Harrisi*."

Everyone knew it was Jenkins's hawk, but no one did anything about it.* Likewise, many in the scientific community realized the "Bird of Washington" must be a fraud, and many dismissed Audubon's claim that the "Small-headed Flycatcher" had been plagiarized by Wilson; but Audubon had become a celebrity, lionized on both sides of the Atlantic, and everyone seemed afraid to confront him.

It's tricky to guess at the thoughts of people who lived so long ago. But I have to wonder about the motivations of friends who went along with Audubon's stories. Edward Harris was a competent naturalist, but he seems never to have questioned his friend's statements. At one point he even claimed a possible sighting of a "Bird of Washington," although of course he didn't manage to obtain a specimen. John Bachman, who became a close friend and collaborator, can hardly have missed some of the inconsistencies in Audubon's tales, but we have no record that he called him out on any of them.

To me, the most intriguing questions surround Charles Lucien Bonaparte and his reactions to Audubon. As an acclaimed scientist and a member of a genuine royal family, Bonaparte had at least as much celebrity status as the bird painter, and no reason to be intimidated. He was also one of the most thorough and reliable ornithologists of that era, and should have been quick to spot dubious claims. He was aware of Audubon's potential for dishonesty—for example, his boast that he had studied painting with the French master Jacques-Louis David, a claim that Bonaparte easily disproved by checking with members of his own family. Yet he seems never to have confronted Audubon directly. Even when it came to the fabulous, fictitious "Bird of Washington," he had little to say. He included it in one of his major publications in 1838, *A Geographical and Comparative List of the Birds of Europe and North America*, noting that it had been named by Audubon and lived in the "northern parts" of North America. A dozen years later in another

---

*Jenkins deserved credit for this notable find. The bird we now call Harris's Hawk is common in southern Texas, but it's only a rare visitor in Louisiana and even more unexpected as far east as Mississippi.

publication, he reduced Audubon's *washingtonii* to a synonym of the Bald Eagle, but without comment.

In failing to challenge Audubon about his Bird of Washington, perhaps Bonaparte was simply being diplomatic. Given his family background, he might have understood diplomacy better than most. Later in his life he would be active in politics in Europe (by then, he could claim the title of prince of Musignano with no complications), but he never ceased his prodigious output on natural science, especially birds. When he died in 1857 he had been working on the second volume of a detailed treatment of the birds of the world.

Bonaparte spent only a few years in the Philadelphia area before going back to Europe for good. But his time there was essential to his foundation as an international expert, and his work contributed to major advances in bird classification on both sides of the Atlantic. Most modern birders, especially in the United States, seem unaware of his historic influence, but that may be partly because his efforts were divided between the two continents.

But he's connected to his temporary American home in one way. There's a small, beautiful species of gull, common and widespread, that we now call Bonaparte's Gull, and it bears the specific name of *philadelphia*. (Formerly in the genus *Larus*, it is now *Chroicocephalus philadelphia*.) It's appropriate and it might seem intentional, but it came about entirely by chance. Bonaparte himself was the first to describe the adult plumage of this bird; but he didn't name it for himself, or for Philadelphia, and he isn't credited as the describer.

Birders today often struggle to identify the many species of gulls. Some of the easiest to recognize are the smaller gulls that develop black hoods in the breeding season. These tend to be distinctive at all ages, and they usually achieve adult plumage at the age of two or three years, unlike larger gulls that may take four years and go through more intermediate stages. But in the early days of ornithology, even the smaller hooded gulls created massive confusion.

Consider two species in which adults have dark hoods in breeding plumage. The Laughing Gull is common along the Atlantic Coast of North America. The Black-headed Gull is common in northwestern Europe. In size, bill shape, and wing pattern, they are easily separated. Linnaeus described and named them in editions of his *Systema Naturae* in 1758 and 1766. The Laughing Gull, which he called *Larus atricilla*, was originally based on the Laughing Gull illustrated by Mark Catesby, but by 1766 he had turned it into a composite by adding details about European specimens. The specific name *atricilla* means "black-tailed," even though the adult pictured by Catesby has a white tail. Linnaeus named the Black-headed Gull (which actually has a dark brown head) *Larus ridibundus*, even though *ridibundus* means "laughing." He got that name from the French ornithologist Brisson, who mistakenly thought the European bird was the same as Catesby's Laughing Gull. As you can see, the seeds for confusion were planted early.

Regardless, the British ornithologist John Latham distinguished these two in his *General Synopsis of Birds* in 1785. He got many details wrong (and mentioned a possible third species, the "Red-legged Gull," guessing correctly that it was a different plumage of the Black-headed), but at least he maintained them as separate species. Three decades later, though, George Ord rejected their distinctions. Ord was preparing the ninth and final volume of Wilson's *American Ornithology* for publication in 1814; Wilson had finished the illustrations for several species, including a fair rendition of a Laughing Gull. Ord wrote a good account of Laughing Gull's behavior and appearance, based on experience along the New Jersey coast—but he called it the Black-headed Gull. "We are inclined to the opinion, that the three Gulls of Latham, *viz.* the Black-headed G. the Red-legged G. and the Laughing G. are one and the same species, the very bird which we have been describing."

It was an understandable mistake, possibly one that Wilson himself would have made. When Ord issued a revised version of volume nine of *American Ornithology* in 1825, he took out the reference to Latham and substituted "Laughing" for "Black-headed" throughout the text. It's not clear whether he recognized the error or had just decided to change the name.

But what about the bird that we now call Bonaparte's Gull? It was still unrecognized at the time, even though C. W. Peale had had a specimen in his museum. Bonaparte's is quite similar to the genuine Black-headed Gull of Europe, with a long white triangle in the outer part of the wing, but smaller and differing in other subtle details. Bonaparte's is also much smaller than the genuine Laughing Gull of North America, which is much darker on the wings. Charles Bonaparte apparently was the first to publish the fact that it was different from both of these birds. He described it in his *Synopsis of the Birds of the United States* in 1828. The name he applied to it, Brown-masked Gull (*Larus capistratus*), already had been misused by the Dutch naturalist C. J. Temminck for a plumage of another bird. But at least Bonaparte had established the existence of a smaller, slender-billed species similar to the Black-headed Gull.

William Swainson and John Richardson wrote the next chapter in this bird's story in 1831, in their *Fauna Boreali-Americana; or the Zoology of the Northern Parts of British America*. In this landmark work on Canadian birds, they described a species they said was similar to Bonaparte's *Larus capistratus*, but not quite the same, and named it in his honor: Bonapartian Gull, *Larus Bonapartii*. With some changes in spelling, this English name has been used ever since, and that scientific name was used until the late 1850s.

So where did the *philadelphia* come from? Oddly, in a roundabout way, that goes back to George Ord. In 1815, just after he had finalized the last two volumes of Wilson's *Ornithology*, he contributed to a publication that's essentially unknown today: *A New Geographical, Historical, and Commercial Grammar; and Present State of the Several Kingdoms of the World*, by William Guthrie. (Yeah, I had never heard of it, either.) Among the miscellany packed into these volumes was a list of birds of the United States, compiled by Ord. Below the list, a footnote described in four brief lines a species new to science: the Banded-tail Tern, *Sterna Philadelphia*.

Banded-tail Tern? Well, Bonaparte's is a small gull, graceful in flight, often suggesting a tern. And when it's young, during its first

winter, it does have a dark band across the tail. Decades later, in 1858, George Lawrence and Spencer Baird decided that Ord's brief notes on this "tern" must have applied to a young Bonaparte's Gull, so his specific name had priority. Henceforth it would be scientifically known as *philadelphia*, and its English name would continue to honor Bonaparte.

Reflecting the importance of Philadelphia to ornithology, two other species besides this gull were named for the city: one warbler and one vireo. Their discovery stories were much simpler than that of Bonaparte's Gull (or the "Small-headed Flycatcher" or "Bird of Washington," for that matter), but the two were found and named four decades apart.

Alexander Wilson encountered the Mourning Warbler within a few miles of Philadelphia in early June, probably sometime before 1809.* When he published its description in the second volume of *American Ornithology* in 1810, he still had not found another individual. During those years Wilson was having a lot of trouble with warblers, including birds he didn't realize were warblers, but he was confident that this one was distinct: "I have now the honor of introducing to the notice of naturalists and others, a very modest and neat little species, which has hitherto eluded their research." Modest and neat indeed, with an olive back, yellow belly, gray hood, and black patch on the chest. Wilson was developing a habit of giving his warblers English names honoring the places he'd found them—Tennessee Warbler, Cape May Warbler, Kentucky

---

*C. W. Peale had collected an individual and had the specimen in his museum, but he thought it matched the Masked Yellowthroat, described previously from South America. Wilson apparently didn't recognize the similarity between his new find and Peale's specimen.

opposite page: Bonaparte's Gulls, two adults in breeding plumage and one young bird, by John James Audubon. The scientific name of this bird (*Chroicocephalus philadelphia*) honors the city of Philadelphia, and the English name honors Charles Bonaparte, who lived in the city for a time. But this convergence of names came about purely by coincidence.

Warbler—but in this case he chose one based on the gray hood and black breastplate, suggesting a bird dressed in mourning. He placed the geographic modifier in the scientific name instead: *Sylvia philadelphia*. It's now *Geothlypis philadelphia*, but we still call it Mourning Warbler.

Today we know that Mourning Warblers are common in summer in southeastern Canada and parts of the northeastern states, spending the winter mostly in South America. Birders regard them as elusive. These warblers tend to skulk in dense low growth and they migrate north relatively late in spring, after the thickets are fully leafed out, making it easier for them to hide.

Far more elusive in a historical sense was the Philadelphia Vireo, which managed to evade Wilson, Audubon, and all their contemporaries. John Cassin introduced it to Western science in a paper about the vireo family that he presented to the Academy of Natural Sciences of Philadelphia in February 1851—only weeks after Audubon had passed away at his home in New York.

Cassin had found this vireo years earlier: "I shot the bird now described in Bingham's woods near Philadelphia in September, 1842, but have never seen another specimen." He decided to go ahead and name it in 1851 because it seemed distinctive—like a Warbling Vireo, but smaller, with a shorter bill and more vivid colors—and because he was writing about vireos anyway. Within a few years, other specimens were found in Ohio and Wisconsin, but it was long considered rare and mysterious.

Birders today will understand how the Philadelphia Vireo escaped notice for so long. It's not rare: its breeding range extends across most of southern Canada, and during the winter it's widespread in Central America. But in migration it passes mostly through the Midwest, between the Mississippi River and the Appalachians, with fewer showing up in the middle Atlantic states, where most early ornithologists were concentrated. (Philadelphia is hardly a good place to seek the Philadelphia Vireo.) And it's almost always outnumbered by two relatives, the Warbling Vireo and the Red-eyed Vireo. As Cassin noted in his original description, it looks very much like a Warbling Vireo. It sounds even

Philadelphia Vireos among foliage of Virginia creeper (*Parthenocissus*), by Kenn Kaufman. This species is widespread as a migrant in eastern North America. Although it was eventually discovered in Philadelphia, it's uncommon there, and it was overlooked by all the leading naturalists based in that city in the early 1800s.

more like a Red-eyed Vireo. Their songs are essentially identical. Even after years of trying, I can't tell the songs of Philadelphia and Red-eyed apart with certainty. These vireos often sing while hidden among foliage high in trees, and since Red-eyeds are abundant, the occasional Philadelphia among them is easy to miss.

With a close view, the Philadelphia Vireo is sometimes mistaken for some kind of warbler. The vireos (family Vireonidae) and American warblers (family Parulidae) were vexing for the first European naturalists exploring our shores. They can still be confusing for birders today, but the two groups are quite distinct.

In North America north of Mexico, about a dozen vireo species occur regularly; warblers are much more varied, with well over fifty species. Curiously, the last full species of warbler in the East was discovered at almost the same time the last eastern vireo (the Philadelphia) was described and named, in 1851. Thereafter the vireos were pretty well understood. But the warblers continued to offer up surprising and complex challenges, much to the consternation and delight of the naturalists who pursued them.

Interlude:
Channeling the
Illustrator

Double Vision

They're everywhere, those Audubons. Most people in the United States (and many all over the world) have seen Audubon art re-productions, whether they realize it or not. The prints are framed on the walls of waiting rooms and dining rooms and office hallways. They adorn the walls in the backgrounds of movie sets. They're copied on tea towels and T-shirts and place mats. In the public domain for more than a century, the more popular ones have been reproduced and sold countless times.

Most people, even if they have stopped to look closely at these prints, aren't aware of one essential point about them: these are not exact copies of the originals. When Audubon was launching his *Birds of America*, no technology existed for making a direct reproduction of a painting. Every method available involved some intermediate step to produce something that could be printed.

Copper-plate engraving was the option considered state-of-the-art at that time. A skilled engraver would copy the details of the painting onto a thin sheet of copper, cutting fine lines and tiny pits into the metal. Ink applied to the copper plate would settle in the engraved spots, and that design in ink could be transferred to a sheet of paper. The resulting print, black lines and dots on white paper, could then be colored in by hand to approximate the look of the original.

Alexander Wilson, preparing his *American Ornithology*, had experimented with engraving his own copper plates in 1805. After assessing his less-than-stellar results, though, he had opted for having the work done by a professional: another Scottish immigrant, Alexander Lawson, Philadelphia's leading engraver during that period. Audubon apparently never even considered doing his own engraving. He had his hands full with trying to find as many bird species as possible and with producing hundreds of paintings; the essential task of engraving could be left to a specialist in that craft.

When Lawson and other engravers turned him down in the United States, it seemed a setback. But being forced to travel to England turned out to be a stroke of great luck. Audubon's rough clothing and mannerisms had marked him as a country rube in Philadelphia. In England they were even more out of place, but they made him interesting, an exotic character. He took advantage of it, leaning into the persona of the American Woodsman, turning himself into a selling point for his drawings. (He would become a master of public relations. In later years, when he headed off to a remote area like Labrador or the Missouri River, he would arrange for friends to send letters about his exploits to the newspapers to keep him in the public eye—essentially sending out press releases.)

Going overseas also gave him a reset as a bird expert. Friends and fans of Wilson in America were already suspicious of Audubon's claims, but British naturalists, dazzled by his artwork, saw no reason to doubt him. He was soon accepted and honored by scientific societies there, making it possible eventually for him to gain such honors in America as well.

Most important, though, in England he wound up working with Robert Havell Jr. of London, one of the most highly skilled engravers in the world at that time. Havell was a brilliant artist in his own right, and his masterful engravings added to the quality of the published plates.

Once they established their working relationship, Audubon often relied on Havell to finish details of the compositions—or more than details. His original watercolor of the Mountain Plover showed just the bird on plain paper, with a trace of shadow under its feet. Havell added an entire mountainous landscape behind it.* Similar collaborations, with Havell providing everything but the birds, produced several of the other color plates. Often these were of western birds that Audubon had never seen in life, drawn based on specimens provided by others, such as the California Quail, Black Oystercatcher, Steller's Eider, and Marbled Murrelet—as if he were less personally invested in these.

Even where Audubon's original was complete, Havell sometimes made improvements. His treatments of water in the background, such as reflections and details of waves, are often much better than in the originals.

However, even when the engraving hews closely to every original detail, differences in the resulting prints will be visible. Almost all the original watercolors for *The Birds of America* have been preserved: the New-York Historical Society bought them from the artist's widow in 1863. Images from the collection can be viewed on the Society's website, and they have been reproduced directly in book form in a couple of different editions. It's possible now for anyone to make comparisons between the works as they came from the artist's own hand and the much-better-known prints based on Havell's engravings.

Viewed closely enough, differences are apparent. In the prints, but not in the originals, narrow black outlines around objects usually can be seen. In the prints, subtle shading from light to dark is accomplished in a variety of ways, and with considerable skill, because Havell was a master of the technique called aquatint as well as regular engraving, etching,

---

*The Mountain Plover, despite its name, is a bird of flat, open grasslands. So Havell's background, though attractive, was misleading. But Audubon had never seen the bird and had only sketchy information about it from Thomas Nuttall, so he wouldn't have known the difference.

Mountain Plover by John James Audubon. In this composition, Audubon painted only the bird, and the entire background was supplied by his engraver, Robert Havell Jr. This was true for many of the plates in *The Birds of America*, especially toward the latter stages of the project, as Audubon came to rely more and more on Havell's artistic skills.

and drypoint; but even the smoothest gradation may show a mottled or stippled effect that differs from the appearance of the original watercolor. Large areas of plain color, such as blue skies or open waters, often look more even and smooth in the prints than in the originals.

When I first began working on my own pseudo-Audubons, trying to imagine how John James would have painted the birds he missed, I had to confront a decision: Should I seek to emulate the style of his originals, or of his universally known prints? The question would make only a small difference in the early stages of each drawing, but a bigger difference in how I finalized them.

In the end, I opted for a sort of compromise, a hybrid approach. I figured it gave me something of a hedge against criticism. If someone looked closely and said that my narrow dark outlines around objects were unrealistic, I could respond that such outlines were features of the engraved prints. If someone complained that part of a background was incomplete, I could claim that this was the way it was done in the original watercolors, and the engraver's colorists would fill it in. It was a cop-out—and I'm inclined to think that Audubon, if he had been placed in the same situation, would have done the same thing.

6

The Fugitive Warblers

For a few weeks every spring, all my friends in Europe hate me.

Okay, "hate" might be too strong a word. It's more like an intense level of envy, and for one reason: warblers. American warblers. Essentially all my friends are birders, and they know I live in one of the best places on the planet to see large numbers of American warblers in May.

The Lake Erie shoreline in northwestern Ohio, where I live today, can seem slow in the grip of hard winter. In spring, though, when migratory songbirds flood northward out of the tropics, they pause in key habitats along the shore, and concentrate in unbelievable numbers. Warblers are the undisputed stars here in May. The most famous place to see them, the boardwalk at a wildlife reserve called Magee Marsh, is just five miles from my front door—hence the jealousy of my British and European birding pals. When my local friends and I call our neighborhood "the Warbler Capital of the World," it's a claim that echoes around the global birding community.

The American warblers could serve as a litmus test to separate avid birders from normal people. Even here in the self-styled warbler capital, the average non-birder has never consciously seen one of these creatures. They are so tiny, so quick, so skilled at hiding behind leaves, that most people have no reason to be aware of them or to think of them at all.

Birders, on the other hand, obsess over warblers, pursue them, celebrate them, want to see them again and again. What accounts for this appeal? I think it's a balance of challenge and reward. Warblers are elusive and hard to see, but their beauty and variety make them worth the effort. More than three dozen species are possible here at Magee Marsh in May, although you never see them all on the same day. Some flit in the highest twigs and some lurk in the undergrowth; most have bright colors and sharp, elegant patterns. Rich yellow is a common theme, but green, orange, blue, chestnut, buff, black, and white also grace the palette. Males and females often look strikingly different. The brilliant colors of many males make them instantly recognizable—when you can see them clearly—but some females are so subtle that identifying them is a challenge.

And notably, many warblers change to a different, duller plumage in fall. That's part of what drives the urge to see them here in May. They pass through in a rush on their way north in spring, with only a few staying for the summer; when they come back through in the fall, they won't add up to such a colorful sensation. In the spring they're at their peak of warblerness, and that's the time to see them.

In Warbler Appreciation 101, it's extremely helpful to have good binoculars and to be well practiced in using them. (I started birding at the age of six but didn't acquire my first cheap binoculars until I was ten. During those first four years, despite my avid interest, I did not identify a single warbler.) It's also helpful to be in a place where these tiny travelers concentrate in spring migration, like certain spots along the Gulf Coast and around the Great Lakes. Thousands of birders flock to places like these to revel in the spring warbler celebration. It's like a daily treasure hunt, but the bright fragments of treasure are not buried in a trunk underground; they're dancing among the leaves, multicolored sparks of life and sheer magic.

Turn back the calendar, though, and a different picture emerges. In the 1920s a leading bird painter of the day, Francis Lee Jaques, quipped: "The difference between warblers and no warblers is very slight." The comment reflected his preference for big waterbirds he could include in dramatic compositions. He was probably also needling his birder friends, who knew that Jaques was happy to join them watching warblers in the spring. But the bird illustrators and pioneer ornithologists of a century earlier might have said the same thing, and they might have meant it in all seriousness.

At the beginning of the 1800s, the concept of bird families was not in use yet, and no one had recognized the American warblers as a group distinct from anything in Europe. When Alexander Wilson called a bird a warbler, he was not anticipating what we would call the American warbler family today. Instead, he meant that the bird should be classified in the genus *Sylvia*, which the Italian naturalist Giovanni Scopoli had established in 1769 for certain small, active, insect-eating birds in Europe.

When they encountered similar birds in North America, Wilson and his contemporaries would try to assign each to one of the genera included in the huge Linnaean order of Passeres. Studying birds we now recognize as American warblers, Wilson would identify them as thrushes, creepers, titmice, (European) warblers, or (European) flycatchers. Since they were unrelated to all of these, they never made a good fit, but Wilson forged ahead because he could see no other way to categorize these creatures.

Wilson's treatment of warblers reflected his overall approach to ornithology. Aware that he was far from centers of learning in Europe and had limited access to published works, he was reluctant to stray from the established framework of classification. Even when a new bird seemed unique, he would find a way to squeeze it into a known genus. Throughout the nine volumes of *American Ornithology*, even as he named many new species, he only proposed one new genus,* and his

---

*For the Red Crossbill, Wilson suggested the genus name *Curvirostra*. This species had been named *Loxia curvirostra* by Linnaeus in 1758, but Wilson objected to having the crossbills, with their unique bill shape, included in *Loxia* along with grosbeaks, finches, and many other thick-billed birds. In a way, later scientists agreed, but the genus *Loxia* now includes only the crossbills and nothing else.

name for it failed to catch on. But contrary to this timid approach on naming genera, he never hesitated to contradict European authorities about other aspects when he thought they were wrong.

And when it came to the birds we now recognize as warblers, he thought they were wrong frequently. Of the Hooded Warbler (which he called Hooded Flycatcher), he wrote: "Why those two judicious naturalists, Pennant and Latham, should have arranged this bird with the Warblers is to me unaccountable. . . . The bill is broad at the base, where it is beset with bristles; the upper mandible notched, and slightly overhanging at the tip; and the manners of the bird, in every respect, those of a Flycatcher." Again, about the warbler called the American Redstart: "Tho this bird has been classed by several of our most respectable ornithologists among the warblers, yet in no species are the characteristics of the genus Muscicapa more decisively marked; and in fact it is one of the most expert Flycatchers of its tribe." Regarding the Black-and-white Warbler, he pointed out that William Bartram originally had called it the Black and White Creeper. "Succeeding naturalists have classed it with the warblers; a mistake which I have endeavoured to rectify." On the other hand, the warbler now called Northern Parula had been considered a type of titmouse by various Europeans: "Notwithstanding the respectability of the above authorities, I must continue to consider this bird as a species of Warbler."

Designating species as either warblers or flycatchers rattled him. The bird he described under the name "Green Black-capt Flycatcher" is the same one we know today, ironically, as Wilson's Warbler. Of the Cerulean Warbler, he wrote: "It has many of the habits of the Flycatcher; tho, like the preceding, from the formation of its bill we must arrange it with the Warblers." Regarding the Blackpoll Warbler: "This bird may be considered as occupying an intermediate station between the Flycatchers and the Warblers, having the manners of the former, and the bill, partially, of the latter." The difficulty is understandable, because none of these species are related to the birds then recognized as (European) warblers or (European) flycatchers. Until ornithologists recognized American warblers as a unique family, disconnected from any in the Old World, it would be impossible for anyone to classify them properly.

Even without knowing to what category they belonged, it was still possible to recognize and name individual species. And Wilson did. Almost one-fourth of all the warblers in eastern North America—nine species—still bear the specific names that he gave them, although all have been shifted to different genera. Some of his "new" warblers were already known to Charles Willson Peale, William Bartram, and others, but hadn't received formal descriptions, so Wilson had the honor of naming them.

And he did clear up some misconceptions about American warblers. The Yellow-rumped Warbler is common enough in the middle Atlantic states that Wilson got to see it in all stages of plumage during spring and fall, and even in winter along the coast. He realized that its seasonal variations in color pattern had misled European authors into giving it multiple identities. "In this beautiful little species we have another instance of the mistakes occasioned by the change of color to which many of our birds are subject," he wrote. After listing three different warblers named by the Welsh naturalist Thomas Pennant, he added, "I am persuaded that the whole three have been drawn from the present species."

Still, Wilson himself was misled by variations in warblers, even though he recognized the special challenges of these birds. On his one trip west of the Appalachians, he named the Tennessee Warbler and Nashville Warbler for the places he had found them, not knowing those birds to be spring migrants on their way to Canada. Around Philadelphia, he realized that many warblers were transients, stopping briefly on their way to or from breeding grounds farther north—and he groused about the lack of data from those breeding grounds. Regarding Black-throated Blue Warblers: "It is highly probable that they breed in Canada; but the summer residents among the feathered race, on that part of the continent, are little known or attended to. The habits of the bear, the deer and beaver, are much more interesting to those people, and for a good substantial reason too, because more *lucrative*; and unless there should arrive an order from England for a cargo of skins of Warblers and Flycatchers, sufficient to make them an object worth speculation, we are likely to know as little of them hereafter as at present."

So he would do the best he could with brief encounters during spring and fall migrations. In the case of the Bay-breasted Warbler, seasonal change led him astray. The adult male of this species in spring plumage is distinctive, with markings of rich chestnut. William Bartram had mentioned it earlier, under the name "Little Chocolate-breasted Titmouse," but hadn't given it a proper description, so Wilson named it in 1810. "This very rare species passes thro Pennsylvania about the beginning of May, and soon disappears. . . . It is never seen here in summer, and very rarely on its return, owing, no doubt, to the greater abundance of foliage at that time, and to the silence and real scarcity of the species." A year later, he described and named the Autumnal Warbler. "This plain little species regularly visits Pennsylvania from the north in the month of October, gleaning among the willow leaves; but what is singular, is rarely seen in spring." Later he added, "These birds doubtless pass through Pennsylvania in spring, on their way to the north; but . . . I have never yet met with one of them in that season; tho in October I have seen more than a hundred in an afternoon's excursion."

The Autumnal Warbler was, as you've likely guessed, the fall plumage of the Bay-breasted Warbler. The seeming abundance of this bird in autumn probably helped to blind Wilson to the fact that this was the same species he considered so rare in spring. Actually, in the fall he was probably seeing a combination of Bay-breasted and Blackpoll Warblers. These two, so different in spring, both change in appearance in late summer, and look similar to each other during fall migration—even experienced birders today have to let some go as "Baypolls" if they're not seen well. For Wilson, laboring without binoculars, they all would have looked the same.

Other warblers gave him trouble for different reasons. The male Black-throated Blue Warbler, as colorful as its name suggests, looks the same all year, even when young, with little seasonal change. Wilson gave a good illustration and account of it in his second volume in 1810, although he claimed the female was very similar to the male. It isn't: the female looks different, dull buff and dark olive-brown, with mere hints of blue. In his fifth volume in 1812, Wilson introduced the female as a brand-new species, the Pine-swamp Warbler. He had found it in "the deepest and gloomiest pine and hemlock swamps of our mountainous regions," he wrote, and he had shot a male and two females.

Since he thought he had male and female specimens of both the Black-throated Blue and the Pine-swamp Warbler, he had no reason to suspect these names applied to two sexes of the same species. A problem for Wilson, and for many later ornithologists, was that the internal sex organs of these little birds can be small, and hard to judge—or even hard to find, especially after the bird has been shot. It's not rare for dead specimens of small birds to be mis-sexed.

So in another case, Wilson shot a Blackburnian Warbler (probably a young male) in Pennsylvania's Great Pine Swamp in summer and described it as a new species, the Hemlock Warbler. He was familiar with the adult male Blackburnian, with its flaming orange throat, and he knew that the female had the orange replaced by yellow; still, he failed to realize the identity of his supposed new bird. Again, after describing the Cerulean Warbler and giving a good illustration of a young male in 1810, he illustrated a female the following year and introduced it as a new species, the Blue-green Warbler. Finally, a bird he described and named the Blue-Mountain Warbler was probably a young female of the Black-throated Green Warbler, a species he already knew.

Given the difficult conditions under which he worked, it's not surprising Wilson went astray on some warbler questions. He seemed to acknowledge the challenges of the group in a comment he made about his Blue-Mountain Warbler: "Several of these solitary Warblers remain yet to be gleaned up from the airy heights of our alpine scenery, as well

opposite page: "Pine-swamp Warblers" by John James Audubon. This is actually the female plumage of the Black-throated Blue Warbler, but Alexander Wilson had described it as a distinct species in 1812, and other writers (including Audubon) followed his lead for more than two decades.

as from the recesses of our swamps and morasses, whither it is my design to pursue them by every opportunity."

As a reflection of Wilson's influence, other ornithologists accepted most of his mistaken new warblers without question for at least two decades after he described them. Charles Bonaparte, in his *Synopsis of Birds of the United States* in 1828, included entries for the Hemlock Warbler, Autumnal Warbler, Blue-green Warbler, Pine-swamp Warbler, and Blue-Mountain Warbler, all presented as full species with no doubts raised. In his *Manual of Ornithology* in 1832, Thomas Nuttall—who always seemed eager to accept any new bird proposed by anyone—included all of Wilson's nonentities, plus a couple of nonexistent warblers that Audubon had introduced by that time, and even a couple that can't be traced to any particular species, just to pad the list.

Audubon's interactions with American warblers were as complicated as Wilson's, but in different ways. At first, he accepted all of Wilson's proposed new species. And not only did he paint them, he also wrote about them as if he knew them well.

So, in Pennsylvania's Great Pine Swamp in the summer, Wilson had succeeded in shooting a single young male Blackburnian Warbler, the basis for his supposed Hemlock Warbler. Audubon went to what he thought was the same locality and reported he "procured upwards of twenty specimens" of Hemlock Warblers in less than a week, but apparently without noticing what they really were. He claimed to have found a pair tending a nest. He described the song of this supposed species: "Its notes are sweet and mellow, and although not numerous, are easily distinguished from those of any other Warbler." (As vague as it is, this description doesn't fit the song of the Blackburnian Warbler.) He went on to mention having seen the species again in Maine and Newfoundland.

Regarding Wilson's Autumnal Warbler—the fall plumage of the Bay-breasted Warbler—his claims were even more extravagant. He reported having seen large numbers migrating through Louisiana in early March, and many breeding in upstate New York in summer, and then gave a description of the nest and eggs. For the Pine-swamp Warbler (the female Black-throated Blue Warbler), he described the song of the male, and gave an account of finding a pair with their nest.

Of course, all those claims were impossible. Migrating warblers in spring don't wear their fall plumage, female warblers don't form pairs and build nests together, and most female warblers don't sing. There's no doubt that Audubon did encounter these birds; his paintings of them, done mostly during the first half of his work on *The Birds of America*, are detailed enough that they are clearly based on specimens. But his text accounts, published in his *Ornithological Biography* in 1831 and 1834, are rife with exaggerations and dubious claims. He wanted to show that he knew more about these rare warblers than Wilson had, and if he didn't have enough observations, he would just make things up.

In an appendix to the fifth and final volume of *Ornithological Biography* in 1839, Audubon did clear up some points about these non-species. He announced that the Black-throated Blue Warbler and Pine-swamp Warbler were the same species (although he mistakenly suggested the latter were young birds, as well as females). He mentioned his strong suspicion that the Blue-green Warbler was the same species as the Cerulean Warbler. But he muddied the status of the Autumnal Warbler further by suggesting it was the young of the Hemlock Warbler, which wasn't a real species, either.

His dealings with Wilson's nonexistent warblers were tangled enough, but just as intriguing were his attempts to discover new species of his own.

Several of his claimed novelties were just slight variations on known birds. Here are some of Audubon's names, with the actual species in parentheses): Selby's Flycatcher (Hooded Warbler), Bonaparte's Flycatcher (Canada Warbler), Children's Warbler (Yellow Warbler), Rathbone's Warbler (Yellow Warbler), Roscoe's Yellowthroat (Common Yellowthroat), and Vigors's Warbler (Pine Warbler). It's possible these were all honest mistakes, since these species can be subtle in their female or immature plumages. But it's hard to avoid noticing that he named all these for people—for individuals who were wealthy potential patrons, influential naturalists, or both. Almost as if, when he wanted to flatter someone, he would whip out another painting of a Yellow Warbler and give it a new name. I would have considered that interpretation far too cynical and unfair before I started delving into the artist's work, but now it seems at least a possibility.

The most mysterious of Audubon's warblers was not named for a person. This was the Carbonated Warbler (*Sylvia carbonata*), presented on plate 60 of *The Birds of America*. Introducing the species, he wrote:

> I shot the two little birds here represented, near the village of Henderson, in the State of Kentucky, in May 1811. They were both busily engaged in searching for insects along the branches and amongst the leaves of a Dog-wood tree. . . . On examination, they were found to be both males. I am of opinion, that they were both young birds of the preceding year, and not in full plumage, as they had no part of their dress seemingly complete, excepting the head. . . . They were drawn, like all the other birds which I have represented, immediately after being killed.

While some of his other mystery warblers were rather featureless, he illustrated the Carbonated Warbler with a strong pattern. Each of the two little birds has a black cap and black face stripe, bright yellow underparts, black streaks on the sides, an olive back with black spots, and broad bands of white and yellow crossing its dark wings. At a glance they look convincing and different from any known bird. Audubon reported he never saw the species again after 1811, and no one else has seen it, either.

opposite page: "Carbonated Warblers" by John James Audubon. A few birds painted by Audubon can't be matched to any species known today. This is perhaps the most distinctive. While most of his bird portraits were drawn directly from specimens, this one apparently was done from distant memory. So even assuming he really did see such a bird, the details in this illustration may not be reliable.

But many have speculated about its identity. Some have pointed out a similarity to a young male Cape May Warbler, although the black cap is too extensive and other details are wrong. Others have suggested a male Blackpoll Warbler with the white in its plumage replaced by yellow, although some essential marks are missing. Still others have said it could have been a hybrid, perhaps with a Cape May or a Blackpoll as one parent. And loyalists have maintained that the Carbonated Warbler was a rare species, now extinct, that would have remained unknown had Audubon not documented its existence.

When the American Ornithologists' Union began publishing an official list of birds in 1886, they relegated the Carbonated Warbler to the Hypothetical List: "Known only from Audubon's plate and description of two specimens killed near Henderson, Kentucky, in May, 1811." In the edition of 1931, they added a note: "As a number of his drawings of birds obtained about this time were later destroyed it is possible that the published plate may have been based to some extent upon memory."

Phrased diplomatically, it was still a direct contradiction of Audubon's claim that these birds were drawn "immediately after being killed." (It was his standard practice to draw specimens while they were still fresh, but he almost never stated this so specifically. In this case it sounds almost defensive: as if to insist that he really had done the drawing first in 1811, and didn't want to admit he'd had to re-create it from memory later.) Other authors repeated the idea that the Carbonated Warbler illustration might have been done from memory, but the first worthwhile comment was published online in 2008 by ornithologist and artist David Sibley.

Unlike anyone before him, Sibley had looked closely at the illustration itself, noting several details that were simply impossible. The median coverts on the wing—the feathers that display the upper wing bar—overlap in a specific direction on every warbler, and indeed on every songbird; but the illustration shows them overlapping in the opposite direction. Another set of wing feathers, the primary coverts, are missing. The feathers above the base of the tail are the wrong shape, and arranged in the wrong way, for any bird. The markings on the back are

All paintings in this section © Kenn Kaufman. This page, *top*: Snowy Egret in my own recent style. *Bottom*: Western Sandpipers. Juvenile *(left)*, winter adult *(center)*, and breeding-plumaged adult *(right)*. In this sandpiper illustration, and in all the drawings on the next seven pages, I was attempting to emulate the style of John James Audubon.

Swainson's Thrushes. Adults.

Gray-cheeked Thrush. Adult.

Philadelphia Vireos. Adults.

Kirtland's Warblers. Adult female *(top)* and adult male.

Snail Kites. Adult male *(top)* and juvenile.

Top: Baird's Sandpipers. Adults *(left and center)* and juvenile.
Bottom: Caspian Tern. Adult.

Top: Thick-billed Longspurs. Breeding-plumaged female *(left)* and male.
Bottom: Clark's Grebe *(left)* and Western Grebe.

aligned in the opposite direction from what they would be on any real bird. Several other points just don't match the arrangement of feathers on any warbler, living or dead.

It's a brilliant analysis, and to me the conclusion seems inescapable: Audubon didn't have any specimen in front of him while he was drawing the Carbonated Warbler. He just wasn't that sloppy in details when he could work from reference materials. In other surviving drawings from around 1811, his treatment of wing structure was sometimes vague, but he didn't leave out whole groups of feathers and reverse the directions of others. I think he made his drawing of this "species" considerably later,* and I'm willing to believe it was based on a bird he had seen at one time, but I don't think we can rely on what's shown in the finished illustration.

Whether the Carbonated Warbler was a hybrid, an odd color form, a product of imagination, or a rare species on its way out, we'll probably never know. But we're on more solid footing with two other species Audubon illustrated and described for the first time: Swainson's Warbler and Bachman's Warbler.

The one he would call Swainson's Warbler was discovered by his good friend, the Reverend John Bachman, in the spring of 1832 or 1833[†] along the Edisto River near Charleston, South Carolina. Swainson's is a relatively bulky, large-billed, dull-colored warbler, brown and white, easily overlooked as it skulks in southern swamps. Bachman found it by voice: "I was first attracted by the novelty of its notes, four or five in number, repeated at intervals of five or six minutes apart. These notes were loud, clear, and more like a whistle than a song." Alerted to this

---

*A point that I haven't seen mentioned anywhere: the drawing of the Carbonated Warbler that was used as the basis for the published color plate was done primarily in watercolor, with the addition of graphite, pastel, black chalk, black ink, and a bit of gouache. Audubon commonly used a variety of media, especially later in his career, but in 1811 he was still working primarily in pastels. So the drawing itself would have been an odd departure from his standard approach at that early date.

†Audubon wrote that he was in Labrador when Bachman found the bird in 1832, but his Labrador trip was in 1833. He frequently misstated dates, but it seems less likely he would be mistaken about where he was traveling at the time.

hitherto unknown bird, he found several more individuals that season, including a female with fledglings. "I have invariably found them in swampy muddy places, usually covered with more or less water. . . . The manners of this species resemble those of the Prothonotary Warbler, as it skips among the low bushes growing about ponds and other watery places, seldom ascending high trees. It retires southward at the close of summer."

It was distinctive and previously undescribed. John Woodhouse Audubon, the artist's younger son—still in his early twenties, but showing promise as an illustrator—made the drawing of the new warbler. Audubon decided to name it in honor of William Swainson, then a leading British naturalist.

He and Swainson had become friends while he was in England in the late 1820s, overseeing the engraving of the first plates for *The Birds of America*. By the time he was describing this new warbler, their friendship had soured. Audubon had asked Swainson to collaborate on the text for his *Ornithological Biography*, but refused the Englishman's reasonable request to have his name listed on the title page. Swainson, understandably, had no interest in serving as a behind-the-scenes ghostwriter. (Ultimately the Scottish naturalist William MacGillivray wound up filling that role.) In honoring Swainson with the name of this new warbler, Audubon may have been trying to mend their relationship. But some variants of the plate have the bird labeled as "Brown headed Worm eating Warbler" instead, as if he had had second thoughts.

It might seem unfair that Audubon named this prize for a distant English naturalist and not for the man who had discovered it. But amazingly, that man had found a second novel warbler at about the same time, so there were enough honorifics to go around.

Audubon had already launched his publications and was already being feted on both sides of the Atlantic before he met John Bachman in 1831. Bachman had known Alexander Wilson, William Bartram, and others when he was a young student in Philadelphia in 1804, reflecting his serious interest in natural history long before he met Audubon.

But it's hard to overstate the powerful impact these two men had on each other. The scholarly Bachman provided Audubon with reams of information about southern birds, took part in his most impressive breakthroughs about cryptic species, and prodded him to become more scientific in his approach.* Audubon, in turn, inspired his friend to intensify his pursuits: Bachman had been living in Charleston for more than fifteen years, but it was only after he got to know the famous bird painter that he went out into the surrounding swamps and discovered two new species of warblers.

His second find was in July 1833. A few miles outside Charleston, probably in an area later known as the I'on Swamp, he collected a female warbler. A more typical warbler than the Swainson's, it was petite and marked with yellow, but didn't look familiar. Continuing to search the area, he found others, including an adult male: more distinctive, with a dark cap and a black throat. Bachman prepared the specimens and saved them for Audubon to paint their portraits and write the formal description.

Audubon's drawings of warblers tend to be among his least dramatic. Often they come across as botanical illustrations, with a bird or two pasted in. His portrait of Bachman's Warbler follows that pattern. A male and female warbler perch quietly, almost inconspicuously, among the luxuriant foliage and flowers of a large blooming shrub. The plant had been painted by John Bachman's talented sister-in-law, Maria

---

*He influenced Audubon in another way that was more negative. A pastor for more than fifty years and a leader in the southern Lutheran church, Bachman was considered somewhat progressive by the standards of Charleston. He would minister to enslaved Blacks as well as to white slave owners, and he argued that, contrary to the opinions of some scientists, all humans belonged to the same species. But he also wrote horrifying things about "the negro," including that "his intellect, although underrated, is greatly inferior to that of the Caucasian. . . . Incapable of self-government . . . he is thrown on our protection. . . . Our defense of slavery is contained in the Holy Scriptures." Such white-supremacist drivel was especially damaging when it came from members of the clergy, making it easier for other bigots to shrug off any twinges of guilt and absolve themselves of moral responsibility. I haven't seen evidence of detailed discussions between Audubon and Bachman regarding Blacks or slavery, but they spent so much time together that they must have been aware of each other's views.

Martin, who produced some of the most beautiful botanical backgrounds for *The Birds of America*; Audubon added the two birds later,
based on Bachman's specimens. At a glance it seems a typical Audubon
warbler plate, but it means more when we know the background of
both the plant and the bird.

The shrub or small tree now called the Franklin tree, *Franklinia
alatamaha*, was first observed by John and William Bartram along
the Altamaha River in Georgia in 1765. Returning to the area in the
1770s, William Bartram noted the plant's oddly limited distribution: it
was common in an area of a few acres, but he never saw it anywhere
else. He took some seeds back to the family gardens in Philadelphia,
succeeded in growing and propagating the species there, and named it
in honor of Benjamin Franklin. A few other plant collectors reported
finding *Franklinia* growing wild as late as 1803, and perhaps later. But
every known individual living today, in scattered gardens and arboreta,
is probably descended from the plants at Bartram's Garden. Presumably
John Bachman had some in his gardens at Charleston, providing the
model for Maria Martin's illustration. The species has been regarded as
probably extinct in the wild for the last two centuries.

And the warbler? It's also considered probably extinct.

After Bachman found the first individuals near Charleston, decades
passed before Bachman's Warbler was found again in South Carolina.
A specimen was collected in winter in Cuba, and a possible migrant
in Georgia. But half a century after its discovery, when the American
Ornithologists' Union published their first list of North American birds

opposite page: Bachman's Warblers, male above, female below, by John James
Audubon. The flowers and foliage dominating this plate are those of the
Franklinia, a southern species that has been considered extinct in the wild for
more than two centuries. It was painted by Maria Martin, who was then the sister-
in-law of Audubon's friend John Bachman. The warbler, discovered by Bachman
and named for him by Audubon, is now also considered extinct. It may have been
briefly abundant in the late 1800s, but its past population levels and its subsequent disappearance are both major mysteries.

in 1886, their comment was: "No recent record of its occurrence." For much of the twentieth century, too, this was a grail bird, almost unknown. The late Roger Tory Peterson, birding all over the eastern United States from the 1920s on, never saw a Bachman's Warbler. After years of only rare and scattered sightings, a few were definitely present in the I'on Swamp in the 1950s and early 1960s, as proven by a handful of photos and sound recordings. But only dubious sightings have been reported in the six decades since then.

If we looked only at these end points, we might conclude that Bachman's Warbler was always rare and that it faded out about 130 years after its discovery. But there is reason to believe it was genuinely common for a while, at least from the late 1880s to the early 1900s.

The American Ornithologists' Union statement of "no recent record" in 1886 was quickly and dramatically rendered obsolete. That spring, a collector and taxidermist shot a single Bachman's Warbler near New Orleans, far to the west of the few previous records. He didn't know what it was, but ornithologist George Lawrence identified the specimen and urged the man to watch for more. He did: the following March he collected six specimens, and in March 1888 he found thirty-one! None were seen there later than March, indicating that these were northbound migrants, just passing through. Meanwhile, in Key West, Florida, J. W. Atkins collected a single Bachman's, clearly migrating south, in August 1887. Primed to watch for more the following year, he spotted as many as two dozen in a day on several dates in late July and August 1888. Again in summer 1889, Atkins saw as many as twenty-five or thirty on a couple of dates in August. In March 1890, ornithologists William Brewster and Frank Chapman took a float trip down the Suwannee River in northwestern Florida to survey the birdlife there; in a two-week period, covering about seventy miles, they found Bachman's Warblers at almost every stop, with up to thirty in a day. Another ornithologist, Arthur T. Wayne, surveyed the Suwannee throughout the spring of 1892 and again found Bachman's Warblers common, but concluded they must be northbound migrants there, not staying to breed. All these observers took some specimens, confirming they knew what they were seeing, but not enough to put a dent in the total population.

Unlike some birds, warblers do not migrate in flocks. Unless they're concentrated by a natural barrier, they spread out across the landscape. For ornithologists to have found dozens of Bachman's Warblers, there must have been hundreds, at least, passing through those regions of Louisiana and Florida. And before long, some breeding areas were confirmed farther north. In the mid-1890s, Otto Widmann reported the species as a common nesting bird of bottomland swamps in northeastern Arkansas and southeastern Missouri. Not far away in southwestern Kentucky, G. C. Embody found twenty-two males occupying territories in two local swamps in 1906. Also in 1906, Arthur Wayne rediscovered the bird in the I'on Swamp in South Carolina, observing several pairs and finding six nests. In 1908, the species was found in two counties in eastern Georgia. Observers spotted other likely breeding populations elsewhere in the southeast.

For a moment, it seemed this warbler was a common bird after all. And then, abruptly, it crashed. No one could find dozens of migrants in a day anymore—it became rare to find even one. Searchers checked former breeding sites and found the birds had vanished. But why? What had happened with this species?

Published records, taken at face value, would suggest this warbler was a rarity that had a brief population explosion before declining to mythical status again. But was it really so scarce before 1886? For many years in the mid-1800s, Bachman's Warbler and Swainson's Warbler were both regarded as rare mystery birds. It was not until the 1870s and early 1880s that records and specimens of Swainson's Warbler began to accumulate, and that happened because naturalists intensified their searches of southern swamplands. No one reported one-day totals of migrating Swainson's to compare to some of the high counts of Bachman's; but Swainson's Warblers lurk in dense thickets, while migrating Bachman's flitted about in treetops, much easier to detect, so comparative tallies are misleading.

It's possible, therefore, that Bachman's and Swainson's Warblers were both historically common, and merely overlooked, prior to the late 1800s. But Swainson's is still fairly numerous today, breeding in swampy woods and dense hillside thickets from eastern Texas to Virginia. Bachman's Warbler is just gone. No one knows why.

The fates of other extinct birds offer few clues. Passenger Pigeons, Carolina Parakeets, and Eskimo Curlews each gathered in dense flocks and were relentlessly pursued by gunners until their populations dropped too low to recover. Ivory-billed Woodpeckers required vast tracts of old-growth forest. Neither of those factors would apply to a small, widely dispersed warbler. Habitat loss is always worth considering, but every other small songbird that shared habitat with Bachman's Warblers is still doing fine. What could have affected just this one species?

The most intriguing suggestion was one proposed in 1986 by ornithologist Van Remsen. In the American tropics, Remsen pointed out, there are several bird species (often quite rare and sought after by birders) that live only in large stands of bamboo. Was it possible that Bachman's Warbler was a bamboo specialist?

Many people don't realize we have native bamboo in the southeastern United States. Giant cane, or river cane (*Arundinaria gigantea*), grows wild from eastern Texas north to Illinois and east to Maryland. In forest understory and in scattered spots along river floodplains it can be noticeable, with tubular stems an inch or more in diameter, standing more than eight feet tall.

At one time, though, the cane grew taller, commonly to thirty feet or more, according to early reports, with stems as thick as a man's arm. It grew in dense stands that stretched for miles along river valleys, a single stand often covering thousands of acres. These canebrakes, as they were called, were dominant features of the south-central and southeastern lowlands. When I was a young boy in the 1960s, reading adventure stories about the past, I often saw casual references: explorers lost for days when they tried to push their way through the canebrake; pioneers setting out to hunt bears in the canebrake; Daniel Boone escaping from the Shawnees by plunging into the canebrake. These places made up a familiar part of the literary landscape. It was years later, after traveling all over the South, that I realized I'd never seen a canebrake in real life. And I hadn't: they're gone. Giant cane as a species is still widespread, but the big canebrakes were destroyed by clearing for agriculture, livestock grazing, fire control, flood control, and other factors, including the odd life cycle of the plants themselves, with mass blooming and seeding events followed by mass die-offs. The canebrake ecosystem has been reduced to less than 2 percent of its original area, and most Americans today have no idea it ever existed.

Swainson's Warblers reportedly were common in the canebrakes, but not limited to them. What about Bachman's? Were they somehow reliant on these big stands of cane, and unable to survive without them? We'll probably never know. But the warblers and the canebrakes both disappeared at about the same time, leaving us behind with more questions than answers.

Swainson's and Bachman's—they were the only two warblers named by Audubon that are still recognized as valid species today. And he never saw either of them alive, because they were delivered to him by John Bachman. But despite all his attempts to discern differences among members of this group, Audubon never discovered a new warbler species himself.

In a way, he was just a little too late, since Wilson had had easier pickings just a few years before Audubon started his own focused search. But the pool of possibilities wasn't quite dry. One eastern warbler remained unknown to Western science during his lifetime.

Audubon passed away in late January 1851. Less than four months later, Charles Pease was collecting specimens on a farm near Lake Erie outside Cleveland, Ohio. The farm was owned by the renowned naturalist Jared P. Kirtland, so it would have seemed a safe bet that the birds there would be well-known already, but Pease shot a warbler that looked unfamiliar. Kirtland looked at the specimen and couldn't recognize it, either. The specimen was sent to Spencer Baird, a rising star in ornithology, who had just begun his career as the first curator at the Smithsonian Institution in Washington. Baird concluded that it was indeed an unknown warbler, and he named it in Kirtland's honor.

Alerted to its existence, the growing numbers of naturalists kept an eye out for Kirtland's Warbler, but it became clear that this bird must be genuinely rare. Two decades had passed when Elliott Coues, in his 1872 *Key to North American Birds*, called it "very rare; only two or three specimens known, from Ohio and the Bahamas. A species I have never seen." It was understood that the Bahamas must be the wintering grounds, and that the Ohio bird must have been a migrant passing through, since no more were found in that region for years. But it would be more than half a century after the species was described before the breeding grounds were confirmed. The first nest was found in July 1903, near the northern end of Michigan's Lower Peninsula.

The bird has been a focus of research and conservation efforts ever since. It's rare because of narrow habitat requirements: it nests only in young jack pine stands of a certain age. It's also a frequent target of parasitic cowbirds, which lay their eggs in the warblers' nests. The total population may have dipped below 350 individuals in 1974 and again in 1987—terrifyingly low numbers for a small songbird. Conservationists have brought Kirtland's Warbler back from the brink by managing and creating new habitat, and by controlling numbers of cowbirds in core areas. The total population is now over four thousand, and breeding is no longer confined to Michigan's Lower Peninsula: there are now outpost colonies elsewhere. Effective conservation science arrived too late for Bachman's Warbler, but Kirtland's seems to be out of immediate danger.

Today, Kirtland's Warbler represents our collective determination

opposite page: Kirtland's Warblers, female above, male below, by Kenn Kaufman. My first thought was to depict this species on a branch of jack pine. But the association of Kirtland's Warblers with jack pine forests in northern Michigan was not discovered until more than half a century after Audubon did his last work; so even if he had encountered a migrant of this species during his career, he would not have known to link the bird with that tree. Therefore, I opted for perching these birds on a random flower, as Audubon often did—in this case, on a spiderwort (*Tradescantia*).

to save endangered species from extinction. In the early 1870s, it represented something else. That such a distinctive bird had remained undetected so long suggested that even in the eastern United States there might be other rare warblers awaiting discovery.

That was the context for William Brewster, born in 1851, the year the first migrating Kirtland's was discovered. Growing up in eastern Massachusetts, Brewster developed a keen scientific interest in birds while very young. By his early teens he was collecting whole series of bird specimens and reading and rereading a copy of Audubon's work that his father had bought. Young Brewster understood that the birdlife of Massachusetts was already well known, but he was open to surprises. So he may not have been shocked when, in 1874, still in his early twenties, he found what appeared to be a new and undescribed species of warbler.

The bird seemed to have the same structure and bill shape as the Blue-winged and Golden-winged Warblers. Its pattern suggested that of the Blue-winged, with a thin black line through the eye, but its throat and underparts were white, not yellow, and its two wing bars were yellow (like those of the Golden-winged), not white. He wrote up a formal description and applied the specific name *leucobronchialis*, or White-throated Warbler. Other naturalists soon honored the young man by referring to his find as Brewster's Warbler.

Amazingly, the very next year, another new warbler was named from another well-studied region. The describer, Harold Herrick, wrote that "I take greater pleasure in recording it, because of its capture in New Jersey, a section already so thoroughly worked up." This new one had the black mask and throat of the Golden-winged Warbler and the bright yellow belly of the Blue-winged Warbler, and was clearly related to those species. But according to Herrick, it was "so clearly and strikingly marked as to preclude the possibility of its being an unusual form of [either of those two], or a hybrid." He proposed naming it in honor of the ornithologist George Lawrence.

So nearly a quarter century after Kirtland's Warbler had seemingly closed the book on new eastern members of the family, naturalists had two new birds to consider, Brewster's Warbler and Lawrence's Warbler.

But doubts began to set in. William Brewster himself, rapidly gaining stature as an ornithologist, published a study in 1881—only seven
years after his original description of his warbler—questioning the status of both Brewster's and Lawrence's Warblers. By that time, at least
a dozen specimens of Brewster's had been found, and at least one more
apparent Lawrence's. As Brewster pointed out, neither bird had any
unique characteristics: Everything in their appearance was "borrowed"
from either Blue-winged or Golden-winged Warblers. And almost all the
specimens had been found in areas where both of those were known to
breed. His conclusion? Blue-winged and Golden-winged Warblers must
be interbreeding occasionally, and Brewster's and Lawrence's Warblers,
far from being rare full species in their own right, must be the hybrid
offspring.

A bold suggestion, it met with resistance. At the time, hybrids between songbird species in North America were practically unknown.
For the next three decades, opinions about the identity of these birds
varied wildly. Some believed that both were good species, others that
Lawrence's was a hybrid but Brewster's was a full species, or vice versa.
Some asked how both could be hybrids when the Lawrence's was so
much scarcer than the Brewster's. Still others suggested that Brewster's
was a color morph of either the Blue-winged or Golden-winged.

Debate still lingered in the early 1900s, when Walter Faxon began
studying warblers breeding in a swamp near Lexington, Massachusetts.
He saw Brewster's mated with Golden-winged Warblers several times.
Finally in 1913 he found what he hoped for: a male Golden-winged
Warbler breeding with a female Blue-winged Warbler. As he had predicted, the offspring of this mixed pair all turned out to be Brewster's
Warblers. Just five years earlier, J. T. Nichols had published a partial
explanation of how Mendelian genetics could account for the scarcity
of Lawrence's Warbler, if it were the hybrid type carrying the recessive
genes. In the wake of these findings, resistance faded, and the hybrid
origin of Brewster's and Lawrence's Warblers was no longer questioned.

Why was the ornithological community so slow to accept this idea?
After all, William Brewster himself caught on to the clues quickly,

helping to sink what would have been a species named after him. Why did others hold out so long? I think it was because ornithologists are human, after all, and everyone in that era had come along just a little too late for the main age of discovery. The thought of a new, rare species was more appealing than the more obvious conclusion about hybrid origin.

Amazingly, in 1939—a full sixty-five years after Brewster had found the first Brewster's Warbler, and eighty-eight years after the first Kirtland's Warbler was collected—two ornithology students in West Virginia, Karl Haller and Lloyd Poland, found a warbler they could not identify. It looked mostly like a Yellow-throated Warbler, with black feathers framing a yellow throat patch, but it differed in some ways that suggested another warbler, the Northern Parula. Its song was like that of the Northern Parula, but doubled. You can already see where this is going, right?

But they collected the singing male and were struck by how distinctive it looked. Intrigued, they decided to search other places in the region where they had heard Northern Parulas before. Two days later and eighteen miles away, they collected a second individual, a female, of the unknown warbler. Haller described it formally the next year under the name *Dendroica potomac*. For an English name he proposed Sutton's Warbler, in honor of the noted ornithologist and artist, George Miksch Sutton.

I have a slight connection to this bird, because I knew Sutton. Born in the 1890s, he was of the old school of shotgun ornithologists: skilled at finding and identifying birds in the field, but a firm believer in taking specimens to confirm everything. He was shooting them for science, for museum collections, but when he had time, he would also paint beautiful watercolor portraits of them. As an ornithologist/collector/artist, he was closer than anyone else I've known to the John James Audubon model, minus the tendency toward scientific fraud.

George Sutton was also a fine writer who produced several books about his adventures in the far north and in Mexico. His writing was beautiful and sensitive, with asides of deep insight, but in recent years his books have fallen out of favor. My guess is that many modern readers just can't get past his frequent and casual mentions of shooting birds.

I was fortunate to meet "Doc" Sutton (as his many students had called him) a few times when I was in my teens and he was in his seventies. Once we even spent a long evening in conversation—amazing generosity on his part, since he was a world-renowned scholar and I was just a crazed kid birder. At one point, I couldn't resist asking about his namesake bird. I'd seen reproductions of a watercolor he had done of the first two specimens in 1939, and I'd read that ornithology had long since come to a consensus, but I wanted his personal take. What was his opinion of Sutton's Warbler?

I expected him to brush away the question and say the bird was a hybrid. And eventually he did. But first there was a hush, a pause, as he turned to look out the window at the winter dusk, and in that silent moment I sensed a wistfulness deeper than words. Yes, he said finally, the evidence of hybrid origin was clear. Then he made light of it with a small joke he'd probably used before: "Hopes dashed, just as for George Lawrence and William Brewster. Not bad company to be in."

Later I would dwell on that momentary pause. What did it mean? Sutton had been born a decade before Roger Tory Peterson, and almost six decades before me, in a time when bird study was different. When he was an avid young naturalist, the status of Brewster's and Lawrence's Warblers was still being debated. When he was in his early twenties he would have read of the discovery of the Cape Sable Sparrow in Florida—it's treated as a subspecies of the Seaside Sparrow now, but at the time it was regarded as a full species. When he was in his early thirties, as part of a museum expedition to Canada, he was the first white man ever to find the nest and eggs of Harris's Sparrow. He was grounded in an era of ornithology when the first great age of discovery was still close enough to taste, when it seemed new species might still be hovering out there, just out of reach.

Maybe the pause reflected that. Nothing about having a bird named for him personally, but a recognition that an exciting earlier age had quietly drawn to a close, leaving him behind.

Everyone agrees now that Sutton's Warbler is just a rare hybrid type. I've still never seen one, but I think about it every spring when I'm reveling in the warbler migration near my home in northwestern Ohio.

At the peak in May, thousands of birders are scattered among scores of migratory stopover sites near the Lake Erie shoreline, seeking warblers above all else. Every year, they find at least a handful of Kirtland's Warblers, en route to their breeding grounds not far away in Michigan; northern Ohio is the best place to find this species in migration, a nice echo of the discovery of the first one there in 1851. Almost every year they find a Brewster's hybrid, and sometimes a Lawrence's. The Sutton's Warbler hybrid must arrive there occasionally. In the way that birders keep their lists, hybrids don't "count" for adding to totals, so I'm afraid many wouldn't recognize this rare thing or realize what a special find it would be.

That's all right. When the warblers are passing through, when every tree may hold surprises, we don't need to find rarities to be satisfied. For the newcomers to birding, each warbler could be an exciting new mystery to solve. For the seasoned watchers, seeing a particular species for the first time this season—or even for the first time today—brings its own sense of delight. It's like a treasure hunt of rediscovery, and if we could, we would repeat it every spring forever.

Interlude:
Channeling the
Illustrator

All Those Plants

Audubon's bird illustrations differ from those of Wilson, and most of his other predecessors, in their elaborate background materials. Large birds are presented against whole landscapes or seascapes, with mountains, marshes, crashing waves, stormy skies, even distant city skylines in the background. Songbirds appear in settings of detailed foliage and flowers. The botanical elements in these songbird plates are not just generic plants; almost all are drawn to depict actual species.

Bird-and-flower motifs were already highly developed in Chinese paintings more than a thousand years ago. Among nature illustrators in the West, their origins are more recent. Mark Catesby, in his *Natural History of Carolina, Florida, and the Bahama Islands* in the 1700s, had positioned most of his birds in clearly identifiable plants—but for Catesby, the plants were essential subject matter, not just places for birds to sit; his work illustrated and described 171 plant species, as opposed to only 109 species of birds. Audubon was different in that his

work was wholly focused on birds, but he took pains to build compositions that included detailed, accurate, real plants.

This tendency added to my challenge when I set out to create my
pseudo-Audubons because I had done very little botanical drawing.
Most of my recent work, including the paintings that had been juried
into art exhibitions, had involved close-up portraits of eagles or other
large birds, or wading birds surrounded by water. Songbirds outnumbered by leaves hadn't been among my subjects. Getting the plants right
was going to take some intense concentration.

There may be some visual geniuses who can draw anything the first
time they see it. Most of us need some familiarity or practice with the
subject. When I draw a bird, I don't have to struggle to see the arrangement of feathers on the wing or around the base of the beak, for
example, because I have drawn those countless times, and now it takes
just a glance to see how they differ from one bird to another.

But plants furnish a whole new set of structural details. How does
each leaf and each flower attach to the stem? Do the flowers all face the
same direction, and are they all open to the same degree? When every
leaf is turned at a slightly different angle, how do I capture the perspective so they look convincing? If I draw perfect leaves, with no holes or
insect damage, won't they look unrealistic?

Years ago I got to know the late Manabu Saito when that great
botanical artist was living in Tucson, and I got to watch him work on a
few of his beautiful watercolors. As I struggled to create my own plant-
based backgrounds for my current project, I tried to remember as much
as I could of his technique. Manabu seemed to draw each flower effort-
lessly, his eyes taking in every detail, his hand producing a perfect outline every time. I knew I couldn't match that without putting in decades
of dedicated practice, but I tried to honor his memory by emulating his
obvious affection for the flowers and his gentle, unassuming style.

One tactic that stayed with me was his approach to greens. Of
course, shades of green will figure in almost every botanical illustration,
but Manabu seldom used commercially produced green paints because
their hues were unnaturally intense—I think he said they were "too

violent." Instead, while I watched, he mixed his own, blending various blues with yellows or yellowish browns. I didn't go that far, but at least I was prepared for the fact that most green paints were too artificially bright, and I would tone them down by adding ocher or reddish brown. Still, I struggled to match the shades of green on many of the plants. And I kept wishing that I had kept more careful notes on Manabu's techniques.

For a while I considered one genuine Audubon approach to the plants: getting someone else to do them. John James almost always painted his own birds—a few were contributed by his son, John Wood-house—but in many cases, other elements, including backgrounds and plants, were provided by others.

The teenage Joseph Mason had taken art lessons from Audubon in Cincinnati in 1820 and had shown a remarkable talent for drawing plants. So in October of that year, he accompanied the artist down the Mississippi to New Orleans, to act as his assistant. (He may have re-garded himself as a collaborator, assuming that the resulting artworks would be credited to Audubon & Mason; in later years he reportedly was bitter about the scant recognition he had received.) Over the next two years, Mason produced at least fifty beautiful, detailed botanical backgrounds for his teacher's birds, and many of these were included in the first volume of *The Birds of America*. In some compositions, the plant life is more detailed and impressive than the birds, such as the tulip tree leaves and flowers that dwarf the Baltimore Orioles, or the lush blooms and flowers of southern magnolia around the Black-billed Cuck-oos. Often, too, the plants and birds are so interwoven that they must have required careful coordination between the artists. It's not clear how the work was divided—Audubon might even have blocked in the plants and left Mason to finish them. Regardless, the younger man's contribu-tion undoubtedly saved him countless hours of work.

George Lehman was already an established artist when Audubon met him in Pennsylvania in the late 1820s, and soon hired him to add plants to several color plates of warblers and other birds. Later he ac-companied Audubon on his journeys to Florida in 1831 and 1832, and spent some time working with him in Charleston. Lehman had a broad range of talent, producing sweeping landscapes behind some of the larger aquatic species as well as fine, delicate flowers to go with some of the smaller songbirds. His work probably appears in more than thirty of the finished plates. (Since Audubon was, to put it mildly, casual about giving credit to others, we can't always be sure about the involvement of background illustrators.)

While visiting John Bachman in Charleston, Audubon was charmed by Bachman's younger sister-in-law, Maria Martin. She had a budding interest in art, so he gave her lessons in drawing and painting. Within a few months of practice, Martin was creating beautiful botanicals—good enough to be incorporated into Audubon's plates, including of some prize birds like Bachman's Warbler, Swainson's Warbler, and the Fork-tailed Flycatcher. In that era there were few chances for women to be involved in natural history in any way, and fewer chances for them to get any credit for it. Uncharacteristically, Audubon went so far as to acknowledge Martin's work in a few accounts in *Ornithological Biography*. In many cases we're left guessing, but she may have contributed to as many as eighteen of the final plates, or even more.

By my estimates, as many as one-third of the botanical illustrations in Audubon's works may have been furnished by others. I considered emulating this approach, saving myself trouble by palming off the most difficult plants on someone else. After all, I'm acquainted with many talented nature artists. But most are swamped with their own projects, and many are bird specialists who don't do so well with plants. And I'm not qualified to teach anyone how to do these botanicals, unlike Audubon, who gave lessons to Joseph Mason and Maria Martin. I decided to follow through as John James did for the majority of his drawings, filling in every leaf, every petal, every blade of grass.

7

Florida on the Edge

"**K** ing Vulture!"
The shout spun us around.

In tropical lowlands of Guatemala, in a clearing hacked out of endless forest, we had been absorbed in history, gazing at ruins and partial reconstructions of Mayan temples that had been left to the jungle a millennium earlier. Absorbed in birding, too, as always, scanning the trees for colorful feathered gems. But the words were enough to snap us to attention.

There it was: the King Vulture! Sailing on broad wings high above the treetops, creamy white against the hot blue sky, with bold black outer feathers on the wings and tail. Through binoculars we could make out some of the bizarre orange, red, and purple colors of its head. A huge bird, dwarfing the handful of Black Vultures and Turkey Vultures soaring nearby, it seemed to live up to its name. Forget those trogons and tanagers in the trees, and look up in awe at this king of the sky, soaring above those silent stone temples where the Mayan priest-kings once stood.

King Vultures are widespread in the American tropics, from Mexico to the northern edge of Argentina, but always uncommon. Black Vultures and Turkey Vultures may gather by the hundreds, and they often come right into city centers; but King Vultures appear as scattered singles or pairs and they seem to avoid humans, holding to those wilder regions where forest still prevails.

I have been fortunate to travel widely in tropical America, on my own and later as a leader of birding tours, so I have seen this species in several countries. But when I think of it, there is one particular place that springs to mind. Where is that? Not the rugged foothills in Panama's Darién Gap. Not the nameless side road in the wide, empty southern transit of Mexico's Yucatán Peninsula. Not southeastern Venezuela at the foot of the tepuis, the fabled highlands that had been the setting for Arthur Conan Doyle's *The Lost World*—a fitting home for a regal wilderness bird.

No, when I think about this bird, the first location that comes to mind is Florida. The Sunshine State. A place where no one has seen a King Vulture in the last two and a half centuries . . . if ever.

The Florida peninsula had been claimed by Spain since the 1500s; but for two decades beginning in 1763 it was considered a British territory, before being traded back to Spain.* During that time, William Bartram made two trips into the region. The first was a foray with his father, the acclaimed botanist John Bartram, in the winter of 1765–66. He returned in the 1770s when a wealthy doctor and plant collector in London commissioned him to travel through the southeastern colonies and Florida to survey the plant life there and send back specimens. William shared the Bartram family passion for botany but he had always had a keen secondary interest in birds, going back to his teenage days in the woods near Philadelphia. He was paying close attention to birds, and taking notes on all that he found, when he journeyed south into Florida in 1774.

Bartram spent a considerable time exploring the St. Johns River region in northeastern Florida, between what would be Jacksonville and

---

*In the cavalier way that European imperial powers treated vast sections of the globe, like pushing pieces around on a game board, Spain had traded Florida to Britain in return for control of Havana, Cuba.

Orlando today. In a book he published later about his travels, he went on at length about the landscape, the plant life, his encounters with alligators, and his observations of other wildlife, especially birds. Ibises, Wood Storks, Sandhill Cranes, and many others are all recognizable in his account.

Then he wrote: "There are two species of vultures in these regions, I think not mentioned in history: the first we shall describe is a beautiful bird. . . . I shall call this bird the painted vulture."* He went on to tell of a big creamy-white vulture with dark flight feathers and with an elaborate, colorful pattern on the bare skin of the head and neck. Apparently he saw multiple individuals, because he went on: "These birds seldom appear but when the deserts are set on fire (which happens almost every day throughout the year, in some part or other, by the Indians, for the purpose of rousing the game, as also by the lightning)." As soon as the fire passed, wrote Bartram, these vultures would join other scavengers on the scorched earth to "gather up the roasted serpents, frogs and lizards."

Some have suggested that what Bartram saw was the Crested Caracara, a hawklike bird that feeds mostly as a scavenger, gathering alongside vultures; it's common in central Florida. I think that's unlikely. Bartram's description includes precise details that are all wrong for the caracara, including the colors of the neck, eyes, and legs, and the appearance of the wattles near the base of the bill. I can't imagine how, in describing a caracara, he could have made so many mistakes that just happened to line up perfectly with a vulture he'd never heard of. No, I think it's almost certain that he did, in fact, find King Vultures in Florida. But no one has been able to find them there since.

---

*As it turned out, the King Vulture had been named by Linnaeus in 1758, based on a specimen from an unknown source. Rare as this bird was, it was too distinctive to be ignored. The second species mentioned in this account by Bartram was the Black Vulture, which is widespread and abundant in warmer regions of the Americas, but was still unnamed at that time. Perhaps it had been overlooked because of its superficial resemblance to the even more widespread Turkey Vulture. Black Vultures have expanded their range northward in the last century, and today they can be found easily near Philadelphia, but William Bartram in the 1770s wouldn't have seen them until he traveled south.

In the third volume of his *American Ornithology* in 1811, Alexander Wilson noted that the King Vulture was "sometimes seen in E. Florida." After all, Bartram was his friend and mentor. But after that, the species generally went unmentioned for years in compilations about North American birds. In recent publications it's sometimes mentioned, but always as something hypothetical or doubtful.

Why should it be doubtful, though? Is it really that unlikely? Consider what we know of the bird's distribution. Although they're uncommon, King Vultures have a wide tropical range, getting as far north as eastern Mexico. If they were in Florida, though, that would indicate a major gap in their range—a gap of 1,300 miles, if measured over land (vultures tend to avoid flying over open water). Is it plausible that a bird could have such an isolated outpost in the peninsula, so far removed from the main range?

Yes. That's similar to the pattern in three other species that U.S. birders have long regarded as "Florida specialties." These are the Limpkin, a loud-voiced brown wader that stalks the edges of swamplands, stabbing large snails; another snail-eater, the Snail Kite, sailing slowly and low over marshes, seeking its lethargic prey; and the Short-tailed Hawk, a small raptor that soars high above forested regions. All three range widely in the tropics, from Mexico to South America; and until recently, all three were known in the United States only from the Florida peninsula. The Snail Kite and Limpkin are also found in Cuba, so they could have arrived from across the water, but the Short-tailed Hawk doesn't occur anywhere in the Caribbean. Its total range is similar to that of the King Vulture—including, if we believe Bartram, that detail of the isolated population in Florida.

And if that enigmatic vulture was there centuries ago, and then vanished, that would fit another kind of pattern. More than any other state, Florida has a history of bird species appearing and disappearing. That history reflects some complicated facts about the geography of life.

The Florida peninsula has been hard to understand, at least for the relative newcomers of the last five hundred years. People lived here at one time who seemed to have worked out how to thrive in this place—the Calusa, the Tequesta, and others—but they are all gone now, and the European-American colonizers are still trying to figure it out.

The popularity of the peninsula has had its ups and downs. William Bartram, looking with a naturalist's eye, described the region in glowing terms in the 1770s. Others who came later disagreed. George Ord visited in 1818, while Florida was still under Spanish rule, and mentioned that cardinals and mockingbirds could be seen daily "around the rude habitations of the disheartened inhabitants, as if willing to console them" for the privations they were forced to bear. Audubon arrived fourteen years later and was more pointed in his comments. "The country around is certainly poor. . . . When the United States purchased the peninsula from the Spanish Government, the representations given of it by Mr Bartram and other poetical writers, were soon found greatly to exceed the reality. For this reason, many of the individuals who flocked to it, returned home or made their way towards other regions with a heavy heart."

However, Audubon added that "the climate during the winter months is the most delightful that could be imagined," and that climate has been enough to override the challenges of living there. Through cycles of land speculation, failed developments, and economic crashes, through cycles of storm destruction and rebuilding, the population has continued to grow. Florida now has the third-highest population of any U.S. state, trailing only California and Texas. It may not be sustainable. Many of the state's politicians deny the reality of climate change, even as rising sea levels begin to flood their coastal cities and salt water seeps into aquifers.

I fell in love with Florida on my first visit at the age of seventeen, and I've been back for the birding there almost every year since. But as with other love affairs, it's complicated.

Three major factors help to make the birdlife of Florida different from that of any other state. It approaches the tropics; it's a peninsula; and its southern end is very close to the Caribbean islands of Cuba and the Bahamas.

A pattern that holds, in a general way, all over the world is that the tropics have the highest bird diversity; polar regions, the lowest. There are more bird species as you go toward the equator, fewer as you go toward the poles. (The huge northern nation of Canada has far fewer kinds of birds than small, tropical Costa Rica.) This trend holds within the United States, with more species in the southern states than in the north. So it's not surprising that Florida, with its subtropical vibe, has more bird species than a large northern state like Maine.

The pattern applies even within large states near the edge of the tropics. In Texas and Arizona, we find more bird species overall as we go south. But that's not the case in Florida. Although it's easy to be distracted by all the big, showy storks, pelicans, egrets, and the like, as we go south in Florida, the overall variety of birds goes down. This is especially true of breeding land birds. In summer, as we go south in the peninsula, various widespread birds of the eastern states begin to disappear: Wood Thrush, Carolina Chickadee, Yellow-throated Vireo, Prothonotary Warbler, Blue Grosbeak, and many more. They fade out, and for the most part, they are not replaced by other species. The southern tip of the Florida mainland has what we could call a depauperate avifauna. Why? Because it's at the end of a peninsula.

Something like this has been observed at many locations around the world and with various groups of animals and plants, with fewer species at the tip of a peninsula than at the base. It's not consistent, and no explanation for it seems to apply everywhere. But it seems to be related to the broad principles of island biogeography: the geographic patterns of living things on islands, and on island-like, isolated habitats. And since the birdlife of southern Florida is so strongly influenced by the proximity of Caribbean islands, we might as well go ahead and segue into that topic.

Island biogeography has been an active field of study since the 1960s. Whole books and hundreds of papers have been published about it, and it would be foolish to try to summarize the subject in a paragraph. But one basic idea is worth noting: islands tend to have fewer

species than mainland areas, and small islands tend to have fewer species than large islands.

This isn't as obvious as it sounds. It's not just a matter of having
enough room. Given a similar climate and habitat, an island will have
fewer species than an equivalent area on a mainland. So, for example,
one hundred square miles on a continental mainland will support more
species than an island with a surface area of one hundred square miles.
An island of ten square miles will support fewer species than any ten-
square-mile section of the larger island. If you could experimentally reduce the size of an island, the variety of resident species would drop
until it reached equilibrium at a lower number.

The tip of a peninsula is, in effect, almost an island, surrounded on
three sides by water. Of course, the connection to a mainland allows
new things to arrive overland, but the habitats out toward the tip might
not allow as many species to persist.

Another aspect that's essential to understanding the situation in
Florida: islands tend to have more turnover than similar areas on the
mainland. Resident species on islands are more likely to disappear; new
species that arrive by chance are, oddly enough, more likely to establish
a foothold.

These elements are doubly relevant in southern Florida. Not only
does the state taper to a narrow peninsula, but it's flanked on the south
by scores of islands, highlighted by the long string of the Florida Keys.
It's like a living laboratory for experiments in island biogeography. And
as our knowledge of the region has accumulated over the years, the patterns revealed have grown ever more fascinating.

I tend to romanticize the idea of going into unexplored terrain
where new discoveries are possible at every turn. After all, that's one
plotline of this book. But there are advantages, too, to coming into the
field after decades or centuries of exploration by others, after vast numbers of data points have been gathered all over the globe. Only then will
subtle patterns start to become evident. The principles of island biogeography couldn't have been deduced by looking at just a few islands.

Today we're unlikely to find undescribed species in our backyards, but we can glimpse magnificent global patterns of life that were hidden to the pioneer naturalists. And we can build on the observations of those pioneers to add depth to modern knowledge.

It's hard to imagine how difficult it was to access southern Florida at the beginning of the 1830s. The southern tip of the mainland was almost uninhabited and almost uninhabitable. The Calusa and Tequesta peoples had mostly been killed or removed, the Seminole were just starting to be driven south into the region, and European-Americans had barely begun to make inroads. Today we can traverse the vast wetland of the Everglades on two major highways that cross the southern peninsula from east to west, or we can join the roughly one million people who visit Everglades National Park every year, driving down the park road to the edge of Florida Bay. But there were few people on the southern Florida mainland then. Even the coastal region, where the continuous metropolis of Palm Beach to Miami now holds six million residents, was practically empty.

Today we can drive south out of Miami to Key Largo and then glide more than a hundred miles down the Florida Keys on the Overseas Highway, with dozens of long bridges linking dozens of islands, all the way to Key West. But Miami didn't exist in the early 1830s, and there were no bridges. The Florida Keys were still wild in more ways than one, but they were far from an untouched wilderness. Pirates and smugglers had hideouts there; boatloads of fishers, turtlers, and loggers from Cuba and the Bahamas regularly scoured the area; new settlements were thriving on Indian Key and Key West. You could explore the Keys if you had the right boat, but the interior of the southern peninsula was a forbidding wilderness.

The major islands of the Caribbean, by contrast, had borne the first major incursion of Europeans, beginning in 1492. By the 1830s the colonies on islands such as Cuba, Jamaica, Puerto Rico, and others were centuries old, with cities and ports and plantations.

To the citizens of the United States and Europe, then, southern

Florida was a wild and mysterious tract lying between the better-known and more civilized regions of the southeastern U.S. and the islands of the Caribbean. This context is important for understanding the value of Audubon's journey to southernmost Florida in 1832. It was probably the most significant exploration of his life. He found two undescribed species there, although in one of those two cases he didn't realize it. He found a number of species that had been previously unknown in Florida, or in the territory of the United States. Most important, though, his observations on the birds of the Keys—those he found, and those he didn't—provided a baseline still valuable for comparison two centuries later.

With the publication of the first volumes of his work, he had gained recognition by officials of the U.S. government as a worthy American scholar and received permission to ride on government ships. The Treasury Department operated a fleet of small, fast sailing ships called cutters, tasked with patrolling coastal regions and ports to collect tariffs and watch for smugglers. Audubon hitched a ride on one such revenue cutter to reach northeastern Florida in the winter of 1831–32. His major expedition, though, was on the cutter *Marion*, traveling down the east coast of the peninsula and throughout the Keys in April and May 1832.

It was an extraordinary opportunity. Audubon had sailed through the straits between Cuba and the Keys on previous occasions, traveling from the port of New Orleans to the Atlantic states or to Europe. Alexander Wilson had followed the same route in July 1810, going from New Orleans to New York, and had observed Sooty Terns and other tropical seabirds offshore; he might have landed briefly on a couple of islands. But no ornithologist had explored the Keys in any detailed way. The captain of the *Marion* took a serious interest in Audubon's work, assigning members of his crew to row the artist ashore at various points and to help with tasks such as carrying equipment and shooting birds. There was local help, too. At Indian Key—a bustling village on the upper Keys then, abandoned now—a local official sent his boat pilot, a Mr. Egan, along to assist for several weeks. (Egan impressed Audubon, and he praised the man's knowledge of the area and his skill with a gun.) At Key West the military commander, Major Glassel, sent along a soldier to help with local explorations. An amateur naturalist in the town, Dr. Benjamin Strobel, offered information about birdlife of the region. With all these advantages, Audubon's few weeks in the Keys were as productive as they could be.

And as exciting. Despite the heat, rain, wind, mosquitoes, and mud, Audubon was in paradise. This was his giddy reaction on first landing at Indian Key: "With what delightful feelings did we gaze on the objects around us!—the gorgeous flowers, the singular and beautiful plants, the luxuriant trees. The balmy air which we breathed filled us with animation, so pure and salubrious did it seem to be. The birds which we saw were almost all new to us; their lovely forms appeared to be arrayed in more brilliant apparel than I had ever before seen. . . . We longed to form a more intimate acquaintance with them."

He would pursue that more intimate acquaintance. The vast expanse of Florida Bay between the Keys and the mainland was so shallow in places that even small boats had to thread their way through channels among sandbars, hidden shoals, and innumerable islets crowned with mangroves. Wading birds and fishing birds swarmed over these shallows. Even allowing for Audubon's tendency to exaggerate, the sheer abundance of birds must have beggared anything we could see today. Egan, the pilot from Indian Key, led the group to one island after another where the nests of pelicans, cormorants, herons, ibises, and other birds covered the mangroves. They landed on exposed flats where, as Audubon wrote, "the flocks of birds that covered the shelly beaches, and those hovering over head, so astonished us that we could for a while scarcely believe our eyes." Time and again he referred to hundreds, or even thousands, of wading birds arrayed across the shallows.

Naturalists of that era seemed fixated on flamingos. Wilson, in *American Ornithology*, had included four pages about the tall pink birds, even though he had never seen one. When Audubon spotted a distant flock in flight, their long necks outstretched, long legs trailing behind them, he was ecstatic: "Ah! Reader, could you but know the emotions that then agitated my breast! I thought I had now reached the height of all my expectations, for my voyage to the Floridas was undertaken in a great measure for the purpose of studying these lovely birds in their own beautiful islands. I followed them with my eyes, watching as it were every beat of their wings." He saw more flocks in the course of his journey, but always at a distance, and commented later that he had not "had the satisfaction of shooting a single individual." He also failed to find a nesting colony. It's not entirely clear whether flamingos have ever nested in the wild in Florida. The flocks that Audubon saw were probably visiting from Cuba, the Bahamas, or the Yucatán Peninsula, just like the few that show up in Florida Bay today.

Another large wading bird in the region, although less colorful, proved more significant. Great Egrets were common in southern Florida, as they had been in many places Audubon had visited before, from Louisiana to New Jersey. Tall and white with yellow beaks, they were familiar enough to be overlooked in a quest for more exotic life. It was the pilot, Egan, who pointed out another white, yellow-beaked wader that was even larger than the Great Egret. This bird was a creature undescribed to science, and Audubon was able to give it a formal name: *Ardea occidentalis*, the Great White Heron. Today there's debate whether this is an all-white subspecies of the Great Blue Heron, or a full species. Either way, it's a spectacular specialty, one of the largest herons in the Americas, more or less restricted to the coastlines of southern Florida, Cuba, and the Yucatán, and it had remained unnoticed before 1832.

The farthest extent of the area patrolled by the cutter *Marion* was around the coral islands of the Dry Tortugas, west of Key West. The Tortugas are still isolated—seventy miles beyond the end of the Overseas Highway—and a visit is still an adventure for birders, who travel there by boat or seaplane. By the time of Audubon's visit, the islands had been known for centuries. Ponce de León had named them Las Tortugas in 1513, for the sea turtles that came ashore to lay eggs. A bigger spectacle was, and is, the huge breeding colony of two species of tropical terns, the Sooty Tern and the Brown Noddy. These two are so widespread in tropical seas that Linnaeus had received specimens of

Great White Heron by John James Audubon. The largest heron in North America, this may be either a full species or a localized subspecies of the Great Blue Heron. Audubon is credited with discovering this bird when he traveled to the Florida Keys in 1832, but it was pointed out to him by a local naturalist.

them, and given them formal names, in the 1750s and 1760s. Audubon recognized them as soon as he saw them: the Sooty Terns starkly black above and white below, the noddies dark brown with white caps, and he spent hours watching their behavior.

Other terns in the Keys were not so easily identified. Even today, equipped with good binoculars and telescopes and field guides, birders often struggle to identify members of this group. Most terns are gray-backed, white-bellied, black-capped birds, graceful in flight, beautiful to observe but often hard to tell apart. I've already described how Audubon failed to notice the Caspian Tern in other places, and he may have overlooked it yet again on this voyage, passing it off as a Royal Tern; Caspians were not found breeding in Florida until 1962, but they were known as regular visitors long before then.

Given the equipment of the day, Audubon had no way of identifying terns smaller than the Caspians except by shooting them. This he proceeded to do, with gusto, and with the willing aid of crew members from the *Marion*. On one of his first such attempts on the Keys, he was astonished to pick up a few of the slain birds and realize they were Roseate Terns. "Beautiful, indeed, are Terns of every kind, but the Roseate excels the rest. . . . I had never seen a bird of this species before, and as the unscathed hundreds arose and danced as it were in the air, I thought them the Humming-birds of the sea, so light and graceful were their movements. . . . Not another individual was robbed of life on that excursion." The Roseate Tern was already a known species, having been described from islands off Scotland in 1813, and it had been found at various points in northern Europe and on the northeastern coast of the United States. But it was assumed to be strictly a denizen of high latitudes. We know today that Roseate Terns live at scattered coastal sites around the world, in climates hot and cold, but at the time it was a surprise to find them on these subtropical islands.

A second tern was surprising in a different way. After approaching a flock, guns blazing, Audubon recorded his reaction. "On examining the first individual picked up from the water, I perceived from the yellow point of its bill that it was different from any that I had previously seen, and accordingly shouted 'A prize! a prize! a new bird to the American Fauna!' And so it was, good Reader, for no person before had found the Sandwich Tern on any part of our coast." Named for the town of Sandwich in County Kent, England, this distinctive tern—larger than most, with a black crest and yellow-tipped black bill—was already known to be widespread in the Old World, but its presence in the Americas was doubted before Audubon found it in Florida.

Great White Herons, Roseate Terns, and Sandwich Terns all can still be found on the Florida Keys. So can various other novelties that Audubon found there, including Gray Kingbirds perching like jaunty sentinels at the tips of branches, throaty-voiced Mangrove Cuckoos slipping through the tangled branches, and dark slaty White-crowned Pigeons flying, in swift flocks, across open channels between islands. But some birds that apparently lived there in 1832 have disappeared, and some other new ones have arrived in the time since. These turnovers reflect Florida's unique position on the edge of the Caribbean, and the dynamic influence of nearby islands.

By coincidence, three birds that have vanished from the Keys all represent the same group, the family of doves and pigeons. For one of these species the story is straightforward, although not easily explained. The other two are more complicated.

Doves were among John James Audubon's favorite birds. His father had told him that when he was a small boy, his first attempt at drawing had involved a stuffed specimen of a dove. Perhaps his fondness for the birds had originated there. Whatever the reason, he was delighted when he found Zenaida Doves on the Florida Keys. He even told of meeting a former buccaneer who had given up a life of piracy in the Keys because he was so touched by the gentle cooing of these doves. "Through these plaintive notes, and them alone, he was induced to escape from his vessel, abandon his turbulent companions, and return to a family deploring his absence. . . . He now lives in peace in the midst of his friends." The far-fetched story may have just reflected Audubon's own reaction to the Zenaida Dove's voice: "Heard in the wildest solitudes of the Keys, these

Zenaida Doves by John James Audubon. Although Zenaida Doves are common almost throughout the Caribbean region, they are only rare visitors to Florida today. In the 1830s, however, Audubon found them nesting on the Florida Keys, apparently in good numbers. Island groups like the Keys tend to see a turnover in bird species more frequently than mainland areas.

notes never fail to remind one that he is in the presence and under the protection of the Almighty Creator."

Zenaida Doves are close relatives of the Mourning Doves that are abundant over most of North America, although shorter-tailed and more richly colored. Classic Caribbean birds, they thrive from the Bahamas through all the major islands of the Greater and Lesser Antilles, but nowhere on the mainland except locally along the coast of Mexico's Yucatán Peninsula. In Audubon's day they were common summer residents, at least, on several of the Keys. In modern times they have been very rare visitors to Florida. And the reasons for this change are unknown. Audubon reported that Zenaida Doves nested only in the interior of certain islands, and always nested on the ground—surprising, since on many Caribbean islands they regularly build their nests in trees. If they were consistent ground-nesters on the Keys, that might have made them more vulnerable. But their disappearance may have just illustrated a point of island biogeography, that populations on small islands are more likely to blink out.

The other two vanished species belong to the odd group known as quail-doves. As the name might suggest, these are chunky, round-bodied, short-tailed doves that spend most of their time walking on the ground; about twenty species live in the American tropics, mostly in dense forest, and all are typically hard to see.

At Key West, on a hint from local naturalist Benjamin Strobel, Audubon went looking for quail-doves. A soldier from the garrison there offered to guide him on the search, and they set off to push their way straight across the island, through the dense, thorny, tangled thickets that covered the interior. After a long and strenuous trek, the soldier, in the lead, spotted a quail-dove ahead and dispatched it with a single shot before Audubon had even had a glimpse. But now he had a specimen to use as a basis for his painting. He apparently did see live individuals later, and the locals assured him they were common denizens of the island.

These birds represented a species undescribed at the time. Audubon didn't realize it, though; he thought he was seeing the Ruddy Quail-Dove,

Key West Quail-Doves by John James Audubon. When Audubon encountered this bird at Key West, Florida, in 1832, it was still undescribed to science, but he didn't realize that; he thought it was the Ruddy Quail-Dove, already known from islands in the Caribbean. Even so, he decided to name it for Key West, and that is still part of its name, although it's no longer a resident anywhere in Florida.

which had been named by Linnaeus decades earlier, based on accounts from Jamaica. Not until 1855 did Charles Bonaparte point out that the Key West birds were much more colorful, and that these brightly hued birds were also found side by side with Ruddy Quail-Doves on some Caribbean islands. So Bonaparte is credited as the formal describer of this species. But Audubon had called his birds "Key West Pigeons," and so strong was his influence that they still bear the English name of Key West Quail-Dove, even though they are long gone from Key West.

The occasional individual still shows up somewhere on the Keys or the south Florida mainland, undoubtedly straying in from Cuba or the Bahamas. Some modern authorities have suggested that Audubon encountered such a stray, and that there was no resident population. I think that's unlikely. Unless he made up the whole anecdote about local intelligence and an intentional search for this bird, the information seems solid. But the story about the other vanished bird, the Blue-headed Quail-Dove, seems a little shakier.

The Blue-headed Quail-Dove is a beautiful bird of dense forest, known only from Cuba today. Linnaeus had named it in 1758, with no information beyond suggesting that it lived in "America." Audubon claimed to have seen a pair feeding on the ground on the west side of Key West—"On our approaching them they ran back into the thickets, which were only a few yards distant"—and later he saw a captive pair, said to have been caught on the nearby Mule Keys. Some have suggested that these captives had been brought from Cuba, that Audubon misidentified the other pair he saw, and that the species has never occurred naturally in Florida. On the other hand, Cuban ornithologist Orlando Garrido argues that a distinct population was resident at Key West in 1832, and I'd like to believe he's right.

In 1941, 109 years after Audubon's visit, Roger Tory Peterson traveled to the Keys. People were not yet calling him the "Twentieth-century Audubon," but thanks to the success of his *Field Guide to the Birds*, Peterson was already well known. The manager of the wildlife refuges around Key West, Earle Greene, took this celebrity birder out in his boat to explore the numerous small islands in the vicinity. The birdlife of Florida, like Roger, was also considered to be already well known; but on one June day, the two men discovered two birds that were new for the United States.

In later years Roger would consistently, and graciously, say that "Earle Greene and I discovered these birds." But by that time Greene, an avid birder himself, had been working in the area for more than two years, and it was the alert and perceptive Peterson who pointed out the presence of these novelties. At the edge of one island, a song like that of a Yellow Warbler came from the mangroves. Yellow Warblers are so widespread and common that birders sometimes ignore them—but it was June, the height of the breeding season, and these bright yellow sprites were not known to nest any closer than northern Georgia. The singer turned out to be a "Golden Warbler," a tropical member of the Yellow Warbler complex previously known only from Cuba. That evening they watched nighthawks coursing about in the sky above Key West, and Roger pointed out that their callnotes were different from those of Common Nighthawks all over the North American continent: a snappy *pitty-pick-pick* in place of the familiar buzzy *pzeeent*. These birds proved to be Antillean Nighthawks, widespread in the western Caribbean, but previously unrecorded in Florida.

Today Antillean Nighthawks are known to be regular summer residents in the lower Keys, sometimes wandering farther north. "Golden" Warblers, now usually treated as a subspecies of the Yellow Warbler, are widespread in the Keys in summer, with some staying all year. How long were these birds present before 1941? Could Audubon have overlooked them a century earlier? Both have expanded their ranges in the Keys since the 1940s, so it's likely they were new arrivals when first noticed. But we can't be certain.

We're more assured about the Black-whiskered Vireo. If you drive down the Keys in mid-May you can hardly avoid hearing this bird, even if you have the windows rolled up and the air conditioner blasting. Its short, loud, emphatic phrases—which lead to nicknames in the Caribbean like "Whip Tom Kelly"—instantly command the attention of any naturalist. I can't imagine Audubon missing this vocal vireo, so I believe it colonized Florida sometime after 1832. It's now found throughout the Keys and halfway up both coasts of the peninsula as a common summer resident.

When it comes to the history of Florida's birdlife, we know less about the southern peninsula than we do about the Keys. But we know that there, too, species can come and go, colonizing new areas or vanishing. Consider the Smooth-billed Ani. This big, black member of the cuckoo family, known by its puffin-like beak and long, floppy tail, lives in flocks around tropical pastures and forest edges. It was only a rare visitor to Florida before about the 1930s, but then a flock showed up and began nesting near Lake Okeechobee, in the state's interior. The species expanded its numbers and range, becoming widespread in the southern peninsula by the 1970s. Then it started declining again. Smooth-billed Anis are now quite local and hard to find in Florida, and they might eventually disappear.

Easy come, easy go—that's how it works in this dynamic region of peninsula and islands. In southern Florida there are now dozens of breeding bird species that were not present in the 1830s, most of them brought in accidentally by humans. These include mynas and bulbuls from southern Asia, orioles from Central America, doves from the Middle East, and a plethora of parrots from tropical regions around the world. They may not draw as much publicity as some other introduced creatures, like the Burmese pythons that now fight with alligators in the Everglades, but they are scattered throughout the southern peninsula, especially in districts with more human habitations. Exotic birds may escape from captivity in any state, but they usually don't last long in the wild. In Florida, they frequently thrive and establish new populations. Florida has more established species of exotic birds than any other state except Hawaii.

Naturalists of the past couldn't have found any of these species that we know to be new arrivals—just as we have little hope of finding any of those that have disappeared. Both of those categories are among the elements that make Florida so interesting. But just as fascinating are a few birds that certainly were present in 1832, even though Audubon missed them.

Although he was fond of gentle doves, Audubon also admired bold predatory birds. He wrote movingly about eagles—including his infamous, fictitious "Bird of Washington"—and about various hawks and falcons. Two beautiful birds of prey, found locally in the interior of the southern peninsula, were among the species that Audubon had essentially no chance of seeing during his visit to the coast and Keys.

One would continue to elude naturalists for another half century. When the first Short-tailed Hawks were found in Florida, around the beginning of the 1880s, ornithologists wondered if they might be strays from the tropics. This was a species easily overlooked before the era of binoculars: when foraging, it generally soars high; when it lands, it tends to perch among dense foliage in trees, not out in the open. If Bartram, Audubon, or other early Florida visitors had seen a Short-tailed Hawk, it probably would have been just an unidentified raptor sailing high overhead, out of shotgun range.

The first Florida specimens created even more confusion at first, because this species has two distinct color morphs. They are all blackish on the back, but the underparts can be gleaming white or a deep chocolaty black. These two forms had been described and named as two different species a few decades earlier, based on specimens from South America and Mexico, and doubts about their status lingered in the 1880s. When W. E. D. Scott found one of each morph sharing a nest as a mated pair near Tarpon Springs, Florida, in 1889, it helped put those doubts to rest. Over the following decades it became clear that Short-tailed Hawks were widespread in the peninsula, in scattered breeding pairs, with a total population of probably fewer than five hundred individuals.

Among Florida birds, the Short-tailed Hawk is the one that comes closest to the geographic distribution of the King Vulture. Both are absent from the islands of the Caribbean; both are widespread on the tropical mainland, from Mexico to South America. Short-tailed Hawks in Florida are cut off from the main range of their species just as much as King Vultures in the 1770s would have been.

At least, that used to be the case. But recently, for no obvious reason, Short-tailed Hawks in the main part of their range have been expanding northward. In southwestern Mexico, the spread may have begun as early as the 1940s; within a few decades they had expanded nine hundred miles to the north, approaching the U.S. border. In eastern Mexico, where they had long been present, no movement was apparent until the 1970s. But by the late 1980s, birders reported a handful of sightings in both Texas and Arizona. By the late 1990s, they were photographed for documentation in both states. Now multiples are found every year in Texas and Arizona, with nesting proven in the latter state, and a few have been found farther afield. If they were to extend their range eastward along the Gulf Coast, which would not seem at all far-fetched, the Florida nesting birds no longer would be isolated, but part of a continuous population stretching deep into the tropics.

Perhaps they had such an extensive range in the past. It's not impossible, and it would explain how the Florida birds arrived there in the first place. And perhaps the same was true for King Vultures. There's no way to prove it, and it might seem unlikely, but thinking about bird distribution in Florida has led me to expect the unlikely.

The other Florida raptor that Audubon missed is common in Cuba, so it could have reached the peninsula by that route, although it's not known for crossing stretches of open water. The Snail Kite, a beautiful and specialized bird of prey, is widespread in the American tropics. It has a thin, deeply hooked beak, specially adapted for removing large apple snails (genus *Pomacea*) from their shells, and it flies low over the marsh with floppy wingbeats and slow glides, since no speed is required to overtake its prey. Adult males have slaty plumage with white accents, red eyes, orange legs, and orange facial skin, while adult females and young birds are boldly blotched with buff and brown. The species was described to science in 1817, based on specimens from the southern end of the range, in Argentina. Audubon's friend Edward Harris added it to the North American fauna when he found one in spring 1844, a year before Florida achieved statehood, along the river in what would be downtown Miami today.

The species proved to be a regular but uncommon resident of south-central Florida, ranging across the broad "river of grass" that makes up the Everglades region. When I saw it for the first time, as a teenager in the 1970s, it was officially known as the Everglade Kite—the name wasn't changed to Snail Kite until the 1980s—and considered an endangered species. Both the name and the perceived status reflected a U.S.-centric view of a bird that's common in more than twenty countries.

But the United States population was genuinely isolated, rare, and declining. It had always been somewhat nomadic within its limited Florida range, shifting around as water levels changed. It would build its nest in a shrub or low tree in the marshes, a few feet above the waterline, and it needed water deep enough to discourage predators, but not so deep that it would flood the nests. Changes in water levels also could hurt the populations of its *Pomacea* snail prey. As humans built more water-control structures from Lake Okeechobee south through the Everglades region, the kite's numbers continued to drop, and conservationists worried that it would vanish from the peninsula.

In Florida, however, nature does the unexpected. Exotic, non-native species become established easily there, and not just popular cage birds and Burmese pythons. Snails can do it, too. The so-called island apple snail, native to South America, had been popular in the aquarium trade, and some apparently were dumped into Florida waterways a couple of decades ago. This species is a *Pomacea*, related to the native Florida apple snail; but it grows to be larger, it tolerates a wider range of water conditions, and it reproduces much more rapidly, laying far more eggs at a time. It has proven to be horribly invasive in several parts of the world—including Florida. As it has spread through the peninsula, it has sparked concern about the damage it could cause to the marshes and to the native apple snail.

But it has also sparked a new hope for the Florida Snail Kites. Over the last few years, their breeding success has improved dramatically, their numbers appear to have increased, and they have expanded their range. Prior to about 2010 they were seen almost entirely south of Orlando. Now they can be seen by the dozens every day over marshes

around Gainesville, one hundred miles farther north. Studies have shown that in many areas of Florida, the Snail Kites are now feeding almost entirely on the invasive island apple snail, not the native snail.

And just to make things weirder—because this is Florida, after all—studies also show that local Snail Kites are evolving larger bills, which will make it easier for them to deal with the larger snails. Such rapid evolution of bill shape in response to changing conditions had been demonstrated before in finches in the Galápagos, but no one expected it in a bird of prey.

If Audubon had seen a Snail Kite in Florida, with its broad wings, sharply hooked beak, and slow, floppy flight, he assuredly would have known it was something different. It would have been one of those "Eureka" moments, when a discovery is immediately apparent—as when he picked up his first Sandwich Tern specimens in the Keys and knew right away they were new for North America. His recognition of the Great White Heron was similarly clear at the outset. And if he had seen a King Vulture sailing overhead, the first glimpse would have grabbed his attention. But many discoveries are not so obvious; it takes longer to guess they might be new, and often much longer to be sure of it. The Short-tailed Hawk might have fallen into that category if Audubon had seen it at all.

Then there's the Mottled Duck, probably widespread in Florida all along. William Bartram likely saw it on the St. Johns River in 1774, and Audubon may have seen it in 1832—he certainly saw it in Texas a few years later, as I'll describe in chapter 9. But it was not formally named until 1874, because it looks so much like the well-known, widespread American Black Duck. Detecting the Mottled Duck would require fine

opposite page: Snail Kites, adult male above, juvenile below, by Kenn Kaufman. This raptor is a resident in the marshy interior of the Florida peninsula, but because of the difficulty of travel in that region, it was missed by early explorers. Audubon's friend Edward Harris found the first record for Florida during a visit in 1844.

discernment, not raw discovery. Ornithologists would need data from throughout the continent to realize that the American Black Duck was a migratory species of northern latitudes, while the Mottled Duck was adapted to live year-round in the blazing climates of Florida and the Gulf Coast.

Information at that level was not available in the early 1800s, and that lack made some types of birds more difficult to identify and understand. The most extreme examples didn't involve these Florida birds, but rather a certain group of long-distance migrants. For Wilson, Audubon, and all their contemporaries, the most exasperating and lingering confusion would revolve around the migratory shorebirds.

Interlude:
Channeling the
Illustrator

The Size of the Challenge

"Of the size of life." "At their natural size." From the beginning, one of Audubon's selling points for *The Birds of America* was his intention to illustrate every species at full life size. Had he attempted his project in Africa, Australia, or South America, it would have been impossible; the ostriches, emus, cassowaries, and rheas would have exceeded the dimensions of any paper commercially available. For North America's avifauna he could pull it off by using the largest standard paper size, the so-called double elephant sheets at approximately 39½ by 29½ inches. Even within these broad surfaces, he had to find inventive poses to fit in tall or long-necked birds like the Whooping Crane, Great Blue Heron, and Trumpeter Swan.

In my own attempt to emulate this approach, I didn't have to accommodate any birds of quite such epic sizes. My largest subjects included the Snail Kite and the big, bold Caspian Tern. Paper size put some limits on their poses—I couldn't show them flying with their wings fully extended—but otherwise it was not a major challenge. I had more trouble with the smallest birds.

I had never drawn birds at life size before, or even thought about it. In the 1980s and 1990s I did many illustrations to show how to identify various birds, but the dimensions of these were never based on the sizes of the bird species themselves. Instead, they were dictated by the size at which these pictures would be reproduced. If an ink drawing of the face patterns of grebes was to be published in a space three and a half inches wide, my original drawing would be six or seven inches wide. If a color illustration of four wrens was to appear on a magazine page in a space more than six inches wide, my painting of them would be at least ten inches wide. Then when my originals were reduced for reproduction, any slight mistakes or uneven spots would be less noticeable. This trick was no innovation on my part; every bird illustrator I've known has done the same.

For my pseudo-Audubon project I had to illustrate some small birds, including the Philadelphia Vireo and Kirtland's Warbler. I had illustrated the Philadelphia Vireo before, but my original paintings of it were done at almost twice life size. To be true to the aim of my current project, I had to paint it exactly life size, no larger, no smaller. This proved to be a nerve-racking exercise. At that tight scale, if a dab of paint landed in the wrong spot by even a millimeter, it would show and that detail would look wrong. I could correct some mistakes, but some would wreck the piece and I would have to start over. For a couple of the pieces in this book, I started over three times.

Dealing with the largest species, by comparison, was not a challenge. To fit two Snail Kites into one composition, I just had to place them unnaturally close to each other, and in slightly awkward poses. And when you're channeling Audubon, such an arrangement almost comes naturally.

8

Strangers on the Shore

Heat haze is heavy in the air along the Delaware Bay shore near Cape May, New Jersey, on this August afternoon. Distant people walking the beach are reduced to shimmering mirages. But I'm focused on something closer: a few dozen small brown or gray birds, right in front of us on the mudflats of this tidal estuary.

Most are not much bigger than sparrows. But aside from size, nothing about them could suggest a bird so earthbound as a sparrow. They walk and run delicately across the wet sand and mud, long toes keeping them from sinking. They pause here and there to pick at the surface or probe in shallow puddles with thin, straight bills. When they raise their wings and take to the air, their flocks sweep out swiftly across the flats, swinging wide over the edge of the surf, then returning to alight near where they started.

"Shorebirds." When American birders use that word, we don't mean just any birds on the shore, like ducks or gulls: it's a group term for these sandpipers, plovers, and a few related families. This is a varied group, with more than 220 species worldwide, of which more than 80 have been found in North America. They mostly lack bright colors, but all have elegant shapes. Some are among the most impressive long-distance migrants in the world.

I am an unabashed fan of the shorebirds; they rank among my

favorite creatures. That wasn't always the case. In my early birding I found them frustrating, and I struggled every year to identify the various sorts. Sometimes I'd think I had some worked out, but then I'd see them again and doubts would surface. The confusion seemed endless.

That was long ago, and now I can name them all with confidence. But looking at these shorebirds on the mudflats near Cape May, I can see reasons why they seemed so vexing in the past. These birds are right out in the open, at close range—not hiding behind treetop foliage, as warblers might—but they are so subtle. At a glance, they all look the same. With a closer study they all look different: like snowflakes, no two individuals alike. Some are a bit larger, some smaller, with shorter or longer beaks. Some are grayer, some browner; some have sharper markings, others look more subdued or blended. They could all be slight variations on the same kind, or every single one might represent a different species.

It's August. For many people, summer vacations are peaking, but these shorebirds are already well into their fall migration. For most, their breeding grounds lie far to the north, on the tundra of Arctic Canada. They wing their way northward in late spring and quickly raise one brood of young if they can; by midsummer, the adults are migrating south again, to be followed shortly by their independent young. The New Jersey shoreline in August is thronged with sandpipers and plovers that already have flown more than a thousand miles south from their nesting territories. These include juvenile birds, arrowing southward on their own, with faith in their navigational instincts and their new, strong wings.

Most shorebirds change their appearance with the seasons, growing new feathers twice per year. Adults in breeding plumage of early summer sport their brightest colors (although "bright color," to a shorebird, means a richer shade of brown) and sharpest patterns of black and white. After molting to winter plumage, most are plainer and grayer. In August, for many species, some adults are still in breeding plumage, some already in winter plumage, and some in patchy transition. Juvenile birds have a distinct plumage, often quite different from any pattern worn by adults at any season.

With a dozen or more species often mingling at the same place, and all the variations within each species, a gathering of shorebirds can present a bewildering variety of different looks. Even though new birders today can start with excellent, thorough, well-illustrated guides for identification, shorebirds still cause them trouble.

In the early 1800s, these birds gave Alexander Wilson a lot of trouble, too. As he recounted in *American Ornithology*, his pursuit of a large shorebird called an oystercatcher "nearly cost me my life." He wrote:

> On the sea beach of Cape May, not far from a deep and rapid inlet, I broke the wing of one of these birds, and being without a dog, instantly pursued it towards the inlet, which it made for with great rapidity. We both plunged in nearly at the same instant; but the bird eluded my grasp, and I sunk beyond my depth; it was not until this moment that I recollected having carried in my gun along with me. On rising to the surface I found the bird had dived, and a strong ebb current was carrying me fast towards the ocean, encumbered with a gun and all my shooting apparatus; I was compelled to relinquish my bird, and to make for the shore, with considerable mortification, and the total destruction of the contents of my powderhorn.

The oystercatcher got away.

In the first six volumes of *American Ornithology*, Wilson avoided shorebirds. He discussed only four species, and botched the identities of three of them. In his seventh volume he tackled the group, putting on a brave face in his flowery introduction: "In prosecuting our researches among the feathered tribes of this extensive country, we are at length led to the shores of the ocean, where a numerous and varied multitude, subsisting on the gleanings of that vast watery magazine of nature, invite our attention; and from their singularities and numbers, promise both amusement and instruction."

Amusement and instruction—and confusion, too, in copious amounts. Aside from his risky plunge after the oystercatcher, most of

Wilson's problems with shorebirds involved trying to classify and identify them. He wasn't alone. No other group of birds in North America
and Europe proved as challenging for the first scientists who attempted
to figure them out. Their early struggles echo today for every bird-
watcher trying to learn to recognize the shorebirds.

Look again at this varied throng of almost-different, almost-the-
same little waders on this tidal flat near Cape May. Imagine we could
step back more than two centuries in time and stand here with Alexander Wilson. Now we have no binoculars, no telescope. Now we have
no illustrated guides, and we know practically nothing about the migrations of these birds, or their striking seasonal changes in color. We don't
even know if all these birds have been described to science yet. (Spoiler:
Some have not.) How are we ever going to sort them out?

A problem for Wilson, and for everyone trying to understand shorebirds then, was the question whether those in North America belonged
to the same species as those in Europe. It was understood that some
aquatic birds lived on both continents. And some shorebirds looked
identical in both regions. The Ruddy Turnstone, a chunky sandpiper
with a harlequin face pattern, short orange legs, and a pointy wedge-
shaped beak, is common on rocky and sandy shores on both sides of the
Atlantic. That was an easy call. But most cases were not so apparent.

Today we can say that almost forty species of shorebirds are seen
regularly in good numbers along the Atlantic Seaboard of the United
States and southeastern Canada. About a quarter of those, nine species,
are also commonly seen in western Europe. But at least another ten are
so similar to related Old World species that they easily could be confused with them—and often were, in the past.

One example was the oystercatcher that almost did in Wilson. The
oystercatchers make up a small family of large shorebirds, about a dozen
species scattered around the world, mostly on coastlines. With long red
beaks, red or yellow eyes, short pinkish legs, and plumage that's either
all-black or patterned black and white, they look as if they should be
unmistakable. Wilson assumed the ones he saw on the New Jersey coast
were the same as those in Europe.

Actually, the American Oystercatcher is distinct. The Dutch zoologist C. J. Temminck described and named it in 1820 as a South American species, thus different from the bird believed to be present in North America as well as Europe. By 1834, in his *Manual of the Ornithology of the United States and of Canada,* Thomas Nuttall suggested that Temminck's bird might be "expected occasionally on the coast of Florida." It was left to Audubon, in the third volume of *Ornithological Biography* in 1835, to assert that oystercatchers along our Atlantic Coast were all of the species described by Temminck. "I have never met with the European Oyster-catcher . . . in any part of the United States. . . . I believe that the American or Mantled Oyster-catcher has been confounded with it by Wilson and others."

And that was one of the easy ones. Most such transatlantic confusions would be harder. Wilson, to his credit, did sort out an error made by Europeans about the Long-billed Curlew. The largest sandpiper in North America, it's similar to an Old World curlew—sort of. Wilson wrote: "This American species has been considered by the naturalists of Europe to be a mere *variety* of their own, notwithstanding its difference of color, and superior length of bill. . . . We do not hesitate to consider the present a distinct species, peculiar to this country."

He had few such successes among the shorebirds. For bird groups he knew well, Wilson was quick to point out where other writers had erred. Species accounts in his *American Ornithology* often began by clarifying mistakes made by the French Comte de Buffon, or the Englishman John Latham, or the Welshman Thomas Pennant, or "European naturalists" in general, or even the great Linnaeus himself. But when it came to the shorebirds, his comments were muted. He didn't have enough experience. He might question what Europeans had written, but seldom was he confident enough to contradict them. Just as often, he perpetuated their errors.

A small sandpiper now called the Dunlin, *Calidris alpina,* breeds on Arctic tundra around the world and winters on coastlines, including all along our Atlantic Coast. Dunlins are notable for the graceful precision of their flocks in flight, with dozens of individuals flying fast, close together, veering and turning in unison. They are also notable for seasonal color change: an adult in breeding plumage has a bright reddish-brown back and a black patch on the belly, while winter birds are mostly a dingy gray-brown with white bellies. Dunlins are common enough in Europe that Linnaeus had described them to science—twice. In 1758, he named the breeding plumage *Tringa alpina*. Then in 1766, he named the winter plumage *Tringa cinclus*. Decades later, both names were still in use, and hardly anyone suspected they applied to the same bird.

In the seventh volume of *American Ornithology*, Wilson wrote about birds under both names. He called the breeding-plumaged bird Red-backed Sandpiper. The drab winter plumage carried the odd name of "Purre," a word already in wide use in England and probably an imitation of the bird's call. His accounts under these headings were separated by a dozen pages and four other sandpipers, and he clearly regarded the Red-backed Sandpiper and Purre as distinct species. Their striking seasonal change in color blinded him to the fact that they were the same in every other way.

The Red Knot was another source of confusion—for everyone. It's another sandpiper with strong seasonal change. Adults in late spring are colored a soft orange-red on their underparts, with spangles of the same on their backs. In winter they're plain gray above and whitish below. Juveniles in early fall are also gray, but with a beautiful pattern of narrow black and white crescents across their back and wings. The Red Knot has a wide distribution, so early ornithologists had plenty of chances to encounter this bird, and name it. And they did. By the time Wilson began his work, Europeans had bestowed no fewer than seven scientific names on this bird.

Did Wilson solve this tangle of seven names? No, he added an eighth. He somehow decided that bright spring Red Knots didn't match any sandpiper already described, so he presented them as a new species: *Tringa rufa*, the Red-breasted Sandpiper. He assigned the well-marked juvenile knots to *Tringa cinerea*, a name that had been coined in the 1760s by the Danish naturalist Morten Thrane Brünnich, and he called

Dunlins, winter plumage on left and breeding plumage on right, by John James Audubon. As with several other kinds of sandpipers, the seasonal changes in plumage of the Dunlin were very confusing to early naturalists. Alexander Wilson and others thought that the breeding and winter plumages represented two distinct species.

it the Ash-colored Sandpiper. In volume seven of *American Ornithology*, Wilson placed the Red-breasted Sandpiper and Ash-colored Sandpiper several pages apart, with no hint that they might be the same.

The Sanderling, one of the most familiar shorebirds, was also perplexing at first. Practically everyone who has been to the beach has seen those pale little sandpipers that dash back and forth at the waterline, chasing the receding waves. Sanderlings wear their pallid gray "winter" colors for most of the year, molting into a rich reddish-brown breeding plumage for only a few weeks in late spring and early summer. The striking change confused Linnaeus and subsequent editors of his *Systema Naturae*, who again described the bird twice. Actually, they described it as two species of plovers—the distinctions between sandpipers and plovers hadn't been worked out yet—and half a century later, books still separated them as Sanderling Plover and Ruddy Plover.

Wilson was among the first to suspect their true identity. In his account of "Ruddy Plover," he wrote: "This bird is frequently found in company with the Sanderling, which, except in color, it very much resembles. . . . I should not be surprised if the present species turn out hereafter to be the Sanderling itself, in a different dress." He was frustrated, though, by the works of Pennant, Latham, and others, who supported the claim of Linnaeus that these birds were distinct. "Naturalists, however, have considered it as a separate species; but have given us no further particulars than that 'in Hudsons Bay it is known by the name of Mistchaychekiskaweshish'—a piece of information certainly very instructive." The sarcasm in the last comment practically drips off the page, but still he wasn't confident enough to contradict the European authorities.

However, Wilson's account of the "Sanderling Plover" introduced a new insight. In the early 1800s, the category of bird families was not in use yet. Instead, plovers were classified in one genus, sandpipers in another genus, snipes (sandpipers with longer bills) in another, and so on, within a very large and unwieldy order of wading birds. Plovers were known for having only three toes on each foot. Sandpipers had four: three toes pointing forward and a small hind toe. The Sanderling (and

Sanderlings, two adults in winter plumage, by John James Audubon. In the early 1800s this bird was often called the "Sanderling Plover," while its breeding plumage, marked with dark reddish-brown, was usually treated as a distinct species called the "Ruddy Plover." Alexander Wilson was among the first to suggest that these birds were really sandpipers, not plovers, and that they represented two stages of the same species.

its alter ego, the Ruddy Plover) lacked that hind toe. As Wilson pointed out, though, everything else about the Sanderling—the structure of its bill, its feeding habits, its voice, and its social behavior—would place it among the sandpipers. And he was right.

A focus on shorebirds' feet sometimes led ornithologists astray. That's reflected in a term used by no one but bird people: semipalmated. The word means "half-webbed," and it refers to partial webbing between the bases of the three forward-pointing toes. Birders get used to the word because it's in the name of the common (but unrelated) Semipalmated Plover and Semipalmated Sandpiper. We usually just call these birds "Semis," we rarely see the toe webbing, and we seldomly think about what the word means.

But for early ornithologists, that bit of webbing was a crucial detail. Among all these similar, variable birds, it was so hard to tell whether an individual matched a vague written description. But holding the bird in their hands, they could check one simple thing: Did it have slight webbing between the bases of the toes, or not? That could be the deciding characteristic.

To see how pervasive this was, look at the shorebird known today as the Willet. This large sandpiper has long gray legs, a bladelike beak, and a ringing cry that sounds like *Pill-will-willet*. When it flies, it flashes a black-and-white wing pattern recognizable from half a mile away. But what did early ornithologists call this bird? Semipalmated Snipe. Yes, this big, flashy shorebird has slight webs between the bases of its toes, and for Wilson, Audubon, and their contemporaries, that was what counted. Eventually that name was abandoned for the simpler, more poetic Willet.* The Semipalmated Plover and Sandpiper are still saddled with that clumsy English modifier, as they have been for two centuries. But in the context of the early 1800s, that name made sense.

The Semipalmated Plover looks almost identical to the Common Ringed Plover of Europe. This similarity fooled Wilson—fooled him twice, but he figured out one of his errors. In volume five of *American*

---

*The reference to its feet survives only in the Willet's scientific name, *Tringa semipalmata*.

Ornithology in 1812, Wilson reported that "the Ringed Plover is very abundant on the low sandy shores of our whole sea-coast, during summer." He described the nesting behavior of pairs on sandy beaches of New Jersey and illustrated a very pale-backed plover. Then he added: "This species is subject to great variety of change in its plumage. In the month of July I found most . . . such as I have here figured; but about the beginning or middle of October they had become much darker above, and their plumage otherwise varied."

The paler birds were a different species, the Piping Plover, undescribed at that point. By the time Wilson was finishing his seventh volume a year later, he was having second thoughts, so he included another text account for the Ringed Plover. "In a preceding part of this work, a bird by this name has been figured and described, under the supposition that it was the Ring Plover, then in its summer dress; but which . . . I now suspect to be a different species." He went on: "The present species, or true Ring Plover, and also the former, or light-colored bird, both arrive on the sea coast of New Jersey late in April. The present kind continues to be seen in flocks until late in May, when they disappear on their way farther north; the light-colored bird remains during the summer, forms its nest in the sand, and generally produces two broods in the season. Early in September the present species returns in flocks as before. . . ."

He had hit on distinctions between two species. Frustratingly, though, the Welsh zoologist Thomas Pennant had seen American specimens and had pronounced the paler birds to be nothing significant. They were, he wrote, faded and degraded versions of the Ringed Plover: "The climate had almost destroyed the specific marks." There it was again, that confounded theory from Buffon, claiming that the unhealthy climate of the new continent caused nature in America to be a degenerate form of the European ideal. Wilson disagreed about the plovers, but wasn't confident enough to name the paler birds as a new species, and he died a few months after completing the seventh volume. George Ord, editing a new edition of this volume in 1824, built on Wilson's observation and named the pale bird *Charadrius melodus*, Piping Plover, the name it bears today.

Ord had, of course, looked at the plovers' feet—the accepted practice. Sure enough, the pale birds had no webbing between the bases of the three front toes, while Ringed Plovers from Europe had slight webbing between the outer and middle toe. Yep, must be a different species. But then Ord pointed out a difference in the supposed Ringed Plovers from North America: they had webbing not only between the outer and middle toe, but also between the middle and inner. It was just a tiny scrap of keratin, but assumed a large significance: "Here then is a diversity, which, if constant, would constitute a specific difference."

A year later, Charles Lucien Bonaparte agreed: "The remark made by Mr. Ord relative to the difference between the union of the toes in American and European specimens, is no less extraordinary than correct; I have verified it on the specimens in my collection." Bonaparte proposed that the American birds be called *Charadrius semipalmatus*, the Semipalmated Plover. Today we know that Semipalmated and Common Ringed Plovers differ in voice and in other details. No one questions that they are separate species. But if not for the difference in their feet, the distinctions between them probably wouldn't have been noticed until decades later.

The other Semi—the Semipalmated Sandpiper—played a role in another confusing complex that took much longer to straighten out. The seven smallest sandpipers, all related, spend their summers on Arctic tundra and their winters farther south, four in the Old World and three in the New. Birders are often stymied in trying to identify them, and may just refer to them under the catchall terms of "peeps" in North America and "stints" in Eurasia. Early scientists also tended to lump them all. Of these seven species, only two had been formally described and named before 1810, another three by 1820, and the last two not until after 1850. It took time for ornithologists to rise to this challenge.

Wilson saw no challenge in 1812. In volume five of his *Ornithology* he recognized only one small species under the name Little Sandpiper, *Tringa pusilla*, a mash-up of four birds from western Europe and eastern North America. But by the next year, in volume seven, he had a novelty to introduce: the Semipalmated Sandpiper, *Tringa semipalmata*.* "This is one of the smallest of its tribe; and seems to have been entirely over-looked, or confounded with another which it much resembles (*Tringa pusilla*). . . . Its half-webbed feet, however, are sufficient marks of distinction between the two." The structure of the feet might not separate sandpipers from plovers, but it was good enough for defining species within the sandpiper group.

"Half-webbed" was an exaggeration, but those slight webs equaled a godsend for ornithologists. By the 1820s, Little Stint and Temminck's Stint had been described from Europe, and Least Sandpiper and Semi-palmated Sandpiper from North America. All were sparrow-sized crea-tures varying from brown to gray, and devilishly alike. The one bright spot was the webbing on the Semi's feet. Held in the hand, this one spe-cies could be named with confidence.

Or so it seemed. But another member of the complex has those same toe webs. As a result, this other bird, the Western Sandpiper, was over-looked among the Semis for decades.

As their English name implies, Western Sandpipers are not common in the East. They breed only in Alaska, and migrate mainly down the Pacific Coast, with tens of thousands gathering at some bays and estuar-ies. But some spread out across the rest of the continent in migration. Even as far east as the Atlantic Coast, they occur regularly in spring and fall. In winter they can be found all along the Gulf Coast and south-ern Atlantic Coast, with some north to New Jersey and Long Island. Meanwhile, Semipalmated Sandpipers are abundant in the eastern states during spring and fall, but essentially absent in winter, when most have gone to South America.

So Wilson and others almost certainly saw Western Sandpipers along the coast in winter. Unfortunately, at that season they are excruciatingly

---

*Today the scientific name of the Semipalmated Sandpiper is *Calidris pusilla*. Linnaeus had introduced *pusilla* in 1766 as the name of a poorly defined small sandpiper, and later authorities decided it probably applied to the Semipalmated. Wilson's earlier reference to "Little Sandpiper, *Tringa pusilla*" had been a composite, but in this paragraph he was evidently singling out the bird now known as the Least Sandpiper.

similar to Semipalmateds. They're subtle enough at other seasons, with Westerns showing some brighter reddish-brown markings in breeding plumage and juvenile plumage. But winter birds of both species are plain grayish-brown above and whitish below, with no notable marks of any kind. Although Westerns average slightly larger and longer billed, they overlap completely with the largest Semis.

It's no wonder they managed to slip under the eastern radar for so long. But for years there were hints the Semipalmated Sandpiper might not be as simple as it seemed. Audubon, in the fifth volume of *Ornithological Biography* in 1839, noted that the Semi varied in size: "There being a very remarkable difference of size . . . I was induced to compare a great number of them. . . . I found differences as to size and proportions enough to induce persons having nothing better than skins, to imagine that several species might be made out of them."

At about the same time (1838), Charles Bonaparte suggested that the Semipalmated Sandpiper, found in "America generally," had a close relative living only in "South and central parts." He even suggested a name for it (*mauri*), but since he provided no description, the name had no official standing. During the 1840s and '50s, the German ornithologist Jean Louis Cabanis and the German-Cuban naturalist Juan Gundlach both struggled with the size variation of "Semipalmated" Sandpipers wintering in the Carolinas and Cuba, suggesting that they might represent two species.

Finally, in 1864, George Lawrence gave the first good description of the larger bird. He declared it distinct and named it *Ereunetes occidentalis*. His diagnosis was based on specimens from the Pacific Coast, in breeding plumage, and he explained their differences from the Semi.*

---

*The Western Sandpiper is now included in the genus *Calidris* with the other smallest sandpipers. By rights it should have the scientific name *Calidris occidentalis* and should be credited to Lawrence. But in the 1850s, after a conversation with Charles Bonaparte and through some shaky reasoning, Jean Cabanis decided that some of the birds he and Gundlach had encountered in Cuba and/or South Carolina must fit under the name *mauri* proposed by Bonaparte years earlier. That decision was mostly ignored for years until

Western Sandpipers, juvenile *(left)*, winter adult *(center)*, and breeding adult *(right)*, by Kenn Kaufman. Most numerous in western North America, this species is nonetheless a regular visitor along the Atlantic Coast during migration seasons and winter. Early naturalists undoubtedly saw it there but mistook it for an abundant eastern bird, the Semipalmated Sandpiper. Their separate status wasn't fully resolved until the 1880s. One surprising source of confusion: scientists of that era, examining specimens in the hand, relied too much on the structure of the birds' feet.

Even then, the scientific community was slow to accept it. Accounts of North American birds through the early 1880s mostly treated it as a subspecies or variety of the Semipalmated Sandpiper. Not until 1886, in the first official list published by the newly formed American Ornithologists' Union, did the Western Sandpiper gain recognition as a full species.

John James Audubon never had a chance with the Western Sandpiper. But in treating other shorebirds, he had major advantages over Alexander Wilson. Like his predecessor, Audubon mostly ignored the shorebirds during the first part of his project; he didn't focus on them until the 1830s, after the first couple of volumes of his paintings and text had been published and after he had spent time along the Atlantic Coast. Waiting gave him the benefit of more information, as facts about shorebirds continued to accumulate in the two decades after Wilson finished his seventh volume.

Much of the new knowledge built on Wilson's foundation, as George Ord and Charles Bonaparte had both published updates and commentaries on *American Ornithology* during the 1820s. And a major step forward was the 1831 publication of *Fauna Boreali-Americana*, volume 2, by Swainson and Richardson. This work on the birds of northern Canada proved invaluable. Richardson's observations helped to confirm that most of those migratory sandpipers and plovers were going to the Arctic to raise their young, even if individuals of some species might linger all along the Atlantic Coast in summer.

Not everything published after Wilson was so helpful. Thomas Nuttall's *Manual of the Ornithology of the United States and of Canada*, published in 1832 and 1834, contained good information on some birds that Nuttall knew well. But when it came to shorebirds, he was out of his depth. Some of his sandpiper accounts are so vague that they can't be connected to any single species. And he uncritically accepted practically

---

American ornithologists essentially dug it out of the wastebasket in the early 1900s and made it official. So today the Western Sandpiper is *Calidris mauri* and credited to Cabanis, not to Bonaparte or Gundlach or Lawrence.

any shorebird that anyone had ever proposed might live on this continent, so that purely Eurasian species are listed alongside those of North America.

So when Audubon started treating shorebirds in his third and fourth volumes, he referenced Nuttall mainly to contradict him. In his account of the Least Sandpiper, he started off by rejecting five species of sandpipers that Bonaparte and Nuttall had claimed as part of the North American avifauna, and then launched into a diatribe:

> The extreme confusion that exists with respect to these species, and many others of the same tribe, is in my opinion caused solely by the anxiety of authors to discover or invent new species, often founding distinctions on slight differences in the length of bills, tarsi, or toes. Now, Reader, if in such large species as the *Grus Americana*, for example, the young has been palmed on the world of science as a distinct species for nearly a century past . . . can we be surprised that in birds so small as the present, opportunities should have occurred of committing errors. My opinion . . . is, that we have in the United States only the diminutive species badly figured by Wilson, and almost as carelessly described by that wonderful man. To enter upon a long discussion as to the identity of the present bird [Least Sandpiper] with any of the small Tringas enumerated by European authors, would be to me quite as irksome as it would prove unprofitable to you, for there scarcely exists a single description of these birds sufficiently accurate to enable one to decide with certainty.

Harrumph.

The whole paragraph is classic Audubon, from the sarcastic dig at "that wonderful man" Wilson to criticism of those who were, like himself, trying to discover new species. And in the midst of these comments about shorebirds, he tosses in a sentence about "*Grus Americana*"—a nod to his bizarre, stubborn, and incorrect insistence that the bird we now know as the Sandhill Crane was just the young of the Whooping Crane, despite the many differences between those two species.

Still, Audubon deduced that others had been wrong in attributing various European shorebirds to North America. And he made correct calls on several questions left unsettled by others. The Stilt Sandpiper, a medium-size but long-legged wader, had been listed under two or three names, but Audubon recognized that they all referred to one variable species. He also chose to ignore multiple species of snipes and godwits that others had proposed, and he was among the first to recognize that golden-plovers in America were different from those in Europe.

Overall, Audubon's treatment of the shorebirds of eastern North America was more thorough and accurate than what Wilson had produced two decades earlier. He still had some major misconceptions about their migratory habits, but at that point, so did everyone else. And he didn't have a complete tally of the species present. No one did.

By the 1840s, question marks on the list of eastern shorebirds involved closely similar pairs of species that couldn't be clarified without more detailed study. Western and Semipalmated Sandpipers wouldn't be fully accepted as distinct species for another fifty years. It would be a full century before scientists could agree on the status of the sandpipers called dowitchers: Were they all one species, or two? (There are two, now known as Long-billed and Short-billed Dowitchers, although both have long bills.) Even in 2023, we are debating whether the Willet (the flashy sandpiper that was called the "Semipalmated Snipe" two hundred years ago) might be a complex of two species. There was no way Audubon could have reached conclusions on questions like these.

However, another sandpiper that migrates through eastern North America managed to evade Audubon, Wilson, Nuttall, and all their contemporaries. It was overlooked even by explorers who collected specimens in the 1840s and '50s without realizing it was different. When it was finally described in 1861, it was named for Spencer Baird, who had been one of Audubon's young protégés two decades earlier. Ironically, the lingering confusion about this bird had been caused partly by Audubon himself.

The bird now called Baird's Sandpiper escaped notice partly because it resembles the bird now called the White-rumped Sandpiper. Both are a bit larger than the smallest "peeps"—about seven and a half inches from bill tip to tail tip, as opposed to about six inches for Least and Semipalmated Sandpipers. Both Baird's and White-rumped Sandpipers have relatively long wingtips, extending past the end of the tail at rest; the long wings reflect their remarkably long migrations. Both are more numerous as migrants through the Great Plains and the Canadian Prairie Provinces than they are along the Atlantic Coast, where the early American naturalists concentrated their efforts.

Although they're similar in size and shape, at all seasons the White-rumped Sandpiper tends to be grayer on the back, while Baird's Sandpiper tends toward a warmer brown. And as reflected in the current name, the White-rumped has white on the rump—more precisely, on upper tail coverts, the narrow row of feathers just above the base of the tail. On Baird's Sandpiper, these feathers are dark brown to black.

Birders often focus on descriptive bird names—complaining, for example, that it's hard to see the red belly on a Red-bellied Woodpecker. We assume that everyone must have been aware of the white rump of the White-rumped Sandpiper. But that wasn't its name in early days, and no one paid much attention to what seemed a minor mark. Audubon, Nuttall, and Bonaparte all called this bird Schinz's Sandpiper, conflating it with a subspecies of the Dunlin. Their descriptions mentioned white on those upper tail coverts, but with no hint that it might be significant. And most bizarre is Audubon's painting, showing two "Schinz's Sandpipers" on a sandy beach. One is standing in profile. The other is flying, turned on its side, so that we see the complete upperside of the wings, tail, and back. The pose could have been chosen to show off that stripe of white—except that it *doesn't* show. Audubon painted those feathers dark brown with gray edges, like all the rest of the upperparts.

Audubon wrote that his painting was based on two birds he shot at St. Augustine, Florida, at the beginning of December 1831. Could one of those birds have been a Baird's Sandpiper, unknown at the time? Maybe. The collection at the Smithsonian Institution in Washington has

"Schinz's Sandpipers" by John James Audubon. This was almost certainly intended to illustrate the bird now called the White-rumped Sandpiper, but Audubon caused long-lasting confusion by painting it without the diagnostic white stripe across the rump. It's possible that the flying bird in this plate was based on a specimen of Baird's Sandpiper, a species that was unrecognized at the time and wouldn't be named until years later.

a few dozen specimens from Audubon, and these do include one White-rumped Sandpiper, but only one.

An odd note in his *Ornithological Biography* may be significant. His description of "Schinz's Sandpiper" mentions the white tail coverts. But at the end of the account he adds a separate sentence: "In some individuals, about six of the middle tail-coverts are black, the lateral barred with white and dusky." That would be true for Baird's Sandpiper, but *not* for the White-rumped. This sentence, isolated like an afterthought, might hint that Audubon was uncomfortable about it. If so, he never mentioned it again; and his painting and description probably influenced others to overlook Baird's Sandpiper as late as the 1850s. It was not until 1861 that a young Elliott Coues, working with the growing specimen collection at the Smithsonian, was able to clarify the differences and formally present Baird's Sandpiper to the world.

Naturalists of Audubon's era had a hazy concept of the migrations of shorebirds. They saw them come and go along the coast or along the edges of rivers, but without a clear idea of which species were present. They saw the migrant flocks swell in numbers and then diminish, but still they struggled to understand the timing of the passage. They knew that many North American shorebird species were shared with Europe, and they gave less thought to the possibility of sharing them with the southernmost reaches of South America. These two long-winged migrants, the White-rumped Sandpiper and Baird's Sandpiper, reflect this lack of understanding.

In the 1830s, even as the White-rumped continued to be overlooked by naturalists in North America, the French ornithologist Louis Pierre Vieillot had already named it as a distinct species in 1819. Vieillot's diagnosis was based on writings by the Spanish naturalist Félix de Azara, who had found these sandpipers in small flocks on wet meadows and the edges of ponds in open country—in Paraguay. On the edge between the tropics and the south temperate zone, Paraguay lies some four thousand miles south of the United States. The White-rumped Sandpipers that Azara saw were not residents there, however; they were mostly transients, just passing through, because most of their wintering

Baird's Sandpipers, two adults (*left* and *center*) and one juvenile, by Kenn Kaufman. Nesting in the Arctic and spending the winter in southern South America, this long-distance migrant moves north through the center of North America in the spring. During the fall, it is uncommon but regular farther east, including along the Atlantic Coast. Overlooked for years, it wasn't described and named until 1861.

grounds are even farther south in Argentina, all the way down to Tierra del Fuego.

The breeding territory of the White-rumped Sandpiper lies entirely north of the Arctic Circle, in northernmost Alaska and the Canadian High Arctic. For this bird to vault the entire span of the Americas, from the northernmost land to the southernmost, might seem bizarre, almost unbelievable. But a number of shorebirds perform similar feats of distance. These include the Baird's Sandpipers that managed to hide in the White-rumped Sandpiper's shadow for years, and many others besides.

We could even describe this as one of the characteristic patterns for the group. From November through February, when it's winter in the northern hemisphere, the shorelines and grasslands of southernmost South America are thronged by more than twenty species of shorebirds that had spent their breeding season no closer than Canada. A one-way journey of seven thousand miles is not at all unusual for this tribe of epic travelers.

Ornithologists of the early 1800s could not conceive of the extent of these migrations. Many had only a sketchy understanding of geography. Few could imagine how brief were summers in the Arctic, or how harsh those lands became when summer ended; it was difficult to realize that some migrants could still be on their way north at the end of May, and others already southbound at the end of June. Naturalists who had traveled would have known that travel, from the viewpoint of an earthbound human, was painfully slow. Would any bird go so far, almost halfway around the world, twice per year? Of course not.

But they do. And it's an element of shorebird magic. When I watch a flock of sandpipers lift off from a coastal lagoon and climb into the sky, it lifts my soul—not only because of the beauty of their flight, but also because I know they might not touch down for a thousand miles. Scientific knowledge of the migrations of these birds, based on years of research, doesn't take away from the sense of magic; it makes it stronger.

Early naturalists all underestimated the travels of shorebirds. When he saw Upland Sandpipers arriving in Louisiana in spring, Audubon assumed they had spent the winter nearby on "the vast prairies of Texas and Mexico." But they hadn't; they were coming from grasslands of southern South America. Wilson and Nuttall both asserted that the sandpipers known as Greater Yellowlegs and Lesser Yellowlegs bred in marshes along the central Atlantic Coast, though neither gentleman had ever seen a nest. But they don't; those birds go on to high latitudes of Canada and Alaska to breed and raise their young.

Every writer on birds in that era mentioned that plovers and sandpipers in early fall were especially stout, but invariably they followed with some comment about eating them. (Nuttall wrote that Sanderlings "are seldom in good order for the table until autumn, when, with their broods, they arrive remarkably plump and fat, and are then justly esteemed as a delicacy by the epicure.") No one ever asked *why* the birds were so fat at that season. We know now that they were bulking up to prepare for their longest migratory flights of the year, putting on fat to burn as fuel during flights that might last for days. With nineteenth-century knowledge, such a mental leap might have been impossible.

It's still surprising that no one questioned another odd pattern of migration that was becoming clear. By the 1830s, Audubon recognized that many shorebirds did go to the far north for the summer. And he recognized that some of those were common migrants along the Atlantic Coast—in fall. He mentioned this for the Pectoral Sandpiper and "Schinz's Sandpiper," and implied it for several other species. But he never seems to have asked: If they migrate along the coast in the fall, where are they in the spring?

Where indeed? It would take a few more decades to work this out, but vast numbers of shorebirds migrate north in spring through the center of the continent. Especially among those that migrate farthest, major flocks move out of South America to come up through eastern Mexico and Texas, and then straight north through the heart of the Great Plains and the Prairie Provinces. The present-day state of Kansas may be far from the popular idea of "shore," but wildlife refuges in central Kansas may swarm in spring with hundreds of thousands of migratory shorebirds. When their return passage southward begins, as early as July for some, many of these same birds shift eastward, appearing along the

Atlantic Coast. It's a pattern of loop migration that we now know to be common. But in spring, if they arrive in a coastal region it will be on the coast of Texas, pausing there before they arrow north through the interior.

If Audubon had had any inkling of this loop migration, he could have taken full advantage of it. By chance, his one visit to the new Republic of Texas in spring 1837 put him in position to intercept this central corridor of migrants. He was there at the perfect time and place to discover both the Western Sandpiper and Baird's Sandpiper—but he didn't. He had no way of knowing that the sandpiper flocks on the mudflats, seemingly so much like flocks on the Atlantic Coast, held subtle novelties just waiting to be revealed. These birds of passage passed him by, and they would hold their secrets for a few years longer.

Interlude:
Channeling the
Illustrator

Materials and Methods

Years ago, when I was reading a lot of science fiction, I ran across a thought-provoking story by Robert Silverberg. The central character was a classical composer who had shown brilliant promise in the 1700s, but then died young. Some music-loving modern scientists develop the technology to pluck this prodigy from the past and bring him into the present, assuming he will continue writing beautiful pieces in classical modes. To their dismay, the revived genius embraces every kind of advanced electronic synthesizer and starts producing heavy techno-pop for the counterculture club scene.

When I read the story I thought, *Well, why not?* Why wouldn't an innovator in one age continue to innovate in another? And this story came to mind as I began working on illustrations for this book. I was trying to imagine how Audubon would have painted various birds. But if he stepped into the present day, would he go back to the methods and materials he had used in the 1800s, or would he try new approaches?

His method of shooting birds and pinning up freshly killed specimens in lifelike postures to serve as models would run afoul of today's legal protections. I assume he'd be working from reference photos instead.

But what artistic materials and techniques did he use? The best account I've seen was in a 1993 essay by Reba Fishman Snyder, who took part in a detailed study of the originals in the collection of the New-York Historical Society. According to Snyder's analysis, Audubon experimented with a remarkable variety of media to achieve his results.

Even on the frontier, even with a perpetual lack of money, he always used the highest quality watercolor papers available—mostly Whatman papers from two mills in England, featuring a very smooth surface, ideal for the intricate details in Audubon's bird portraits. On this fine paper, he consistently began with a detailed pencil drawing, often putting every major feather and leaf vein in place before beginning to add color.

And for that color, he would try anything. Audubon's earliest surviving bird drawings were done largely in pastels, which had been very popular in Europe when he was a boy. Later he used mainly watercolors. But Snyder's team found that most of the originals for *The Birds of America* incorporated a variety of media, used in varied ways. Sometimes Audubon brushed on layer after layer of watercolor, for deep, rich hues. Often he added some pastel on top of the watercolor, sometimes adding it while the paint was still wet. He might add white gouache for detail, although he would also create white areas by scraping away paint to expose the paper beneath. Black ink appeared in some cases for fine detail. Often he drew with pencil on top of watercolor, adding short, fine lines to mimic the texture of feathers. Rarely he added metallic paint, or added background in oils, which doesn't necessarily work well on watercolor paper. He added glazing selectively on top of some colors.

It was daunting for me to try to emulate this mixed-media mastery. The Whatman company no longer produces watercolor paper (although they did so as late as the 1950s). For a worthy replacement, I settled on Arches watercolor paper, produced in France. Their hot-pressed papers had the smooth surface I needed, and the largest of their standard sheets were close to the size of Audubon's largest compositions. But I had done my earlier bird painting in acrylics, and then for many years in gouache, and then in oils. I'd done little with regular watercolors, and I'd never used pastels at all. Regardless, I set to work, studying high-resolution images of the originals from the New-York Historical Society, and trying all the media and all the techniques that Snyder had described.

Many of the top bird illustrators today work mainly in gouache—not just white gouache for accents, but the full range of these opaque watercolors. Having used it extensively myself, I understand why. In transparent watercolor it may take several layers of paint to achieve a particular hue, but in gouache it's possible to mix up just the color you want and then apply it directly in one layer. Some shades of brown wind up with a bothersome "milky" look in gouache, but it's possible to overcome this, and it's possible to create both fine details and broad areas of flat color when necessary.

Also available today is a brilliant range of colored pencils, and some bird illustrators get superb results with these. Given Audubon's early use of pastels, I suspect he would find colored pencils easy to adopt, and he might use them with pastels and other media.

What about acrylics? These versatile paints weren't available until the middle of the twentieth century. They're often compared to oil paints because they can produce similarly rich colors, but they dry more quickly, and many consider them easier to use. Audubon didn't paint in oils much, and when he did, it was to produce one-off paintings for sale, not illustrations for his published works. It's hard to picture him switching over to acrylics as a primary medium for *The Birds of America*, but he might have found ways to incorporate the use of them along with other media.

The questions that vexed me the most involved computer graphics. By the early 2020s, some talented bird painters had briefly put aside their brushes to experiment with digital illustration, drawing with a stylus on a graphics tablet to create images on the computer monitor that could then be saved as digital files. This approach requires as much skill as traditional media, but it has the huge advantage that images can be endlessly changed and repaired. With watercolor (as I experienced many times), it's easy to mess up so badly that you have to start over. With most media, if you decide after finishing that some basic detail is wrong, you have to start over. With digital illustration, you can go back and change anything: rotate that bird's position, move its eye higher on its face, make those feathers darker or lighter, make that wingtip shorter.

I confess this method tempted me. I told myself that Audubon would have jumped on this opportunity when he was under time pressure to produce hundreds of bird portraits. Instead of pasting bits of white paper over mistakes or painting over them, as he sometimes did, he could have made those changes digitally. He could have emailed files back and forth with those who assisted him, like Maria Martin or Joseph Mason: *Here, you paint a flowering shrub and send it back, and I'll add a couple of warblers.* It would have simplified his work immensely. It would have simplified my task, too, especially since I already had the equipment and had used it for digital editing of photos.

In the end, though, I put aside the temptation to take the easy way out. I would stick to classical methods after all, and push through to the end of my pseudo-Audubons with materials replicating, as closely as possible, those that would have been available two centuries ago.

9

Lost in Texas

The state of Texas looms gigantic in my personal history of birding. Sure, it's a big state, but its influence goes beyond that.

I visited Texas for the first time at the age of seventeen, hitchhiking south out of January chill in Kansas, through blizzards in Oklahoma, then down the long ribbon of Interstate 45 to Houston and beyond to reach the Gulf Coast. The southward shift took me from bleak winter to a land where flowers bloomed, butterflies flitted, and flocks of songbirds foraged through groves of live oak. It felt like magic, like springtime in January. I worked my way south along the Texas coast, awed by myriads of waterbirds of all shapes and colors. As I approached the southern tip of the state, new birds of subtropical affinities appeared: flashy Green Jays, unbelievably gaudy in green and yellow and purple. Great Kiskadees, brightly patterned and noisy, utterly abandoning the modest color themes of their flycatcher relatives. Plain Chachalacas, drab in color but bizarre in structure, like skinny tropical turkeys. And so many more. The avian novelty and abundance captivated me.

After that first visit I was back in the state almost every year, sometimes for weeks at a time. It was such rich ground for diversity. I came on my own and with friends, and later as a leader of birding tour groups. I taught bird-identification workshops on the coast in winter. After the first birding festivals launched around 1990, I came back as a speaker and field trip leader. And I always tried to be on the upper Texas coast in April, when it was one of the best places in the world to observe spring migration.

My friend Victor Emanuel, a lifelong Texan aside from a few years at Harvard, grew up in Houston and later moved to Austin. In the late 1970s he founded one of the first professional birding tour companies; soon his guides were taking groups all over the world, but they always had plenty of offerings in his home state. For several years, Victor and I taught a spring migration workshop together every April on the upper coast. We would give evening presentations on different aspects of migratory bird science, and during the days we would range over the area from Houston and Galveston east to the Louisiana border, trying to connect with the peak flights of migrants.

It was a magical season. So many avian travelers were passing through. The marshes and tidal flats thronged with shorebirds, many of them coming from South America and heading for Arctic tundra. Migratory songbirds gathered in every grove of trees, some moving a short distance up out of Mexico, some coming from deep in the tropics. Birding was good every day, but throughout the workshop, Victor and I watched the weather forecasts, waiting and half-hoping for the phenomenon of a fallout.

Research in the twentieth century had established that vast numbers of spring migrants fly directly north across the Gulf of Mexico, leaving the Yucatán Peninsula and powering straight north across the water to reach the Gulf Coast of the United States. Even though it's roughly an eighteen-hour flight for the average songbird, most of these migrants don't land as soon as they reach the coast; instead, most keep flying until they're inland by a hundred miles or more. At least, that's the case as long as the weather is good. They take off from Yucatán under fair skies and southerly breezes, and if those conditions persist, they fly high above the U.S. coastline and continue toward the more extensive forests of the interior, with only a few coming down to the coastal woodlots.

But that's only when the weather stays good. If those migrants get

most of the way across the Gulf and run into a storm from the northwest, they're in trouble. Already depleted by the flight, they must battle
the winds, beating low across the water to the first land. Every tree
near the shoreline, every hedge, every patch of tall grass fills up with
warblers, buntings, orioles, tanagers, thrushes, vireos, flycatchers, and
more, exhausted from the struggle, stopping to rest. That's the classic
migrant fallout. It's rough for the birds, so we can't, in good conscience,
hope for it to happen. But it's a natural occurrence and it's going to happen just about every spring; and if it's going to happen, we want to be
there to witness the power of nature and the temporary abundance of
grounded travelers. So Victor and I, with the benefit of years of experience and decades of published research, would study the weather maps
to try to pinpoint when and where a fallout might take place.

Most people who don't live in the immediate area have never observed one of these major fallouts. But even without such an event, everyday birding is good all year in Texas, and the state remains wildly
popular with the binocular crowd. Take a poll among birders anywhere
in the United States and you'll find that Texas is among their favorite or
most-wanted destinations. But that recognition was a long time coming.
Texas got off to a slow start in the annals of North American bird study.

By dumb luck, John James Audubon made his only visit to Texas at the
perfect season for finding novelties, and in one of the best regions. He
encountered a number of things that should have qualified as new discoveries. But he overlooked all of them, somehow, and came away with
no idea what he had missed.

Up to that time, the region had received scant ornithological attention. Early Spanish and French explorers had made passing mention of
birds seen there, including turkeys, geese, and herons, but no systematic
lists. Texas itself was an ill-defined region well into the 1800s, part of
the vast territory known as New Spain, which encompassed much of
what is now the western United States, Mexico, and Central America.
Nominally it was all ruled by Spain. In reality, northern Texas was ruled
by Comanche warriors, who had acquired horses from the Spanish and

soon became the greatest horsemen on the continent. After Mexico achieved independence from Spain in 1821, the new government encouraged settlers from the United States to move into the new state of Coahuila y Tejas, partly to serve as a buffer against the Comanches. The strategy backfired; the growing numbers of American colonists in Texas soon fought for, and won, their independence from Mexico in 1836.

Audubon made note of these changes in political status. By early 1836, more than three hundred of the color plates for his *Birds of America* had been engraved and printed, and three of the five volumes of *Ornithological Biography* had been published, but still he was on the watch for more bird species to include. Texas was still not part of the United States, but it was now separate from Mexico and governed by English-speaking American immigrants. To Audubon, it was beginning to look like a legitimate area to explore. None of his rivals or contemporaries had visited Texas—not Wilson, not Townsend, not Nuttall, certainly not George Ord. The region held promise of the possibility of new discoveries.*

In early 1837, joined by his son John, his friend Edward Harris, and his pointer dog, Dash, Audubon traveled overland from Charleston to Mobile, Alabama, and then by boat to New Orleans. He had been promised transportation on a U.S. revenue cutter from New Orleans west along the coast to Texas, but the cutter was delayed for about three weeks, and for a while the travelers doubted they would ever make it. Eventually the cutter did show up, and the party headed west, finally reaching Galveston on April 24.

As we know now, this timing put them there at the peak of spring migration—right at the season when modern birders descend on this region every year. It was perfect timing. But they didn't know it.

By that era, naturalists were beginning to understand the basic outlines of bird migration. Only a century and a half earlier, in the 1680s,

---

*Two competent naturalists, Jean-Louis Berlandier (Swiss-French-Mexican) and Thomas Drummond (Scottish), explored areas of southern Texas in the 1820s and '30s. Both focused mainly on plants, and it's doubtful that Audubon would have heard of them by 1837.

it had been possible for an English scientist to suggest in all seriousness that many birds flew to the moon for the winter. A long-standing myth about swallows, that they would dive into marshes to spend the winter hibernating under the mud, had lingered in the minds of some through the end of the 1700s.* But by 1837 it was recognized that large numbers of birds in the northern hemisphere would breed and raise their young during summer at northern latitudes and then spend the nonbreeding winter season in warmer climates, migrating between their summer and winter ranges during the spring and fall.

Audubon understood this basic pattern. But many details of migration were still unknown, to him and to everyone else. And he held some odd misconceptions, probably dating from his time in Louisiana in the early 1820s, that may have led him to misinterpret what was happening on the Texas coast.

Around New Orleans, and in other areas just inland from the U.S. Gulf Coast, an odd pattern applies to the spring passage of land birds. Migrants arriving from across the Gulf may come down in a fallout on the immediate coast in bad weather, or keep flying far inland in good weather. In between these options—between the shoreline and the forests of the interior—is a gap, a kind of coastal hiatus, where trans-Gulf migrants seldom stop over in large numbers. New Orleans, lying about fifty miles north of the outermost coast, falls in that gap.

During his time in Louisiana, Audubon never made the long and difficult slog out to explore the edge of the sea; he only glimpsed the shoreline from shipboard as he headed out the mouth of the Mississippi River from New Orleans to sail to England. He was never in a situation to see a migrant fallout on that coast, and he had no reason to expect such a phenomenon when he went to Texas years later.

As for daytime migrants like swallows and Eastern Kingbirds, Audubon saw those around New Orleans, often moving along the river

---

*Alexander Wilson discussed this claim about hibernating swallows in volume five of *American Ornithology* in 1812, and Audubon alluded to it in a journal entry from New Orleans in February 1821. Both were refuting the idea, but that they mentioned it at all is a reflection of how long the myth persisted.

or along the edge of Lake Pontchartrain. His observations of them
may have played a part in a peculiar use of language he adopted later.
Throughout *Ornithological Biography*, when he discussed spring migrants, he often described them as moving east. Not north, but east. He
wrote of Little Blue Herons leaving Florida "on their way eastward" to
Georgia and the Carolinas. He wrote of the Rose-breasted Grosbeak
in Louisiana in March "making its way eastward." Of the Blackpoll
Warbler in the spring, he wrote, "Its migrations eastward follow the advance of the season."* Of course he knew the difference between north
and east, and knew many migrants were headed for northern breeding
grounds. But he used the same odd terminology to describe geography.
In his writing, Kentucky was east of Louisiana, Georgia was east of
Florida, New Jersey was east of the Carolinas, and Maine was east of
Pennsylvania. These statements weren't exactly false; but practically
anyone looking at maps would give the direction as northeast, or even
north, rather than simply east.

On the upper Texas coast in April 1837, again, he referred to migrants moving eastward as well as northward. Some probably were,
because in addition to the massive flights that go north across the Gulf
there are many species and populations that fly around it, skirting north
along the coastline of Mexico and Texas and then angling toward the
east. Since the trans-Gulf flights were unknown then, it would have
been reasonable for Audubon to assume all the birds were doing that.
Under that assumption, many of the migrants he and his companions
saw around Galveston and Houston would have been on their way east
toward his old home in Louisiana, giving him no reason to expect much
of novelty among them.

It's possible he witnessed a fallout of trans-Gulf migrants almost
as soon as he reached the area. His original journals from the trip are
lost, but as quoted years later in the biography published by his widow,

*Blackpoll Warblers spend the winter in South America and enter the U.S. in spring
mainly through Florida. As they advance toward their northern breeding grounds, which
extend west to Alaska, most individuals are traveling toward the northwest. No aspect of
their spring migration moves them eastward.

Lucy, he wrote at Galveston Bay: "April 25. A heavy gale blew all night, and this morning the thermometer in the cabin is 63°, and thousands of birds, arrested by the storm in their migration northward, are seen hovering around our vessels, and hiding in the grass, and some struggling in the water, completely exhausted."

Was that a genuine fallout? The scant details suggest that it was. Migrants that had left the north coast of Yucatán at dusk on the twenty-third, reaching the northern Gulf during early afternoon on the twenty-fourth and running into northwest gales, would have stopped at the coast to wait out the storm. That situation could produce a morning scene on the twenty-fifth of thousands of birds hovering around the ship, hiding in the grass, and even struggling in the water.

With the benefit of what we know two centuries later, we can say: migrants must have been present that morning in great numbers and variety, and the explorers should have gone ashore and headed for the nearest trees, to mine this rich vein of feathered gems. But they didn't— at least, not right away. The biography by Lucy mentions a few shore excursions in the following days, including two days after the apparent fallout, when they found "many interesting birds." Most of the excerpts she deemed worth publishing focus on observations of the local humans, including a meeting with Sam Houston, the first president of the Republic of Texas. Audubon was already taking victory laps, enjoying the contact with famous men, rather than focusing all his attention on finding new birds.

Finding new birds: that had been the goal of this expedition from the start. By that measure, the trip was a failure. Writing about it the following year, in volume four of *Ornithological Biography*, Audubon tried to put a positive face on it: his visit to Texas "has enabled me to speak with more confidence on the migratory movements of a good number of species which visit us from southern climes during the breeding season." He acknowledged the diversity he had seen: "In the course of my last journey in search of information respecting the birds . . . I observed so vast a number of them in Texas, that I almost concluded that more than two-thirds of our species occur there." (This was an

underestimate.) But the conclusion was: "In the course of our long journeys through woods and over plains, and of our sinuous sailings along
the many bays, creeks or bayous, which we visited on this expedition,
notwithstanding all our exertions and constant anxiety, we did not discover a single bird not previously known."

Not a single new bird. He almost discovered several. He was close,
so close. But his assumptions let him down.

His assumptions, and the limits of the hospitality of the U.S. government. The Treasury Department had already done Audubon a favor
by sending a revenue cutter over to pay a diplomatic call on the new
Republic of Texas and giving him free passage. It would have seemed
an extreme overreach to send the cutter farther southwest down the
coast. Few settlements of any kind existed there at the time, and the
exact border between Texas and Mexico was still under dispute. Going
farther along the coast apparently was never an option, and Audubon
apparently never felt any regret about that.

His brief visit to the upper coast seems to have convinced him that the
birdlife of Texas was just like that of Louisiana. Based on what he saw, it
was a reasonable conclusion. Texas, in its current boundaries, is almost
eight hundred miles across from east to west, but Houston and Galveston
lie close to the Louisiana state line. The selection of bird species changes
only a little when you go west from New Orleans to Houston.

But if you leave Houston and head southwest, parallel to the coast,
more changes become apparent. The eastern hardwood forest begins
to disappear, reduced to groves along rivers, with drier open woodland
between. Birds that a traveler would have seen over half the continent—
Blue Jays, Barred Owls, American Crows—fade away. Common eastern
birds are replaced by others: the familiar little Downy Woodpecker disappears, and another black-and-white tree-climber, the Ladder-backed
Woodpecker, takes its place. The noisy Red-bellied Woodpecker gives
way to the equally noisy Golden-fronted Woodpecker. The perky and
acrobatic Tufted Titmouse is replaced by another perky relative, the
Black-crested Titmouse. New and unique creatures show up, too, including the Greater Roadrunner, dashing about like a caricature of itself.

If Audubon and his party could have followed the coast another two hundred miles southwest beyond Galveston, they might have connected with all these birds. Although most had been described and named before 1837, from Mexico or California, none were known to be anywhere near Texas. But prior experience had given Audubon no reason to suspect he might find so much novelty by going that short distance. Nowhere else in eastern North America was there such an abrupt change in birdlife from north to south. Moving south in Florida five years earlier, with the peculiarities of bird distribution on a peninsula, he hadn't noticed many new birds until he reached the different surroundings of the Keys.

It's easy for us to look back today and say that of course he and his companions should have gone a little farther south in Texas. At the time, there was no way he could have guessed that. But even in the limited areas they visited on the upper coast, they missed some birds that would have been fine additions to *The Birds of America*. To see how close they came, consider Audubon's treatment of the American Black Duck.

The sleek, elegant American Black Duck is common in the northeastern United States and eastern Canada, and was abundant there at one time. Around 1813, Alexander Wilson called it "the most common and most numerous of all those of its tribe that frequent the salt marshes" along the central Atlantic Coast. "Numbers of them remain during the summer, and breed in sequestered places in the marsh. . . . Vast numbers, however, regularly migrate farther north on the approach of spring." He added: "They are extremely shy during the day; and on the most distant report of a musquet, rise from every quarter of the marsh in prodigious numbers, dispersing in every direction."

Audubon, too, knew this bird well. He had painted its portrait in the early 1830s, and had found nests in Maine and on his Labrador trip. But he didn't write about it until the fourth volume of his *Ornithological Biography* in 1838. There he took pains to point out that, "strange as the fact may appear," he had found this common northern species breeding in Texas in late April 1837. He reported that his son John had found a nest on Galveston Island, and the group had seen many

American Black Ducks by John James Audubon. Formerly abundant in northeastern North America, this duck was a familiar sight to early naturalists. When they traveled south to the Gulf Coast, they encountered a very similar bird, the Mottled Duck, but failed to notice its differences. The separate identity of the Mottled Duck wasn't worked out until the 1870s and 1880s.

individuals in the area, some showing the obvious behavior of females
that had nests nearby.

The presence of nests should have appeared strange. Most of the
ducks in North America are northern breeders. Marshes near the Gulf
Coast teem with vast flocks of waterfowl during the winter, but the
overwhelming majority of the ducks depart before winter ends, heading
for ponds on the northern prairies, lakes in the boreal forest, even Arctic tundra. By the middle of spring, southern waters seem eerily empty,
with only scattered stragglers from winter's abundance. So it would be
odd if American Black Ducks, characteristic of cold northeastern coasts,
were nesting on the Texas Gulf Coast.

These southern birds, present year-round in Florida and along the
western Gulf Coast, are now recognized as a distinct species, the Mottled
Duck. That recognition was slow in arriving. Robert Ridgway described
the Florida population in 1874 as a variety of the American Black Duck,
but by 1880 he had decided it deserved the status of a full species, to be
called the Florida Black Duck or Florida Duck. Then in 1889, George
Sennett described the Texas population as yet another new species, the
Mottled Duck. By 1895, the American Ornithologists' Union had concluded that the latter two forms represented the same species and that it
was distinct from the American Black Duck, a more northerly bird. But
hardly anyone commented on the fact that Audubon had had this new
species within reach and had failed to discern it.

This wasn't the only example. The Glossy Ibis, a dark, sickle-billed
wader, is a common sight today up the Atlantic Coast as far as Maine
and westward along the Gulf Coast to Louisiana and beyond. But this is
the result of a major range expansion that didn't begin until around the
1940s. In the early 1900s it was a localized Florida specialty, and in the
early 1800s it was rare anywhere in the United States. Audubon implied
he had seen the bird in Florida. His painting of the species, apparently
done around 1836 or 1837, supposedly was based on a Florida specimen, but not necessarily one that he took himself.

However, he wrote this about the Glossy Ibis in *Ornithological Biography*: "In the spring of 1837, I saw flocks of it in the Texas; but even

there it is merely a summer resident, associating with the White Ibis, along the grassy margins of the rivers and bayous, and apparently going to and returning from its roosting places in the interior of the country." This sounds matter-of-fact, not like the kind of language he used when he was simply making things up, so it's reasonable to think he did see flocks of dark ibises there.

But were they Glossy Ibises? No. That species was recorded in Texas for the first time in 1983, and not until the 1990s did it begin to show up there as more than scattered singles. What Audubon saw undoubtedly were White-faced Ibises: a close relative, common in the western United States and Mexico, and still much more numerous than the Glossy Ibis on the upper Texas coast today. This species had been described in 1817 by the French ornithologist Vieillot, based on specimens from Paraguay and Argentina, but no one realized it was also in North America until Robert Ridgway figured it out in the 1870s.

Should Audubon have noticed it? White-faced and Glossy Ibises are both rich chestnut all over with glossy green reflections, and at a distance they look identical. But in peak breeding color—as they should have shown during that spring visit in 1837—adult White-faced Ibises have bright red bare skin on the face, surrounded by a ragged border of white feathers, while adult Glossy Ibises have dark slaty facial skin with a narrow blue edge. The difference is obvious if you look closely. But the group saw no reason to look closely; they assumed they knew what these birds were.

Beyond these two—the Mottled Duck and White-faced Ibis—we don't know with certainty about any other birds that Audubon overlooked in Texas. His journals from the trip are lost, so clues are scattered.

But Edward Harris kept notes as well, including a thorough bird list. Harris's trip list of birds identified between the mouth of the Mississippi River and Galveston Bay comes to almost two hundred species—quite a respectable showing, especially for that era. There are some duplicates on the list; MacGillivray's Finch and Seaside Finch are both references to the Seaside Sparrow. And Harris listed both the Hooded Warbler and

"Selby's Flycatcher," even though the latter was just Audubon's mistaken name applied to a young Hooded Warbler years earlier. Overall, though, the list is reasonable, reflecting a good percentage of the species that should have been expected.

That might be the key to the results of their expedition: they saw the birds they expected to see. Clues to some they might have missed can be found among the other birds on Harris's list. He noted seeing the "Florida Cormorant" at several places. This is just a southern subspecies of the widespread Double-crested Cormorant, although Audubon considered it a distinct species at the time. However, at least some of those around Galveston may have been Neotropic Cormorants instead. That species was known to be in Texas by the 1850s, and it was probably there all along, overlooked.

Harris also noted five species of plovers. But the group didn't pick up on the Snowy Plover, which should have been scampering across every sandy beach near Galveston in 1837; it wasn't recognized in North America until the 1850s. They probably overlooked it because it's the same general color as the Piping Plover, which Audubon had already painted. His list included almost every small sandpiper known at the time, but not the Western Sandpiper or Baird's Sandpiper—undoubtedly both were present, but they hadn't been described and named yet.

And this was probably another time when Audubon could have noticed the Caspian Tern, but didn't. Harris's list included "Cayenne Tern"—the bird we now call the Royal Tern—along with six other tern species. Audubon definitely had seen Caspian Terns in Labrador in 1833, passing them off as Royal Terns, which seldom visit those cold northern waters. He probably had seen both species together in Florida in 1832 without noticing the differences,* and the same probably happened again in Texas. Royal Terns are very common along the coast there: big white and gray seabirds with thick orange beaks, standing in flocks on the sand. Caspian Terns are a little less numerous: slightly

---

*Caspian Terns have expanded their range in the Southeast since the 1960s, but it's unlikely that they were absent there altogether in the early 1800s.

Royal Tern, adult, by John James Audubon. This big tern is common along the southeastern coastlines of the United States.

Caspian Tern, adult, by Kenn Kaufman. This is the largest species of tern in the world, and it had been described to science as early as 1770 based on specimens from the Caspian Sea. But in the early 1800s, no one realized that it also occurred in North America. Audubon undoubtedly saw this species in Labrador in 1833, and probably saw it elsewhere, but he failed to notice that it was different from the Royal Terns he had seen along beaches in the Southeast.

bigger white and gray seabirds with slightly thicker, redder beaks, standing with the Royal Terns. Easy to spot, with a careful look, if you expect
them to be there. Easy to overlook if you don't.

It's easy, too, for us to look back now, with two centuries' worth
of accumulated knowledge, and say the early naturalists should have
noticed all these things. But is it fair? Would I have done any better?
Probably not.

It's a bittersweet fact of life for naturalists that we can take to the
field eagerly, primed for discovery, and walk right past things that
would have been new. In most cases, we'll never know what we missed.
A human lifetime is so short that we can't even begin to grasp the diversity of nature. But even our attempts will fill our days with delight.

When I think about Audubon and his group surrounded by diversity on
the upper Texas coast in the spring, it brings up memories of teaching
bird migration workshops with Victor Emanuel in the same region and
season.

A slim, alert man with irrepressible energy, Victor combines deep
knowledge of birds and nature with an almost childlike sense of wonder.
Let a bright orange Baltimore Oriole pop up into view, and even though
you know he's seen half a million Baltimore Orioles before, he will gasp
out, "Wow!" under his breath. And he'll mean it, too. He hated the
phrase "Been there, done that" that was current for a while, countering
with "If you've been there, if it was great, you can do it again!" His was
the perfect attitude for teaching about bird migration, a topic with endless potential to delight and amaze.

Although Victor lives in central Texas now, he still spends part of
every spring birding on the upper coast east of Houston, as he has since
he was a boy. Recently we were talking about changes in the overall
birdlife of that region, and I reminded him of something he had said at
one of our workshops. It was during a serious group discussion about
conservation issues. One participant mentioned that a friend of hers had
stopped birding altogether because he saw how bird populations had
declined, and it was too depressing. She asked, "How do you choose

which way to react? Do you focus on the problems, or do you brush them aside and enjoy the birds?"

Victor leaned forward. "We don't have to choose," he said. "We can do both. We *should* do both. I think we should celebrate and enjoy the amazing, wonderful variety of birds that we have all around us. And that should inspire us to do what we can to preserve them for the future. These two things can enhance each other. We'll appreciate what we still have even more, if we acknowledge what we've lost."

He was silent then for an uncharacteristically long moment, and I looked at him; he seemed briefly far away. *Acknowledge what we've lost.* I wondered if he might be thinking of a special bird he had seen just down the coast from here many years ago, when he was still a teenager—a bird of mystery and magic, a bird that none of us will ever see again.

10

Abundant Life

Curlew. It's a beautiful word, an imitation of the cry of one European species, but curlews as a group are found around the world. Classified as members of the sandpiper family, they're not usually seen on sand—they are just as likely to be on Arctic tundra, open grasslands, or rocky shores, wherever they have a wide view of the sky. On average they are larger than most sandpipers, elegant in shape, with thin, downcurved bills. They fly with power and grace. On their breeding grounds they sing in flight, with breathy, mournful whistles that linger above the barrens. Their migrations span continents and hemispheres; some are among the longest journeys known for any bird. Curlews are children of the wind.

Early naturalists in eastern North America knew three kinds of curlews. The largest was the appropriately named Long-billed Curlew, all brown and buff, two feet long from the end of its short tail to the tip of its slender scimitar beak. It nests on grasslands in the interior of the West (although the naturalists didn't know that yet), and nonbreeding birds could be seen all year along southeastern coastlines. A second bird, the Hudsonian Curlew (now called the Whimbrel), was medium-size, averaging just under a foot and a half in total length, and a grayer shade of brown. It nested in Arctic regions, and large flocks could be found migrating along the Atlantic Coast in spring and fall, some staying through the winter. Both can still be found readily by birders, albeit in smaller numbers than those of two centuries ago.

And there was a third curlew. It was often confused with the Whimbrel, but it was a bit smaller, with a shorter bill and feather tones of cinnamon brown. Explorers had taken a few specimens at high latitudes of British America (Canada) in summer, and observers reported flocks gathering near the coast in southeastern Canada and the northeastern United States in early fall, after which they would disappear—evidently heading far to the south. This bird was a mystery. One certainty was its presence in the high Arctic in the summer, so naturalists called it the Eskimo Curlew.*

During the mid-1800s, more details came into focus. At most times and places in North America, Eskimo Curlews would not be seen at all; but when they did appear, they might appear in large numbers. Great flocks would arrive in Texas in early spring, covering acres of ground on prairies near the coast. As the season advanced those flocks would move north through the Great Plains and the Canadian prairies, heading toward the tundra of the high Arctic. Then in late summer, even larger flocks would arrive near the coast in eastern Canada and the New England states, where they would spend a few weeks fattening up on crowberries and grasshoppers before vanishing out over the ocean. Eventually scientists were able to say that these big flocks of small curlews were flying directly to South America, going all the way to the southern end of that continent, to spend the winter on the windswept pampas of Argentina.

When John James Audubon was compiling his *Ornithological Biography* in the 1830s, much of this was still unknown. He had never seen a live Eskimo Curlew before his Labrador trip in 1833, but fishermen working the coast told him to expect migrating flocks around the end of July. When they arrived, Audubon's descriptions of them bordered

---

*At first they called it the Esquimaux Curlew, using the French spelling. None of the European-American scientists could have guessed that "Eskimo" by any spelling would come to be regarded as offensive, a dismissive catchall for a variety of peoples and their cultures in the far north.

on the poetic: "The birds at length came, flock after flock, passed close round our vessel, and directed their course toward the sterile mountainous tracts in the neighbourhood. . . . Wherever there was a spot that seemed likely to afford a supply of food, there the Curlews abounded. . . . When the birds were in search of these feeding-grounds, they flew in close masses, sometimes high, at other times low, but always with remarkable speed, and performing beautiful evolutions in the air."

Almost two centuries later, as we read these lines about a phenomenon no living person will ever see, one haunting sentence stands out: "They evidently came from the north, and arrived in such dense flocks as to remind me of the Passenger Pigeons."

I saw those words for the first time when I was a boy in my early teens, just a little too young to travel, doing all my exploring in the library. That sentence sent a pang straight to my heart because I saw the unintended irony of what it foretold.

Passenger Pigeons are extinct. Famously so. As recently as the early 1800s they had been among the most abundant bird species in the world, with a population running into the billions, ranging all across eastern North America. These big, long-tailed pigeons were colored in steel blue and flame orange, but they turned the sky black when their enormous flocks went hurtling overhead. That abundance had crashed with shocking speed and the last known individual, the very last, had toppled from her perch to the floor of her cage in the Cincinnati Zoo in September 1914. By the time I started birding half a century later, no one questioned the fact that the Passenger Pigeon was gone.

There were plenty of questions about the Eskimo Curlew. Its abundance had crashed also, but not to zero—at least, not quite. Certainly it had come close. The immense flocks that had carpeted the prairies in Texas in spring and swarmed over the bluffs in Labrador in fall dwindled and disappeared around the 1880s, and by 1900 the curlew had become hard to find. Between 1905 and 1945 there was not a single reliable record in Texas. There were scattered sightings elsewhere, but they were almost always tinged with doubt—after all, there was a history of confusion between this species and the Whimbrel. The young Roger Tory Peterson, seeking birds all over North America in the first half of the twentieth century, never saw a definite Eskimo Curlew. The closest he came was on the coast of Massachusetts one autumn afternoon when a strikingly small curlew flew past, a tantalizing, silent silhouette, continuing in a straight line until it passed out of sight.

For decades, every sighting was like that: plausible, not certain. Then in late March 1959, a young birder named Ben Feltner found a small curlew foraging with golden-plovers and other migrants in fields of Galveston Island, on the upper Texas coast, historically a major stopover for Eskimo Curlews.

In those days, away from a few hotbeds of birding like Boston and New York, there were no hotlines for rare bird reports. But Feltner called his younger friend, Victor Emanuel, to tell him about it. Just nineteen years old, with a heavy schedule of classes at Rice University, Victor couldn't go to seek it right away. Not until early April did he and some friends drive to Galveston Island to look around.

A few miles from where Feltner had seen his bird, they stopped to scan a pasture where many migratory shorebirds were foraging. American Golden-Plovers were there, and Upland Sandpipers, and Whimbrels, and Long-billed Curlews, and—and with them was a smaller curlew, brighter buff-colored than the Whimbrel, with a shorter bill. There was no question what it was.

In the sixty years since, Victor Emanuel has traveled the globe and seen thousands of bird species, including some of the world's rarest. But when he speaks of the Eskimo Curlew, his voice goes quiet and he simply says: "It was the bird of my life."

That wasn't the last sighting. Victor came back to see it again and show it to others. Several local experts saw it, and all agreed on its identity. At least one bird returned the next spring, and the next. In 1962 at least two Eskimo Curlews showed up and someone finally took diagnostic photos, providing the first solid evidence that the species still existed.

In spring 1963, no one could find one at Galveston Island. But that

Eskimo Curlews by John James Audubon. At one time this was an abundant bird, migrating annually between a summer range in the Arctic and wintering grounds in southern South America. Its population crashed in the late 1800s. Definite sightings persisted into the 1960s, but the species is almost certainly extinct now.

fall produced the most solid evidence of all: in early September a hunter shot an Eskimo Curlew on the island of Barbados, in the eastern Caribbean. Recognizing it as something unusual, he saved the specimen and eventually it wound up in a museum.

A short note about the Barbados bird appeared in *Audubon* magazine just a couple of years later. By coincidence, that was among the first new issues of the magazine I received as a kid in the Midwest who had decided to join the Audubon Society. As I read about the curlew's recent history, it dominated my dreams for weeks. Surely the Barbados individual couldn't have been the very last Eskimo Curlew. Surely the photographer on the Texas coast and the gunner in the Caribbean could not have connected with the same individual bird—that would be too absurd a coincidence. In the vastness of the hemisphere, in a migratory route that spanned two continents, these encounters had to be just hints of a larger population. There had to be more curlews out there. I waited for the news of the next definite sighting.

Six decades on I am still waiting, and there has been no documentation of the continued existence of the Eskimo Curlew. Today there are legions of birders in North America, and in South America and the Caribbean also, and a high percentage of us carry good cameras and we document every unusual bird we see. No one has been able to find the enigmatic curlew, and the last photos are still those taken in 1962. But we don't seem able to let it go; the species is still classified as "critically endangered," not extinct.

Apparently that's how we do it now. Earlier extinctions, like the Passenger Pigeon and Carolina Parakeet, are accepted without question, but not the more recent ones. In the continental United States, where birders are everywhere and we should know the status of everything, Bachman's Warbler has not been documented since the 1960s, but it was not declared extinct until October 2023. The noisy, flashy Ivory-billed Woodpecker was last seen with certainty in the 1940s, but a whole culture has grown up around blurry photos and pixelated videos, and true believers refuse to regard the Ivory-bill as extinct. The more we lose, it seems, the more we cling to the shreds of what we used to have.

A focus on the finality of extinction is understandable. And it has led to some heroic conservation efforts. In North America the Whooping Crane, California Condor, and Kirtland's Warbler all have come frighteningly close to disappearing within the last century, but serious, sustained efforts have pulled them back from the brink. They may not be out of danger, but their positions are no longer so precarious, and they're still with us.

But with birds such as the Passenger Pigeon or Eskimo Curlew, we didn't just lose single elements of diversity, or single players from the play. We lost a level of abundance that was part of the defining character of this continent.

In the late 1800s, as populations of Passenger Pigeons were crashing in the wild, a few zoos held small groups. Some of them were reproducing, raising young in their cages. Pigeons and doves in general are not hard to breed in captivity—witness the common city pigeon, which has been domesticated for thousands of years. With some careful management, it should have been possible to create a substantial captive flock over time. If that had happened, we could all go to the zoo today and see a living, breathing Passenger Pigeon, just as citizens of Cincinnati could do before September 1914. Maybe some could have been released to the wild, too, and maybe they would have established some sustainable populations there.

Would that have been a conservation success story? Barely. In my view, that would have been the slimmest of victories. To me, the essence, even the *meaning* of the Passenger Pigeon was in its jaw-dropping abundance. Those enormous flocks that filled the sky from horizon to horizon for hours as they swept overhead, the multitudes that caused trees to crack and buckle when they settled in to roost for the night, the temporary nesting colonies that would fill every tree in whole square miles of forest . . . no epic conservation measures could have saved those phenomena, and they probably could not survive in the North America of today.

Don't get me wrong. I am not shrugging off the extinction of the Passenger Pigeon. The diversity of life is important to me, at a level that's spiritual and not just academic, and I grieve for every loss. Having a few living individuals of a species would be vastly better than having none at all. But still it would be only the palest shadow of what we have lost. The mere existence of a species isn't the only thing that matters.

We may take it for granted today that a major goal of wildlife conservation is preventing the extinction of species. But the idea of extinction is a fairly recent concept. It would have been alien to most of the naturalists of the late 1700s.

In that era, only a few scientists had hinted at ideas like evolution or extinction. The general assumption was that all species on Earth resulted from an original act of creation, and it was unthinkable that any might disappear. Thomas Jefferson, in his *Notes on the State of Virginia* in the 1780s, gave a good summary of the prevailing view: "Such is the economy of nature, that no instance can be produced of her having formed any link in her great work so weak as to be broken."

By that time, fossilized bones of mammoths and mastodons had been discovered. But like others, Jefferson assumed they must represent some large animal that still walked the Earth—somewhere. (When, as president, he sent the Lewis and Clark expedition westward in 1803, he instructed Meriwether Lewis to keep an eye out for these huge mammals as he traversed the interior.) As more fossils of amazing beasts emerged in the early 1800s, the French naturalist Georges Cuvier convinced the scientific community that extinction was a natural process. But for Wilson, Audubon, and their contemporaries, it still would have been a relatively unfamiliar idea. Extinction was something that might have happened, occasionally, in the ancient past, not something that could be possible amid the overflowing abundance of this new land of America.

Nothing represents that abundance better than the massive numbers of Passenger Pigeons that swept over the eastern half of the continent. Alexander Wilson, not a person given to exaggeration, wrote that the pigeons occurred "in such prodigious numbers as almost to surpass belief; and which has no parallel among any other of the feathered tribes, on the face of the earth." After carefully observing a flock that filled the sky for hours between the Indiana Territory and Kentucky in spring 1810, he calculated that the flight had encompassed more than two billion individuals. Audubon later published a calculation that a single flight could contain more than one billion.* Scholars consider such estimates plausible; the pigeons often were highly concentrated in a few areas and mostly absent elsewhere, and their total population may have been as high as five billion.

If you seek out accounts written during the late 1700s and early 1800s and read them with care, you may get a sense of the birdlife of eastern North America during that time—not just the species present, but a visceral sense of their abundance across the landscape. And not just the Passenger Pigeons, either. When the pigeons arrived their numbers were too staggering to ignore, and people wrote about them, of course; but they commented less often about numbers of other birds that were around all the time. It's hard to guess what was considered normal then, but there are hints that birds in general were far more numerous than they are today.

The Red-headed Woodpecker is still widespread in eastern North America, and locally common in some areas, but two centuries ago it wasn't described that way. Alexander Wilson wrote: "There is perhaps no bird in North America more universally known than this. . . . Almost every child is acquainted with the Red-headed Woodpecker." Audubon claimed that the habits of the species were so familiar that it hardly seemed necessary to describe them, but then he did, at some length. After telling of their depredations in orchards and cornfields, he added: "It is impossible to form any estimate of the number of these birds seen in the United States during the summer months; but this much I may safely assert, that a hundred have been shot upon a single cherry-tree in one day."

Is it still possible to see one hundred Red-headed Woodpeckers in a

---

*Audubon's estimated total was *exactly* half that of Wilson's: 1,115,136,000, as opposed to 2,230,272,000. This wasn't a coincidence; he copied the other man's formula and just changed a couple of parameters. Apparently when it came to Wilson, Audubon just couldn't help himself, and he had to get in his digs wherever he could.

day? Yes—these are daytime migrants, and if you stand in the right spot along the lower Missouri River on the right day in September, you might see more than that flying past. But anywhere else, if you claim even fifty sighted in a day—let alone fifty visiting one tree—you'll be doubted. I've rarely had a daily total of more than ten.

Unfortunately, reports of historic abundance usually take the form Audubon used here, of the numbers that could be killed. The Clapper Rail, restricted to salt marshes of the Atlantic and Gulf Coasts, is good at staying out of sight as it slips stealthily through the tall reeds. It's still fairly common in some places. In the early 1800s, though, no one would have used a term like "fairly common." Wilson called it "a very numerous and well known species," and said that after storm tides had flooded their coastal haunts, he had sometimes seen thousands walking about in the flattened salt meadows. Audubon wrote that "the abundance of the birds themselves is almost beyond belief." In the marshes of New Jersey in the summer, he said, "it forms almost a regular occupation to collect the eggs of this bird. . . . In fact, it is not an uncommon occurrence for an egger to carry home a hundred dozens in a day." He also described a hunt for Clapper Rails during the highest winter tides in coastal marshes of South Carolina. As boatloads of gunners floated up the creeks on the same rising tide that drove the birds from shelter, the shooting commenced. "In a few hours," he wrote, "hundreds have ceased to breathe the breath of life." Birders who have gone looking for Clapper Rails in modern times would find such a huge and grisly harvest impossible to imagine.

Such accounts of shooting sprees are all too common in Audubon's *Ornithological Biography*, although only in some cases does he give estimates of the numbers killed. One striking example involved a great flight of American Golden-Plovers at New Orleans on March 16, 1821. Local gunners invited him to join them for an expected passage of plovers, based on weather conditions that matched an event six years before. "At the first appearance of the birds early in the morning, the gunners had assembled in parties of from twenty to fifty at different places, where they knew from experience that the Plovers would pass.

. . . When a flock approached, every individual whistled in imitation of the Plover's call-note, on which the birds descended, wheeled, and passing within forty or fifty yards, ran the gauntlet as it were." By evening, one man seated nearby had killed sixty-three dozen plovers. Audubon calculated that two hundred gunners were there, and if each man on average shot twenty dozen, the total haul for the day would have been forty-eight thousand plovers. In a dry understatement, he added that "the next morning the markets were amply supplied with Plovers at a very low price."

Today at New Orleans, even a count of one hundred golden-plovers would be phenomenal. The route of their spring migration mostly passes farther west, through southwestern Louisiana and Texas, but even there the peak counts are now in the low thousands. Even if Audubon's figure was off the mark, the species must have been far more abundant in 1821 than it is now.

Reading the old accounts becomes more jarring when we know the current status of these birds. Most birders today don't see Greater Prairie-Chickens without a special trip to spots where they still live: tiny areas in coastal Texas, southern Illinois, and central Wisconsin, a couple of points in Missouri and Iowa, and a scattered range from northern Oklahoma to western Minnesota. But historically the picture was different. Wilson's account focused on the population along the Atlantic Coast (which would become restricted to offshore islands like Martha's Vineyard by 1870, and extinct by 1932). Audubon wrote that when he first moved to Henderson, these grouse were so numerous that locals were tired of eating them: "no 'hunter of Kentucky' deigned to shoot them." They swarmed by the hundreds in the immediate vicinity. Prairie-chickens would come into town in winter, perch on top of houses, and forage in farmyards with domestic poultry. But their numbers declined rapidly after that as their range receded westward, and I don't know anyone alive today who ever saw a prairie-chicken in Kentucky.

Most historic accounts focused on species that were large and conspicuous. Thomas Nuttall wrote this regarding the Whooping Crane:

In the month of December, 1811, while leisurely descending on the bosom of the Mississippi, in one of the trading boats of that period, I had an opportunity of witnessing one of these vast migrations of the Whooping Cranes, assembled by many thousands from all the marshes and impassable swamps of the north and west. The whole continent seemed as if giving up its quota of the species to swell the mighty host. Their flight took place in the night, down the great aerial valley of the river. . . . The clangor of these numerous legions, passing along, high in the air, seemed almost deafening; the confused cry of the vast army continued, with the lengthening procession, and as the vocal call continued nearly throughout the whole night, without intermission, some idea may be formed of the immensity of the numbers now assembled.

An amazing story, but not credible. In 1811 there still would have been Whooping Cranes migrating up and down the Mississippi Valley between nesting territories in the upper Midwest and wintering grounds in Louisiana, but cranes generally don't migrate at night. And biologists don't think this species was ever that numerous; their total population half a century later, in the 1860s, has been estimated at under two thousand. So what was Nuttall writing about? Unlike Audubon, he recognized Whooping and Sandhill Cranes as separate species, and included both in his *Manual*, so his account probably didn't refer to the much more numerous Sandhill Cranes (which generally don't migrate at night, either). I'm willing to believe he saw and heard some great migration of large birds, but what kind?

For smaller or more elusive birds, information is even more fragmentary. There are questions even about those that live in the open, like swallows. Consider the Bank Swallow, a brown-backed sprite that swoops about chasing insects in midair, like others of its family, and digs nesting holes in dirt banks.

By all historic accounts the Bank Swallow was abundant, more so than today, nesting in large colonies along every river. Audubon claimed also to have seen large flocks in winter in Florida. Based on what we know now, that seems unlikely: most of our Bank Swallows go to South America for the winter, with few stragglers as far north as Florida. But was it different in the 1830s? Wilson, Audubon, and Nuttall all wrote that this was the earliest spring migrant among the swallows in the middle Atlantic states. That isn't true today—it shows up, on average, well after Tree Swallows and Purple Martins, and somewhat later than Barn Swallows—but it could have been reasonable if Bank Swallows were spending the winter much farther north than they do now. But were they really the earliest migrant swallows then? Much of Nuttall's account seems paraphrased from Wilson, and Audubon borrowed from Wilson on any topic for which he had scant data; so it's possible that Wilson was mistaken and that the other two men copied his error. Looking back, it's so hard to be sure of details.

Lacking binoculars, lacking a full idea of what species were present, pioneer ornithologists left many birds uncounted because they were unidentified, or misidentified. We can't look to their writings for any idea of the numbers of treetop birds or forest-interior songbirds like warblers, thrushes, or flycatchers. But from everything I've read, I'm inclined to believe that birds, in all their glorious diversity, filled the woods and fields and skies of this continent in much higher numbers during the early 1800s than they do today. I have even wondered if the naturalists might have missed a few species simply because there were just *so many* birds to sort through.

What happened to that abundance? Well, we happened. People happened. Settlers, especially from Europe, changed the face of the continent, and it can't support as much wildlife as it did once.

In describing North America during that time, we must avoid the trap of calling any part of the land a "pristine wilderness." The continent had been inhabited by humans for many thousands of years—new studies continue to push back human arrival to earlier dates—and the population as of 1492 had already numbered at least in the low millions, with cities, villages, farms, and various forms of land management. Few areas of the continent remained untouched by people. It's true that by the early 1800s, large regions had been largely depopulated, after smallpox and other diseases brought by Europeans had raged through Indigenous civilizations. Some areas may have been in the process of reverting to something like wilderness, after millennia of being more densely inhabited. But I don't think the abundance of birdlife and other wildlife at the time was temporary.

When the first humans arrived in the Americas, they may have hastened the extinction of mammoths and some other megafauna. But as their civilizations grew more sophisticated, most of them developed sustainable ways of interacting with their surroundings. Of course they hunted Passenger Pigeons when flocks were nearby, but they didn't wipe them out. Of course they hunted bison on the plains, but they didn't reduce the vast herds to tattered remnants. Of course they farmed the land, and conducted large-scale habitat management such as controlled burns, but they didn't eliminate the local populations of wildlife that provided part of their livelihood.

Indigenous land-use practices couldn't be applied in most parts of North America today. But we'd be wise to try to adhere much more closely to their unspoken principles of sustainability. With good choices, we could have modern conveniences and healthy wildlife populations at the same time.

Recently I talked with an inspiring group of young supporters of bird conservation. Barely out of their teens, engaged and well-informed, they glowed with optimism and with their determination to make a positive difference. They agreed that their grand, overarching goal was to restore bird populations to historic levels. They recognized that some species were gone and they weren't considering laboratory schemes of de-extinction; but for birds that remained, they wanted to build them back up to their past abundance.

I paused for a very long moment while I considered how to respond. Their goal was admirable but impossible: populations of most bird species simply can't be raised back to levels of the past. Even the most intense and dedicated efforts would be stymied by the reality of carrying capacity.

A given area of habitat will support only so many individuals. To give one example, census work has shown that a square mile of eastern forest might hold as many as 200 Scarlet Tanagers during the breeding season, although totals of 40 to 120 are more typical, depending on forest type and other variables. Cut down half of that square mile of forest, and the tanagers won't just move into the remaining half; it doesn't have the resources to support them. Cut down the whole forest and those tanagers are simply removed from the population. They can't just go elsewhere, because all the good habitat for them is presumably filled already. Turn that forest into farmland and it will support some birds of other species, but not nearly as many. Pave it over and it will support no birds at all.

Within the historic range of the Scarlet Tanager, within regions that were once covered by mature forest, the cumulative area of paved parking lots, roads, and hard roofs now adds up to thousands of square miles. Thousands more are occupied by farms.* The land's capacity to support Scarlet Tanagers has been reduced accordingly. Whatever their original population was (and we don't know that), their current population (which we don't know either) must be lower by at least a million or two. And unless my young friends intend to clear away massive numbers of farms and towns and cities and highways and replant them all to forest, there's no way to bring that tanager population back up to former levels.

I thought about saying all that, but then I stopped myself. Sober realism is essential in wildlife conservation, but idealism is important, too, and it's a precious thing. These young people would run into setbacks and disappointments soon enough. I didn't want to be the source. Why should my reasonable old-guy logic dampen their youthful fire? I should be listening to them instead. I should rekindle the anger I had felt as a boy in the library, thinking about those who had destroyed the wonders I would never see. Those destructive men are long gone now, vanished

---

*Likewise, much forest has been cleared in the wintering range of the Scarlet Tanager in South America, but that's a different aspect of this issue.

like the beautiful abundance of wild pigeons and curlews and others they had slaughtered; but their brand of piggish stupidity is still alive, still selfishly bringing harm to all life on Earth in more insidious ways. We are right to be furious and focused when we think of the wonders of nature we still stand to lose.

So I didn't try to lower the expectations of these young activists. I praised their dedication and wished them well. Then we spoke of the challenge of inspiring people to act on bird conservation. We can't do it, I said, by focusing too much on what has been lost already, even though it's tempting to slip into that hopeless mode. Beyond the tragedy of extinctions, there are so many subtle depletions. Clapper Rails no longer wander New Jersey marshes by the thousands. Red-headed Woodpeckers no longer swarm over every tree in Pennsylvania. Flight lines of golden-plovers won't bring tens of thousands past New Orleans in a day, no matter how favorable the winds.

Is the glass half empty? At least. But what's left in the glass is still extraordinary. There are still avian treasures all around us, and I think it's best to lead with that message. Get outside and look around, or even look out the window—there are birds out there, probably more than you expect, intense little sparks of life. And at the right times and places, they can still occur in astonishing numbers.

If you go to the upper Texas coast in April—no, you won't see flocks of Eskimo Curlews carpeting acres of prairie. You won't see even one lone individual. That hope has faded. But you might see close to two hundred other kinds of birds on any given day, both residents and migrants, from tiny hummingbirds to huge pelicans, a dizzying galaxy of warblers, orioles, vireos, flycatchers, buntings, sandpipers, rails, tanagers, thrushes, and more. . . . Beautiful birds, in numbers beyond counting. We should celebrate this varied abundance that remains, and fight to hold on to it for the future.

11

The Big (Small) Do-Over

I f you were alive and watching tech trends in the 1990s, you might remember the brief heyday of the CD-ROM. The acronym stands for compact disc–read-only memory, and for a while this format was a big deal. A flat disc could be written with large amounts of words, pictures, and even sounds and videos, which could then be read on a personal computer. An early entry in the mid-1980s was an entire encyclopedia on one CD-ROM. At first it contained only words, but it had a lot of them, and it was impressive at the time. Improved versions and other products soon followed. By the 1990s, computer manufacturers were shipping millions of personal computers with built-in CD drives, and several companies were producing content on CD-ROMs to feed the growing interest.

Houghton Mifflin was a long-established book publisher, not usually a trendsetter, but in the early 1990s a team there started developing a CD-ROM version of the Roger Tory Peterson bird guide. They would use Roger's paintings and text from his basic field guides to birds, and add photos, sounds, a few videos, and lots of text about the behavior of the birds, beyond their simple identification. They faced one early problem: no ready source existed for that text about bird behavior. I already had a connection to Houghton Mifflin—they had published my first book, the *Peterson Field Guide to Advanced Birding*, in 1990—and

I was hired to write short, standardized accounts for all seven-hundred-plus species to be included on the CD-ROM.

It was a fascinating challenge. An old series of birdlife-history studies, edited by Arthur C. Bent, was decades out of date by that time, and it was incomplete and anecdotal. My friends in Philadelphia at the Academy of Natural Sciences were just launching a new series, Birds of North America (BNA), with highly detailed life histories for a few species at a time, and I was helping to edit and fact-check them—but only a few accounts would be finished before my deadline. For more than a year I haunted the science library at the University of Arizona, digging through books and ornithology journals to compile information about the feeding habits, nesting habits, migrations, and every other aspect of the lives of all these bird species.

The Peterson Birds Multimedia CD-ROM was popular for a while, into the early 2000s, and you can still find used copies of it, but hardly anyone today has a computer that will run it. It's old technology now. A website can hold more information than any number of discs, and it can be updated continuously.

And what of the text I wrote, more than three hundred thousand words, describing the behavior of every species? I got lucky—Houghton Mifflin decided to publish it in book form. I spent another year revising it and adding to it for that format, and it was published in 1996 as *Lives of North American Birds*, a volume of almost seven hundred pages.

That book had a pretty good run. Eventually, like the Peterson Birds CD-ROM, it went out of production—and for some of the same reasons. Technology played a part: as more people gained access to high-speed internet, more of them were happy to look up bird information online instead of buying a text-heavy book. But another factor was more universal: every reference book on birds, no matter how current it is at publication, will soon go out of date.

I've faced this problem for years. In the decades since my *Advanced Birding* in 1990, I've written several more field guides to birds (and other creatures). All have been out of date, at least slightly, by the time the ink has dried. Birds are reclassified and renamed, their patterns of distribution change, new facts about them are discovered constantly.

In the case of my *Lives of North American Birds*, I got lucky again. In 2014, the National Audubon Society (for whom I serve as a field editor) started work on a new online field guide and mobile app for birds. Once again, they wanted concise information about the habits of each species, and again there was no obvious source. My *Lives* was just going out of print, and we licensed huge chunks of the text for use on the Audubon website and app.

But again—and this is a key point—I had to revise the text extensively before it could be used. So much had changed and so much had been learned since 1996 that I spent weeks going through each species account, making alterations or additions to almost every one, and even writing whole new accounts. And since the online guide and app launched, we have had to continue making changes in the content every year.

Looking back, it's easy to think of ornithology volumes in the 1800s as a few monumental works that were complete and unchanging once finished, frozen at one space in time. That's not accurate; many of those publications were revised and updated repeatedly, and other, less-monumental works came out during the same period. Even though fewer people were studying birds then, so much remained unknown that it took only a slight effort to make any reference work obsolete.

Even as Alexander Wilson was working on early volumes of *American Ornithology*, he was updating some of his data. His volume five contained a serious error about seasonal change in the bird he called the Ringed Plover, but he corrected this in a new account in volume seven. In another case, he included the Savannah Sparrow in volume three and then added another account in volume four, to describe and illustrate what he thought was the male. (It wasn't; the sexes look alike; what he had was a different regional form of the same species.) I'm sure he would have continued to correct or amplify his own texts if he had lived longer.

Since he didn't, others took on that task. George Ord arranged to have the volumes reprinted and updated in the 1820s, and Charles

Lucien Bonaparte published four volumes of supplementary information. These works by Ord and Bonaparte were just the beginning. Starting in the 1820s and continuing for decades, numerous editions of *American Ornithology* appeared, under the direction of various compilers and publishers. Even in the 1870s, "new" editions were still coming out—still credited to Wilson and Bonaparte, but with the contents rearranged, and with the addition of things like a complete list of the birds of the United States, prepared by Spencer Baird in 1858.

And Wilson knockoffs weren't the only bird books appearing. In 1832 and 1834, Thomas Nuttall published *A Manual of the Ornithology of the United States and of Canada* in two relatively compact volumes. It contained some original information—after all, Nuttall had discovered a few birds new to science, including the Olive-sided Flycatcher—but much of the text was paraphrased directly from Wilson. And like Wilson's work, Nuttall's later appeared in revised editions.

So when John James Audubon launched his *Birds of America* in 1828 and his *Ornithological Biography* in 1831, they were hardly appearing in a vacuum. *The Birds of America* was spectacular, of course. With paper measuring more than two feet by three feet, eventually gathered in four huge volumes with a total of 435 bold color compositions, it was just too massive to ignore. No one could compete with that. But almost no one could afford it, either. It was a luxury item for the wealthy (and a few public institutions) on both sides of the Atlantic. The *Ornithological Biography*—five volumes of text, with a few black-and-white illustrations of technical details—was less expensive, but without pictures of birds, it also had less general appeal.

With the publication of his large work, Audubon had created a sensation, transformed himself into an international celebrity, gained entry to the leading scientific societies, and blunted the barbs from his rivals and critics. But he hadn't made the fortune for which he'd hoped. In the end, only about 176 complete sets of the original *Birds of America* were printed. Profits from these allowed his family to live comfortably in the latter stages of the project, but wouldn't be enough to support them in the long term.

So even before the large works were finished, Audubon was plotting his next move: a more compact version, combining the color plates and text in smaller volumes that could be mass-produced at prices within reach of a much larger audience.

The plan was driven partly by economic need. But as ever, a sense of competition seems to have been at play. Thomas Nuttall's inexpensive two-volume manual seemed to be doing well. And in 1838, John Townsend announced a plan to produce a compact, multivolume work on American ornithology, combining text and illustrations—and he even invited Audubon to collaborate with him. By that time Audubon and his sons were already secretly working on their own similar project, but he pretended to consider the invitation, apparently stalling for time, possibly to sabotage the other man's work. In the end, Townsend produced a sample covering a handful of species in a few pages, failed to get subscribers, and abandoned his idea.

Meanwhile, the Audubon family was moving ahead on the publication that would become the Royal Octavo Edition of *The Birds of America*: seven volumes containing a total of five hundred color plates, issued between 1840 and 1844. The work was printed on paper measuring about ten inches by seven inches, a far cry from the roughly thirty-nine inches by twenty-nine inches of the double elephant folio* of the original plates. And while the original work had presented bird species in a random order, the Royal Octavo Edition arranged them taxonomically, separated out by families, the first volume beginning with the vultures and then the hawks.

And just as in the current era, advances in technology would change the way the work was published. All the illustrations would have to be reduced for the new paper size. That's an easy process today, but before the development of photography and photocopying technology, there was no automatic way to do it. The solution was a device called a

---

*It was common in the 1800s to refer to books by their paper size, such as octavo, royal octavo, quarto, folio, and so on, with elephant folio and double elephant folio being the largest sizes commercially available at the time.

camera lucida, invented around 1807. It consisted of a prism on an adjustable stand, with the objects to be copied in front of it and a flat piece of paper below it. Looking through the eyepiece of the prism, an artist could see the paper and the objects at the same time and could essentially trace the objects onto the paper, adjusting the stand to achieve the desired size for the drawing. The younger of the two sons, John Woodhouse Audubon, had been experimenting with a camera lucida. Now he began using it to transfer his father's paintings to the new smaller size, sometimes taking out elements to keep the smaller plates from being too crowded.

When Audubon had begun work on his original *Birds of America*, copper-plate engraving had been the gold standard for producing illustrations; he had been lucky to connect with Robert Havell Jr., one of the world's best at that craft. But by the late 1830s, Havell wasn't interested in taking on another big bird project; he would soon leave London for New York, where he would make his living mostly as a painter, with only a little engraving on the side.

And copper-plate engraving itself was going out of style, replaced by a newer method. The process of lithography had been invented in Germany in the 1790s; it involved drawing directly on a smooth, flat piece of stone, applying ink to the drawing, and then transferring the ink to paper. Several years' worth of experimentation and refinements were necessary before lithography became a viable approach to printing in the United States. The big advantage of this method was in the initial drawing, which didn't require as much technical skill and training as the engraving of copper plates, making the process less expensive up front.

By the late 1830s Audubon had his pick of several competent lithographers in the United States. He chose John T. Bowen of Philadelphia, who would go on to oversee printing of all the color plates for the seven volumes of the Royal Octavo Edition between 1840 and 1844.

The work was a tremendous success. The initial edition attracted more than 1,200 subscribers, and after it was completed, Audubon's sons continued to have more copies printed and bound as needed. Then they brought out another edition, with only slight changes, in 1856; and at least eight more editions were produced before 1890. By nineteenth-century standards, this work was a bestseller.

Audubon had been established as a celebrity by his original *Birds of America*, but the many printings and versions of the Octavo Edition made his work widely known to the American public. Paradoxically, the latter work has been almost forgotten today. Search the online collections of Audubon's art on the websites of the New-York Historical Society or the National Audubon Society and you'll find no indication that he ever illustrated the White-winged Dove, Yellow-bellied Flycatcher, or Harris's Sparrow. But he did—for the Octavo Edition. In the seventh volume, published in 1844, he included several new species (or species he thought were new) that had been described, by him or by others, since the late 1830s. Thousands of Americans had these illustrations on their shelves in the late 1800s, but today hardly anyone knows them.

In composition and artistic appeal, none of the new illustrations in the Octavo Edition rank among Audubon's best. Some of his earlier masterpieces still look dramatic, even when sharply reduced for this edition, but the new ones all seem subdued, as if constrained from the outset by the smaller page size. That may be part of the reason for the lack of enduring interest in this publication. Most of the limited commentary* I've seen about the Royal Octavo Edition has focused on its visual appeal compared to the original work, and it suffers in the comparison.

But I prefer to view it in a different way. Knowledge of North America's birdlife was advancing throughout Audubon's life, including the decade between the launch of his *Ornithological Biography* and the time of the Octavo Edition. How much of that new knowledge did he include in the latter? Did he take the opportunity to enhance and correct the scientific content, or was the new publication purely a commercial enterprise?

Some people, I'm sure, will assume that factual edits were no

---

*A notable exception is the book *Audubon's Great National Work: The Royal Octavo Edition of The Birds of America*, by Ron Tyler (1993), a thorough and well-researched treatment.

priority. We know Audubon committed scientific fraud, plagiarizing some points and inventing others; why would he suddenly start caring about accuracy? This view strikes me as one-sided. The man's lapses into dishonesty are undeniable, but he also put forth extraordinary effort in seeking knowledge. Can we give him credit for the good work he did, while acknowledging all that was wrong?

Today we seem to look at historical characters as through a high-contrast lens, blowing out every shade of gray, reducing everything to black or white. We treat some individuals as icons of greatness, holding them up as heroes for years—and then find out more about them, and scorn them as villains. We don't seem able to recognize middle ground. In truth, many who do great work also do some terrible damage. I'd rather see a version of history that acknowledges these individuals for who they were and what they did, without either celebrating or vilifying them. That's my goal in analyzing the Octavo Edition. Regardless of Audubon's motivations, did these volumes provide new or more accurate information, compared to his previous work?

One major step forward was in arranging all the birds into an organized sequence. In *The Birds of America* and *Ornithological Biography*, as in Wilson's original *Ornithology* and some earlier European works, the species had appeared in random order, reflecting little more than the author's convenience. For the Octavo Edition, they would be treated in taxonomic order, separated out by family and genus.

But whose taxonomic order would that be? Several different classifications had just been proposed. Audubon even scoffed at this proliferation of systems, in an October 1837 letter to John Bachman: "[Bonaparte] is about to publish an ornithological system! Swainson has published about half a Dozen.—Vigors has given one to the World, and is about hatching another.—Dorbigny and Temminck will also astonish us very soon with their lugubrations of these matters—and I feel so very sickened at all these puerile attempts, that I cannot reconcile myself to attempt anything of the Kind." He soon changed his mind, though, and in 1839 he published *A Synopsis of the Birds of North America*. It was written at least partly by his Scottish collaborator and ghostwriter,

William MacGillivray, who had penned much of the text for *Ornithological Biography*. MacGillivray, in turn, probably leaned on works by some of the European taxonomists that Audubon had mocked. Regardless, the *Synopsis* was valuable, serving as an index to the two previous works and laying the foundation for the Octavo Edition.

It's remarkable how far the classification had advanced in just a few years. As I described in chapter 6, the American warblers had caused massive confusion in the early 1800s, as naturalists tried to fit them all into genera established in Europe. By the late 1830s, however, William Swainson and Charles Bonaparte had named new, distinct genera to accommodate these distinctly American birds. In a landmark 1838 publication, *A Geographical and Comparative List of the Birds of Europe and North America*, Bonaparte presented the American warblers in a separate family, Sylvicolinae, and placed them in six genera, divided along lines that are recognizably similar to how the family (now called Parulidae) is arranged today. Audubon, in his *Synopsis* and in the Octavo Edition, also used the family Sylvicolinae* and some of the same genera.

Bonaparte was a better and more perceptive scientist than Audubon, and his classification was closer to what is recognized today. He realized that the brown, ground-walking species called waterthrushes belong with the warblers. Audubon, who had considered them to be actual thrushes earlier, now moved them into the wagtail family, and continued to deny that there were two waterthrush species. But overall the classification was moving in the direction of a more comprehensive and realistic view.

So within this improved framework, did Audubon raise the level of his ornithological game? In some cases, yes, but not in most. As usual with him, it was a mixed picture.

Given his stubborn pride, it's not surprising he continued to insist on the reality of most of the nonexistent birds introduced in his earlier

*In zoology today, the names of families end in "-idae," while the ending "-inae" is used for subfamilies. This usage was not formalized until the mid-1840s.

works. The Small-headed Flycatcher made another appearance, along with the continuing claim that Wilson had copied it from him. The Carbonated Warbler was still there, now renamed the Carbonated Swamp-Warbler, but with the rest of the account unchanged. Also appearing again were Rathbone's Warbler (just another plumage of the Yellow Warbler), the Wood Wren (just a House Wren, although he claimed subtle differences), and Bonaparte's Flycatcher (a young Canada Warbler). And of course the infamous "Bird of Washington" was still featured, now called the Washington Sea-Eagle, but accompanied by the same shameless fictions about finding a pair of adults at their nest and later collecting a specimen.

Aside from these accounts of species that never existed, he perpetuated some errors regarding real birds. His strangest delusion was his insistence that Sandhill Cranes were merely young Whooping Cranes, even though they were gray instead of white, had different voices, and traveled in separate flocks. He may have planted this idea in Alexander Wilson's mind when they went hunting together near Louisville in 1810, but he didn't make much headway in convincing anyone else. By the 1840s, even as he continued to lump the two, most naturalists understood that Whooping and Sandhill Cranes were two distinct species.

Despite these refusals to change his stance in cases where he was wrong, Audubon had already corrected some of his own earlier errors. In an appendix to the last volume of *Ornithological Biography*, he had already published the conclusions that his "Winter Falcon" was a young Red-shouldered Hawk, that his "Petit Caporal" was a small male of the falcon called a Merlin, and that his "Stanley Hawk" was a young Cooper's Hawk.* So these raptors received no separate treatments in the Octavo Edition, and their names appeared mostly in the fine print.

---

*Cooper's Hawk had been described and named by Charles Bonaparte in 1828, while Audubon didn't publish his description of his Stanley Hawk until 1831. However, in the appendix to volume five of *Ornithological Biography*, Audubon claimed that Bonaparte had seen his painting of the bird much earlier, before receiving a specimen of it from William Cooper, and suggested that he should have received credit for discovering it first. He did not repeat this accusation in the Octavo Edition.

Similar realizations and revisions in the same appendix had taken out "Children's Warbler" (a young Yellow Warbler), "Vigors's Warbler" (a young Pine Warbler), "Roscoe's Yellow-throat" (a young Common Yellowthroat), and others. He had also corrected other errors—for example, his earlier claim that the Summer Tanager had no song. With these self-corrections completed in the back pages of his previous work, he could avoid mentioning them in the popular Octavo Edition, where more readers would have seen the admissions of error.

It's easy to become cynical about Audubon's ornithology and the motivations for it, but he did make real discoveries and contributions, and took part in disseminating knowledge turned up by others. A fascinating example of the latter involved the diving ducks called scaup.

North America has two species of scaup ducks. In both, males are black and white with pale blue bills, females brown with a white patch on the face. They're known today as Greater Scaup and Lesser Scaup, but their size difference is barely noticeable even when they're together. Other differences between them are equally slight. Even before anyone suspected the existence of two species, one difference in winter habitat preference had been noted unconsciously. Alexander Wilson, based in Philadelphia, claimed that scaup spent the winter mostly on coastal bays. John James Audubon, living in Kentucky, argued that scaup were abundant in winter on larger rivers of the interior. They were both right: Wilson was seeing mostly Greater Scaup, while Audubon's flocks were mostly of Lesser Scaup. The Lesser Scaup was finally described by two different authors, in 1838 and 1839. Audubon realized, belatedly, that this was the bird he had been seeing all along, the one he'd painted and written about earlier. So he added an account for Greater Scaup in the final volume of his Octavo Edition.

Greater Scaup is widespread in the northern hemisphere, while Lesser Scaup is restricted to the New World. This contributed to early confusion about them. Naturalists were focused, as frequently happened in those days, on the question whether the scaup in Europe and America represented the same species. The answer was "yes and no," but the debate hid the presence of two species on the American side. Something similar happened with swallows, but in that case Audubon himself was involved in solving the mystery.

In the preceding chapter I described some questions about the former abundance of the brown-backed, white-bellied Bank Swallow. It's common in Europe—where it's called the Sand Martin—as well as in North America, but there was early debate as to whether these were the same species. Wilson had made up his mind: in the fifth volume of *American Ornithology* in 1812, he included an account for the "Bank Swallow, or Sand Martin," and made a point of expressing his opinion that the European and American birds were the same.

Not everyone was convinced. Some European naturalists, including Louis Jean Pierre Vieillot, continued to question whether the North American birds might be distinct after all. The source of the confusion: This continent has two species of brown-backed swallows that dig tunnels in vertical banks. One is the Bank Swallow, the same as the Sand Martin of Europe. The other, slightly larger, is now called the Northern Rough-winged Swallow, and Audubon described it for the first time in the fourth volume of his *Ornithological Biography* in 1838—but didn't illustrate it until the first volume of the Octavo Edition in 1840.

Was Audubon the discoverer? Sort of. He didn't describe the species until after his friend John Bachman wrote in the mid-1830s from South Carolina: "Two pairs of Swallows resembling the Sand Martin, have built their nests for two years in succession in the walls of an unfinished brick house at Charleston, in the holes where the scaffoldings had been placed. It is believed here that there are two species of these birds." At that, Audubon belatedly recalled having encountered this other swallow in southern Louisiana in October 1819. That would preserve his pride in being the first to notice it. A flaw in the story is that he wasn't anywhere near southern Louisiana in the fall of 1819; but he often mixed up dates in his writings, so it's possible he did find Rough-wings in some other year, prior to the heads-up from Bachman.

Be that as it may, John Bachman also contributed to two other discoveries that rank among Audubon's most impressive: the Carolina Chickadee and King Rail. Both are widespread in eastern North

America, and both had been overlooked by Wilson, Ord, Bonaparte, Nuttall, and others before Audubon described them in 1834 and 1835.

How were they overlooked? First, the chickadee. An almost identical species, the Black-capped Chickadee, is one of the most familiar birds in forests of eastern Canada and the northeastern United States. It had been named by Linnaeus in 1766, as a Canadian species, based on a description from the French scientist Brisson. Early writers on American birds remarked on the ability of the Black-capped Chickadee to survive in cold northern climates, but they had little to say about its southern limits, because birds that looked just like it were found all the way to the Gulf Coast and northern Florida. When Audubon painted chickadees near Natchez, Mississippi, in May 1822, he assumed they were of the Black-capped species.

Eleven years later, in May 1833, he stopped in Maine on his way to Labrador. A friend there showed him a chickadee specimen he had just obtained, and as Audubon later wrote, "The large size of his bird, compared with those met with in the south, instantly struck me." That fall he visited John Bachman in Charleston, and when he mentioned his impressions of chickadee sizes, Bachman "immediately told me that he had for some time been of the same mind. We both went to the woods, and procured some specimens." When they compared these to specimens from farther north, it was clear these chickadees in South Carolina were smaller, and showed less white on the face and less white edging on certain wing feathers. Audubon described these as a new species under the name *carolinensis*.

Birders today recognize Black-capped and Carolina Chickadees as distinct species, replacing each other along a line that stretches from Kansas east to New Jersey. Along most of that line, the boundary between the two has been gradually shifting northward for many decades. Carolina Chickadee breeding territory now includes the entire Philadelphia area—the Black-capped is only a scarce winter visitor—and extends thirty or forty miles farther north, with Black-cappeds taking over north of Allentown. We don't know where the dividing line was in the early 1800s, but it must have been near Philadelphia, right under the noses of the top ornithologists of the day. Audubon, with help from Bachman, deserves credit for sleuthing out the difference.

The King Rail case was a variation on the same theme. Rails are marsh birds, heard more often than seen. The Clapper Rail, one of the larger species, about the size of a small chicken, lives in salt marshes all along the Atlantic and Gulf Coasts, and apparently it was much more numerous two centuries ago. Perhaps because Clapper Rails were so familiar, ornithologists seem to have paid little attention to them. Alexander Wilson noted their preference for salt marshes, but added that they were "occasionally found along the swampy shores and tide waters of our large rivers." He also wrote that young birds in their first year were more grayish brown or ash-brown, while older adults were more reddish brown on the underparts.

The more reddish rails were of a different species, living in freshwater marshes of the interior, and unrecognized at the time. Audubon claimed to have shot one in Kentucky in 1810, and later he was aware that hunters found such birds in fresh marshes of inland Louisiana, but in neither case did he follow up on the significance of these findings. Evidently it was John Bachman, again, who prompted him to look more closely. Bachman had noticed rails in the interior of South Carolina that were different from the abundant Clappers near the coast: larger and more colorful, and consistently in fresh water. Audubon decided his friend was right. In describing how his predecessors had missed the King Rail, he could hardly contain his glee: "Always unwilling to find faults in so ardent a student of nature as Wilson, I felt almost mortified when, after having . . . carefully examined the habits of both species . . . I discovered the error which he had in this instance committed." But the discovery had been at least partly guided by Bachman, and it's not at all clear he would have detected this species on his own.

Bachman and Audubon were beginning a collaboration on a major treatise on mammals, *The Viviparous Quadrupeds of North America,**

---

*The live-bearing, four-footed animals of North America. The word "mammal" had been coined by that time, but it wasn't in very common use yet.

King Rails by John James Audubon. Although Audubon is usually credited with "discovering" this bird (which he called the "Fresh Water Marsh Hen"), his friend John Bachman may have been the first to convince him that it was different from the Clapper Rail of salt marshes along the coast.

which would be issued in multiple parts between 1845 and 1848. Like the Octavo Edition, this project would become a family enterprise, with Audubon's sons playing big roles: Victor handling many of the business aspects, John Woodhouse creating many of the illustrations.

Between the quadrupeds and the Octavo Edition, these projects would keep the sons busy throughout the decade. And the mammal work would distract Audubon senior from his bird focus—partly, but not entirely. He was still, in a sense, wrestling with Alexander Wilson's ghost, trying to treat as many bird species as he could, to outdo his absent rival. For the Octavo Edition he'd had to subtract some of his hypothetical birds, like the Winter Falcon and Roscoe's Yellowthroat, when they proved not valid. He needed more birds to bring the total back up.

The Carolina Chickadee and King Rail had been defined, with Bachman's help, in time to be included in the original *Birds of America* and *Ornithological Biography*, and the Northern Rough-winged Swallow at least had made it into the text. Now the Octavo Edition would introduce other new species that hadn't appeared in an Audubon publication before.

Not the brown thrushes, though. These birds that had confused everyone from Mark Catesby onward were still a mess. In the Octavo Edition, Audubon would treat the Hermit Thrush as two species, and would include no mention of Swainson's Thrush or the Gray-cheeked Thrush. Those two were both described (from the Pacific Coast and from South American wintering grounds) during the 1840s, but the status of all the brown thrushes in eastern North America would not come into focus until the late 1850s. That clarity would come about because ornithologist Spencer Baird, working at the recently formed Smithsonian Institution, could compare large series of specimens and begin to sort them out into groups.

The same person and the same method—Spencer Baird, comparing series of specimens—had already led to a breakthrough with another confusing group, the small flycatchers. And it happened in time to add names to the Octavo Edition.

The little flycatchers now classified in the genus *Empidonax* create challenges for birders even today. Five species are migrants or summer residents in eastern North America, and they're so similar that a single description could apply to all: very small, grayish to greenish above, whitish to yellow below, with two pale wing bars and a pale ring around each eye. Early descriptions were no more detailed than that, making it almost impossible to tell which of the birds was being referenced. It's no wonder only two of the five eastern species had been named at the time Audubon finished his *Ornithological Biography*.

The methodology of the era didn't work for these birds. A lone naturalist out on the frontier, wherever that might be—Wilson in Philadelphia in 1808, Audubon on the lower Mississippi in the 1820s—shoots a specimen of a small, drab flycatcher, and then tries to match it to a vague description or poor illustration. Perceived similarities or differences might result from limitations in reference materials. Trying to sort out subtle creatures this way, studying one individual at a time, was a losing approach.

Spencer Baird would not go that route. As a boy in Carlisle, Pennsylvania, about a hundred miles west of Philadelphia, he focused on nature at an early age. By the time he was in his mid-teens, in the late 1830s, he was beginning a correspondence with John James Audubon and collecting bird specimens.

He and his brother, William, made a point of pursuing the small flycatchers that passed through Carlisle in spring migration, observing their behavior, and collecting representatives of each kind. Between 1839 and 1843, Spencer and William Baird built up enough of a series that they could make comparisons and point out key differences among four distinct species. Two of these were the "Traill's Flycatcher" (now called the Willow Flycatcher), which Audubon had described in 1831, and the Acadian Flycatcher, known since the days of Wilson. The other two were unnamed. The Baird brothers wrote them up in a paper for the Academy of Natural Sciences of Philadelphia in 1843: Least Flycatcher and Yellow-bellied Flycatcher. Not settling for mere descriptions, they detailed how each differed from all known flycatchers. It was solid work, and these two species are recognized today as common migrants through the eastern states, even though they had gone undetected for so long.

Spencer Baird was only twenty years old when he and his brother described the Least Flycatcher and Yellow-bellied Flycatcher, but he would go on to become a leading American ornithologist in the latter half of the nineteenth century (and an authority on mammals, reptiles, and fishes as well), describing more species and clarifying the status of many others. Hired at the Smithsonian in 1850, at the age of twenty-seven, he rapidly built up the specimen collections there. With this resource at hand, Baird could lay out long series of birds, assess their similarities and differences, look for patterns of geographic variation, try to determine if color differences were related to age or season. He could get a clear overview that wouldn't have been possible for old-time naturalists, pursuing single birds outdoors. It was a modern, analytical approach, and it reflected a shift in the practice of ornithology.

John James Audubon was happy to encourage the teenage Baird when their correspondence began. Later, in the final volume of his Octavo Edition in 1844, he would be happy to include Least Flycatcher and Yellow-bellied Flycatcher, and credit his young friend for their discovery. But he would not live to see ornithology transformed by the rise of major study collections, and in any case, he might not have been able to adapt to that new era. He still thought of himself as the American Woodsman, the rugged individual pursuing knowledge on the edge of the wilderness.

He would have one more venture out to that frontier. The vast northwestern reaches of the Louisiana Purchase, stretching through what are now the Dakotas and eastern Montana, were still mostly untouched by white settlers; but an active fur trade was thriving in that region, with Native tribes bringing furs of beaver, bison, and other animals to exchange for manufactured goods at outposts far up the Missouri River. Steamboats were now plying the upper Missouri, making travel to that region far easier than it would have been a generation earlier. John Bachman encouraged Audubon to visit those relatively unexplored lands and seek out new mammal species they could include in their *Viviparous Quadrupeds*.

He would go there—but not with the tight focus on quadrupeds that Bachman might have preferred. Shooting big quadrupeds for sport, yes, there would be a bit too much of that. But for scientific inquiry, birds would still garner most of his attention. In a last great adventure out on the Great Plains, he would revel in the illusion of a wilderness where a lone naturalist could still make grand discoveries, a young America where anything was possible.

12

A Shifting Horizon

North Dakota winters can be brutal. Temperatures often hover around zero Fahrenheit. Bitter Arctic winds, sweeping down unimpeded across the Canadian prairies, can push the wind chill to forty or fifty below, often with blinding blizzard conditions.

At least, that's what I've heard. But try as I might, I can't imagine the state that way. In my mind, this land is suspended in time at a different season, poised at that point when spring opens up to early summer. The prairies are green, flowers and birds are everywhere, the land is alive with possibilities. Everything is fresh and new and young. That was how I saw North Dakota for the first time, and I will always see it that way.

I was a teenager when I first visited North Dakota. It was 1973, an era when legions of young people trekked around North America by hitchhiking; as an avid but impoverished birder, I had logged tens of thousands of miles that way, back and forth across the continent. When the American Birding Association—a fledgling organization, formed just five years earlier—scheduled their first-ever convention for June in Kenmare, North Dakota, I had to go.

Kenmare struck me as the most beautiful small town I'd ever seen. The locals took pride in their community, from the clean and modern high school building (where the birders' convention was headquartered) to the neatly kept yards and houses. The town perched on a bluff over-looking a long, marshy lake, part of the Des Lacs National Wildlife Refuge. Elegant black-and-white Western Grebes swam on the lake, and their reedy, croaking cries floated up on the breeze, background music for summer evenings.

With just two small motels, Kenmare was hardly set up for an in-flux of almost two hundred birders. Some people stayed as guests in the homes of local families; others, like me, spread out sleeping bags on the floor of the high school gym. But no one complained about the choice of location for the convention. After all, we were there for birds, and the region offered up a bevy of specialties. Most special of all was Baird's Sparrow, a sweet-voiced gnome of the tall grasses. A local couple, Ann and Robert Gammell, had monitored this uncommon songster for years. Every summer, visiting birders would call to ask them where to find it, as well as other prairie birds. When the leaders of the American Birding Association called on them, the Gammells mobilized the whole town to act as hosts.

The three days I spent at the convention stand out for me as a bright memory that will never fade. The birds were wonderful—the promised Baird's Sparrows, smartly patterned little Chestnut-collared Longspurs, aerial singers like Sprague's Pipits and Upland Sandpipers, and more. And the presence of so many other birders made the experience shine. Up to that time, my perpetual birding had been mostly solo, or in the company of a few friends. This gathering was by far the largest massing of avian fans I'd ever encountered, and they included many of the most avid experts, luminaries of the field.

From the age of nine I had idolized the work of Roger Tory Peter-son, the so-called "Twentieth Century Audubon," and here he was in person—accessible, unassuming, looking at birds with the rest of us, but still awe-inspiring in his deep level of experience and knowledge. He was in his mid-sixties then, and like me, he had been birding since boyhood, so he had witnessed historic changes in our shared pursuit. Whenever I could, I tried to stay close enough to hear what he had to say, soaking up fragments of wisdom. And one of his comments captured my imagination because it touched on bird study in the past, back far beyond his own lifetime.

I had been happy just to hear anything Peterson said. But some people, it seemed, were more eager to make him listen to them. Gentle and patient, he would listen, tilting his head as a shock of unruly whitening hair fell across his forehead, and sometimes adopting what others had dubbed his "faraway ornithological look." I happened to be listening when he was pinned down between two notably loquacious fans.

One was in an extended rant about the National Audubon Society, complaining that they had gone too far into conservation work, with too little emphasis on birding. The other was exulting that she had seen her two most wanted birds, Baird's Sparrow and Sprague's Pipit, that morning in the same section of prairie near Kenmare.

"He found both of them, you know," Roger interrupted.

"What?"

In later years I would get to know Peterson pretty well, even collaborating with him on some projects, and I would come to recognize these lateral movements of his mind—he had a genius for taking two separate topics and highlighting their connections. But at that moment, I was mystified. I echoed the other two. "What?"

"Audubon," said Roger. "The man, not the society. Audubon discovered the Baird's Sparrow and Sprague's Pipit. Here on the northern plains. He described them to science."

By the standards of the nineteenth century, John James Audubon was already advanced in age by the time he set foot in the land we now call North Dakota. It was 1843. A decade had passed since his last rigorous expedition, to Labrador in 1833, and he was now fifty-eight years old. But now steamboats plied the upper Missouri River, all the way to the far-flung outpost of Fort Union. Audubon could realize his dream of glimpsing the American West.

It was a dream long delayed. As early as 1821 he had heard rumors of a government survey party going cross-country to the Pacific Coast, and had desperately tried to get a place on the expedition as naturalist and artist, even writing to President James Monroe to offer his services. At the time, he was in New Orleans, struggling to stay afloat financially while beginning to work in earnest on the paintings for his great work. Even so, he dreamed of the new and unknown birds he might discover in the vast, largely untapped West. Such a westward jaunt in that era would have been a multiyear prospect, leaving his original project in limbo and leaving Lucy and their two young sons alone in Kentucky. He was probably lucky that nothing ever came of the plan.

In subsequent years, as he alternated between seeking new birds in eastern North America and going to England to oversee publication of his work, Audubon could never have found time for such an extended journey. He watched enviously as younger naturalists traveled to the Rocky Mountains or the Pacific and back, and he added various western species to his *Birds of America*, based on specimens brought back by John Townsend and others. Those dried bird skins, tantalizing and mute, gave him only hints of the living creatures and landscape of the West, and it galled him that he could not travel to see these for himself.

Writing to John Bachman, he complained that he had received a long letter from Townsend, "but alas containing so very little, that I cannot understand how he spent his whole days and years at Fort Vancouver. . . . That he saw many new birds which he has not procured I am now certain but good God, what a pity that you or I, or [Edward] Harris had not been there, oh what might we have done, that he has left undone. . . . But who Knows? I may yet ransack that country!!"

Now he had earned some breathing room, and might have time to ransack that country after all. His *Birds of America* and *Ornithological Biography* had been brought to triumphant completion, and his sons were directing production of the smaller, more affordable version, the Royal Octavo Edition. And now he had another reason to go west: his project with Bachman to write and illustrate *The Viviparous Quadrupeds of North America*. It was the perfect excuse to light out for the territory, seeking different mammals to paint for the new work.

And, of course, going into new country, he would seek birds new to science. Alexander Wilson had been dead for thirty years, but Audubon still felt his hovering shadow, still felt a need to outdo Wilson's count of species by as wide a margin as possible. There were still unknown birds in the West, he was sure of it; and he intended to discover some of them.

No longer would such a journey require joining a government expedition or making an exhausting overland trek. Trade was opening up the West. Fur companies had established outposts, not to displace Native Americans or settle on their lands (at least, not at first), but to do commerce with them.

At the invitation of the Hohe (Assiniboine) people, the American Fur Company had built their flagship trading post, Fort Union, near the confluence of the Missouri and Yellowstone Rivers, at what would be the western border of North Dakota today. Representatives of the Hohe and other tribes brought pelts of beaver, otter, mink, bison, and other animals and went through ceremonial sessions of bartering them for metal tools and cooking utensils, guns, fabrics, glass beads, and other goods. The American Fur Company sent their own steamboats up the Missouri from St. Louis, ferrying trade goods to Fort Union and bringing the furs back to be sold in the eastern United States and Europe. The trade had been well established since 1832, and other artists, naturalists, and dignitaries had already stayed as guests at Fort Union. It was the perfect opportunity for Audubon to visit the West without the rigors of wilderness camping.

His companions for the journey were all considerably younger. His good friend Edward Harris, the wealthy farmer and naturalist from New Jersey, was forty-three. Isaac Sprague, an artist from Massachusetts, and taxidermist John G. Bell, from New York, were both thirty. A young man named Lewis Squires, a neighbor of the Audubon family estate on the Hudson River, was invited along to act as secretary for the expedition. Also invited was Audubon's young friend, Spencer Baird, from Pennsylvania. Audubon had been mentoring him through correspondence for three years, and hoped to give him the golden opportunity of this western journey. In later years Baird would be recognized as a leading ornithologist. But he would not go on this expedition. He was only twenty years old, and his family considered the trip too dangerous.

From the East Coast, the party traveled overland by train and stage-coach and then by a series of steamboats down the Ohio River and up the Mississippi to St. Louis. There they had a delay, because even though it was the end of March, the Missouri River was still largely frozen; the *Omega*, the steamboat of the American Fur Company on which Audubon had booked passage, would not be leaving for almost four weeks. But on April 25, the *Omega* cast off its lines and headed west up the Missouri River.

This was all new territory. Audubon had been a little farther west on the Gulf Coast in the spring of 1837, but he had never been west of St. Louis in the interior. As the *Omega* chugged upriver, it was as if John James had reverted to his younger self, filled with energy and excitement at the prospect of discovery.

Even before they left St. Louis, newspaper reporters had noted Audubon's seemingly youthful aura. One wrote: "Although an old man with silver locks and the weight of years upon him, he retains all the freshness, elasticity, and energy of youth, and is as ready to endure the toils and deprivations of long and tedious journies through savage wilds and uninhabited territories, for the purpose of pursuing his favorite study, as he ever was in his juvenil days."

Now as they steamed up the Missouri, it seemed the country was younger, too. When Audubon had gone out to Kentucky with his young bride in 1810, that land was still the wild frontier. He had seen so many changes since. Settlers pushing west, the banks of the Ohio and Missis-sippi Rivers converted from wilderness to towns and farms, the wolves and bears and the herds of elk retreating ahead of the advance of civili-zation. But here there was still wilderness. Audubon's companions were awed by the size of the tall trees growing along the riverbank; coming from the Northeast, they had never seen anything but second-growth forest. They saw Carolina Parakeets along the river, too. As early as 1831, Audubon had written that "Our Parakeets are very rapidly di-minishing in number; and in some districts . . . scarcely any are now to be seen." But now, a dozen years later, the brilliant green parakeets with yellow-orange heads still flew in noisy flocks along the Missouri.

Forward into the West, backward into the past, the aging bird painter gazed at a shifting horizon as he relived his own youth in the young America. He was back on the frontier, where anything was possible. Not that he had run out of possibilities farther east; even at his new home in New York, if he had paid enough attention to migrants passing through, he might have detected several species that were still undescribed and unnamed at that time. But maybe he was tired of looking in those well-settled regions, or unwilling to go through the painstaking process of amassing and comparing long series of specimens of subtle birds. Or maybe he had drifted into the dulling assumption that everything was known there. No such assumption could apply on the Missouri River. Around every bend, he expected novelty.

Audubon and his companions were hardly the first naturalists of European descent to enter the Great Plains. The Lewis and Clark expedition in 1803 to 1806 had brought back bird specimens, and some had been described and named by Alexander Wilson. Thomas Say and Titian Peale had found several new species on the Stephen Long expedition to the Rockies in 1820. John Townsend and Thomas Nuttall had crossed the plains and explored the Pacific Northwest in the 1830s (although Audubon had groused about how few novel birds they brought back). And a decade before Audubon's Missouri River trip a German naturalist, Prince Maximilian of Wied, had traveled the same route and spent a couple of weeks at Fort Union, one of the first celebrity guests there. Most of Wied's specimens and notes were lost when the steamboat carrying them back toward St. Louis exploded and sank. Discouraged by the loss, he didn't publish much about the birds there until years later. If not for this misfortune, Wied might have claimed some of the species that remained undescribed in 1843.

But Audubon was hopeful. Every time the *Omega* stopped for more firewood for the steam engines, he and especially his younger companions hiked inland to seek bird specimens. In a letter home on May 5, he wrote: "We are all perfectly well, and when we ever go ashore, our

Guns tell wonderful tales." Near the present-day location of Kansas
City, John Bell shot a vireo that turned out to be undescribed, and Edward Harris shot a sparrow that Audubon proclaimed to be new also.
It wasn't, but they didn't know that, and it added to their sense of being
on a grand voyage of discovery.

Novelties aplenty awaited the group, if they would pay enough
attention. Almost forty years earlier, ascending the Missouri with the
Corps of Discovery in 1805, Meriwether Lewis had noticed the local
meadowlarks looked like those on the East Coast but sounded different,
with a fast, bubbling warble in place of the eastern birds' clear whistles.
No one had done anything with that information; in that era, species
were defined by visible characteristics, and it would have been a radical
idea to separate one out by its voice.

Audubon's party began noticing these meadowlarks in late May,
in what would be central South Dakota today. John Bell was the first
to detect the distinctive song, and he pointed it out to Edward Harris.
Eventually even Audubon heard the diagnostic notes. Studying specimens they had collected, he latched on to what he thought were physical
distinctions from the eastern birds. Most of these weren't actual differences, aside from the pattern of the central tail feathers, but they were
enough for him. To reflect this bird's history, he gave it the species name
neglecta.

They would continue to hear the throaty warbling of Western Meadowlarks for the rest of the summer, part of the avian chorus of the vast
open plains. Visually, they were distracted—and awed—by larger creatures. Part of the stated purpose of the trip was to gather information on
mammals for *The Viviparous Quadrupeds*, and mammals were present,
and visible, in numbers unlike anything we can hope to see today.

As they proceeded up the Missouri, the travelers encountered their
first mule deer, like rangy, big-eared versions of the white-tails they
knew back east, and their first prairie dog towns, with the cheeky ro-
dents chirping and scampering across acres of mounds and burrows.
Elk were everywhere, and herds of the dainty, fleet-footed pronghorns,
which the men called antelopes. Bighorn sheep appeared where there

were steep bluffs or rocky hills. Wolves prowled along the riverbanks and howled from the ravines at night. And then there were the bison, or buffalo—magnificent, shaggy beasts, lords of the plains, by the scores and then by the hundreds, and even by the thousands on some days before the steamboat reached Fort Union on the twelfth of June.

Audubon's party would stay at the fort a full two months before starting back downriver in mid-August. Throughout this time, they never lost their fascination with the bison. It would be nice to think that as naturalists, they were simply captivated by the sight: far across the rolling hills of grass, the tawny brown of the young bison calves a counterpoint to the burnt brown of the old bulls, the animals spread out and grazing calmly as they all moved unhurriedly in the same direction, the vast herds creating a spectacle of abundance.

However, they were also captivated by the challenge of prairie hunting. John Bell and Edward Harris, in particular, seemed eager to emulate the skills of hunters based at Fort Union, pursuing the bison on horseback and then shooting them at close range. Many of the group's excursions out onto the prairie devolved into little more than recreational shooting contests with bison as the targets. Audubon, no longer as spry as the others, skipped some of these adventures and merely observed others. In one instance, Harris came close to being trampled by an enraged and injured bison bull. He described the event in detail in his journal. Audubon was several miles away, fishing, when this happened; but he copied Harris's account almost word for word, substituting himself for Harris in the story, and this episode later appeared in volume two of *The Viviparous Quadrupeds*. Far from decrying the slaughter of these animals, he couldn't resist placing himself, fictionally, in the thick of the action.

Here, as ever, Audubon comes across as complex and contradictory. In one sense he was just seeking adventure, out with the boys for one last hurrah in the Wild West. But at the same time, his zest for discovery and his endless passion for birds could not be denied. He wanted to see new birds—new to him, or better yet, new to science. And he had a ready outlet for publishing any new finds: the seventh and last volume

American Bison from *The Viviparous Quadrupeds of North America*. Audubon's trip up the Missouri River in 1843 was partly intended to gather material for this work on mammals, but he and his party got distracted by birds—and by the macho excitement of buffalo hunting. Although this portrait was probably completed by John James Audubon, many of the mammal plates were the work of his younger son, John Woodhouse Audubon.

of his Royal Octavo Edition of *The Birds of America* was not slated
to be published until the following year, and any new species could be
formally introduced and named in those pages.

And indeed, the trip turned up significant finds, including five birds
that are still recognized today as full species and that were previously
undescribed in the written annals of Western science. They also ran
across six species that Audubon assumed were unknown, and that he
continued to believe were new even after returning home months later.

He gave a full description of a bird he called Brewer's Blackbird
(*Quiscalus brewerii*), which he and his companions had found along
ravines through the prairies near Fort Union. He noted its similarity to
the Rusty Blackbird (or "Rusty Grakle"), but pointed out that the males
were more glossy blue around the head, and lacked any of that bird's
brownish feather edgings. He added that "they do not evince the pert-
ness so usually accompanying our other birds of this family, but look
all the while as if unsatisfied with their present abode and longing for a
farther removal northward."

In fact, this bird wasn't new; it had been described in 1829 by the
German zoologist Johann G. Wagler, based on specimens from Mexico,
with the specific name *cyanocephalus* (meaning "blue-headed"). Wagler's description clearly had priority, so his specific designation is still
used in the scientific name. But so influential was Audubon's work that
his English name for the species, Brewer's Blackbird, has been used ever
since.

The person honored was Dr. Thomas M. Brewer of Boston, an
expert on birds and their eggs. Naming a species after a person—that
is, giving the species an eponymous name—was nothing new. Audubon had done this many times in his work on *The Birds of America*
and *Ornithological Biography*: forming an eponym to honor a friend
or colleague, or to repay someone for a favor, or to win the favor of
some wealthy or influential person who might become a benefactor. He
had even, infamously, named his imaginary eagle the "Bird of [George]
Washington" to gain publicity when his publications were just launching. But on his Missouri River trip he seemed fixated on eponyms, and

he named almost all their new finds after people, including Bell's Vireo, Sprague's Pipit, and Baird's Sparrow.

The honorific naming spree extended to several birds that turned out not to be new after all. In addition to Brewer's Blackbird, these included Smith's Longspur, Harris's Sparrow, and LeConte's Sparrow.* Remarkably, even though these species all had been described earlier and Audubon's scientific names for them didn't have priority, his designations of their English names proved more durable. Almost two centuries later, their official English names still honor Brewer, Smith, Harris, and LeConte. Only his name for "Shattuck's Bunting"—which had already been recognized as the Clay-colored Sparrow by practically everyone, it seems, including members of his own expedition—was quickly forgotten.†

Even though Audubon's expedition turned up birds that were new to science—and others he thought were new—he was also pleased about

---

*The bird now known as LeConte's Sparrow had been described under a different name in 1790 by John Latham, based on a winter specimen from Georgia. But the specific name Latham used (*caudacuta*) had been given to another species as well, the bird now known as the Saltmarsh Sparrow. So to resolve that conflict, Audubon's name applied half a century later has been accepted as official, despite its lack of priority, and the bird is now *Ammospiza leconteii*, LeConte's Sparrow. This is an example of the tangled complications we find when we delve into the history of bird names.

†There's an interesting twist to Audubon's experience with the Clay-colored Sparrow (*Spizella pallida*, which he called Clay-colored Finch, *Emberiza pallida*). It had been described to science in 1832 by William Swainson, based on specimens from the prairies of Canada. Audubon had painted it for plate 398 of his *Birds of America*—or so he thought. But what he painted was a faithful portrait of a specimen brought back by John Townsend from what is now south-central Wyoming, and Clay-colored Sparrows don't live there. Instead, this specimen was an example of Brewer's Sparrow (*Spizella breweri*), which was unknown to science at the time, and would be described and named by John Cassin in 1856. Clay-colored and Brewer's Sparrows are similar, but Brewer's are much plainer and duller overall. So when Audubon traveled up the Missouri and saw real Clay-colored Sparrows for the first time, they were so much more distinctly marked than the bird he had painted that he assumed they must be new. Accordingly, they became the basis of what he named "Shattuck's Bunting." But expedition member John G. Bell, in his notes of June 20, 1843, listed various birds he had shot that day, including "several clay coloured buntings"—undoubtedly referring to the same bird we now call the Clay-colored Sparrow. So Audubon may have been alone in misinterpreting the sparrows they saw on the upper Missouri River.

meeting some in life after knowing them only as dead specimens. He had painted dozens of western species for *The Birds of America* on the basis of skins loaned by John Townsend, Thomas Nuttall, and others, but it had galled him to write about them for *Ornithological Biography* without having direct experience. It clashed with his image of himself as the American Woodsman who did research in the wilds. Now, finally, he was catching up with many of those western specialties: sky-blue Lazuli Buntings singing in the willows; Spotted Towhees scratching on the ground under thickets; Chestnut-collared Longspurs fluttering over the plains. Now he could claim proper acquaintance with these creatures.

He seems to have been especially taken with the Chestnut-collared Longspurs, mentioning them repeatedly in his journals (although as often happened, he carelessly referred to them by various names, including Ground-finch, Prairie-bunting, and Prairie Lark). They were pretty enough to catch his attention even on days when he was engaged in macho hunting exploits with the guys. In his journal entry for July 21, for example, before and after accounts of hunting bison and pronghorns, he mentioned finding a nest of Chestnut-collared Longspur and then wrote that the male "flies much like a Lark, hovering while singing, and sweeping round and round, over and above its female while she sits on the eggs on the prairie below."

Before my first visit to North Dakota at the age of nineteen, I had seen Chestnut-collared Longspurs, but only on their wintering grounds in the Southwest. There they were drab sparrow-sized birds, ranging in flocks over arid grasslands, flying ahead with squeaky chattering calls, and hard to see well. Watching them here in the peak of their breeding season was a different experience, almost like what Audubon must have felt when he graduated from dried specimens to the living bird.

On the prairies near Kenmare, male Chestnut-collared Longspurs were as conspicuous as Audubon had described, "hovering while singing, and sweeping round and round," showing off their bold patterns of black and buff and chestnut, their tails flashing mostly white in flight. I was enchanted by them. And I was even more excited on the last day of the birding convention, when I saw McCown's Longspurs for the first time.

It was a stroke of luck for me. As an impoverished hitchhiker, I couldn't afford to register for the convention, so I had just shown up to hang around the edges. But the generous and welcoming people of the American Birding Association had invited me to go for free on the Sunday bus trip down to Theodore Roosevelt National Park, a three-hour ride from Kenmare. On the way, the local leaders took us on a detour to a known stakeout for McCown's Longspurs.

Like their Chestnut-collared cousins, the male McCown's sang in flight, pouring out a short, tinkling warble as they hovered or circled over the grass. Like them, they wore patterns featuring black and chestnut, and their tails flashed mostly white as they spread them in flight. Up to that time I had been frustrated by McCown's Longspurs on their wintering grounds on the plains of Texas and the Southwest, never sure I was identifying them correctly in their drab winter plumage. Here they were distinctive and glorious. And in my mind they were linked forever with my impressions of beautiful North Dakota and of the continent-wide birding community that had made me feel so thoroughly welcomed.

The place near Arnegard where we saw the McCown's Longspurs was less than forty miles from Fort Union, where Audubon and his party had spent the summer of 1843. So, in theory, they could have discovered the species then. But they didn't. That would be left to Captain John P. McCown of the U.S. Army, an amateur ornithologist, who shot two individuals on their wintering grounds in western Texas about eight years later. He sent the specimens to George Lawrence in New York, who described the species as new and named it in McCown's honor.

Did Audubon and his companions just miss this bird? Probably. Historical data are sketchy, but all evidence suggests that McCown's Longspurs were widespread across North Dakota in the 1800s, extending east to the edge of Minnesota. So they should have been somewhere within a day's ride of Fort Union. But undoubtedly they were outnumbered by Chestnut-collared Longspurs, as they are almost everywhere today; and they were similar enough to those common birds that the pioneer naturalists, lacking binoculars and distracted by the allure of buffalo hunting, simply overlooked them.

An explorer going to North Dakota today would miss McCown's Longspurs for another reason: they're gone. Their range has contracted in a major way since the 1800s. They were already quite localized by the 1970s, when I saw them for the first time. By 2018 they were down to one known breeding site in the southwestern corner of the state, and when I visited again in 2022, no one was aware of any McCown's Longspurs anywhere in North Dakota.

Our perceptions are shaped by the names and definitions we apply to things. North Dakota holds a special place in my heart, but it would have meant nothing to Audubon: Dakota Territory didn't exist yet in 1843, and the boundaries of North Dakota as a state weren't fixed until 1889. Similarly, perceptions of longspurs have changed since Audubon's day. Four species of longspurs (so named because of their long hind toes, helpful for walking on uneven ground) are recognized, with McCown's the last described to science, in 1851. By that time it was agreed that longspurs were related to the Snow Bunting of northern latitudes, which has a similar foot structure. But no one was quite sure where to fit them among larger groups. Audubon and his contemporaries had been uncertain whether to classify them with the buntings, finches, or larks, and that level of confusion diminished only a little in the years that followed.

When I was a teenager, the longspurs and Snow Bunting were tacked on to the end of the American sparrow family. That general arrangement held in the following decades, even as sparrows were shifted around in the context of other groups, and it seemed to make sense; longspurs were small and partly brown, and they had short, seed-crunching bills like sparrows. I just accepted this classification, and didn't think about it much.

But then, beginning in the 1990s, scientists began looking deep into the DNA of many birds to find clues to their real evolutionary relationships. When they got to longspurs, they found something remarkable:

These birds were highly distinct. They were not related to sparrows at all. In 2011, the committee that handles classification and nomenclature for the American Ornithologists' Union made it official. Henceforth the longspurs and Snow Bunting would be recognized as constituting their own separate and unique family.

When I read about this taxonomic change at the time, it altered my whole perception of these birds, and I began to focus on just how distinctive they were. None of the typical American sparrows acted like longspurs. None were so buoyant in flight, so quick to take to the air. None gathered in flocks that would sweep low over the plains or circle high overhead, winter-season nomads of endless, restless wandering. None performed such sprightly, lively flight songs, flashing their bright colors in the sky above their breeding territories. I had known of these differences all along, but they hadn't seemed so important until the longspurs were reclassified. The shift in the name of the family changed my view of the birds themselves.

And a few years later, our perceptions of McCown's Longspur would be shifted in a different way. At issue this time would be its English name.

In the early days of ornithology, there were no "official" common names for bird species. Wilson, Audubon, Nuttall, and others might casually use multiple names for the same bird, even within the same written account. And even the scientific names of species, despite the rules of Linnaean taxonomy, could be open to debate. As the field expanded, it became imperative to have a standardized set of names so researchers could be sure they were communicating about the same kinds of birds.

When the American Ornithologists' Union was formed in 1883, one of their first projects was to provide those standardized names. A committee of experts produced a "code of nomenclature and check-list" of North America's bird species in 1886. A standing committee has continued to update that document ever since. They're still informally known as the "checklist committee" (though it's doubtful anyone uses the list to check things off anymore), and they still provide an agreed-upon set of names for communicating about avian species. The name of the

Thick-billed Longspurs, female *(left)* and breeding-plumaged male *(right)*, by Kenn Kaufman. The flowers depicted are globemallow (*Sphaeralcea*). In 1843, Audubon and his group visited the breeding range of this bird on the northern Great Plains, but they failed to notice it. The first specimens would be taken about eight years later, on the wintering grounds in Texas. Until 2020, this bird was known as McCown's Longspur; the change in its English name reflects a new movement away from naming birds for individual humans.

organization itself has changed, from American Ornithologists' Union to American Ornithological Society, but the mandate of the checklist committee remains the same. If a bird book published recently mentions a "Yellow-throated Warbler," for example, it means the species *Setophaga dominica*, not just any warbler with a yellow throat. The checklist committee's rulings make sure we are all on the same page at any given time.

The committee doesn't initiate most of these changes. Instead, they solicit proposals. A researcher might write a detailed proposal claiming, for example, that a certain variable finch is really a complex of two species, or that a certain sparrow should be classified in a different genus. The committee's members, all respected experts, vote on these proposals, and publish the results of their deliberations once a year. It was through this pipeline that a student, Robert Driver, submitted a proposal in 2018, suggesting they should change the English name of McCown's Longspur.

This was during a time when the American public was grappling with the meaning of symbols like the Confederate flag and statues of Confederate leaders from the Civil War era. To some, these always had been taken for granted as reflections of southern heritage. To others, they represented a bloody war to preserve the practice of slavery, so that every such monument was a slap in the face to every Black person. Emotions had been simmering on both sides for many years, but they heated up after about 2015. In a series of high-profile acts of violence, white supremacists embraced the Confederate flag, leading to a growing reaction against such symbols. As an indication of how far-reaching the backlash was, by 2020 NASCAR—the National Association for Stock Car Auto Racing, popular throughout the U.S., but incredibly strong in the rural South—had banned the Confederate flag from all their events.

Reading accounts of people for whom bird species had been named, Robert Driver had run across this fact: Ten years after John McCown shot his longspur specimens in Texas, he had resigned from the U.S. Army to join the Confederacy in 1861. He had served as a major general in the Confederate army during the Civil War.

As a university student in North Carolina, Driver was aware of the competing and shifting viewpoints about the Confederacy. He had heard both sides, such as they were. But he had also read statements from organizations claiming they wanted to make bird study more inclusive and welcoming to people from all backgrounds. Having a longspur named for southern General McCown could be considered the avian equivalent of a Confederate monument. Why not take it down by simply renaming the bird?

This wasn't the first time the checklist committee had been asked to change a bird name deemed offensive. There was a diving duck of the far north, known for its long tail and for the far-carrying, semi-musical cries, *Ow-owdle-ow,* heard from winter flocks. The British have always called it the Long-tailed Duck, and that was the name used in North America at first. Audubon painted it under the name of Long-tailed Duck, but his text noted that "owing to their reiterated cries these birds are named 'Noisy Ducks'; but they have various appellations, among others those of 'Old Wives,' and 'Old Squaws.'" By the time the first American Ornithologists' Union list of birds was published in 1886, their committee of white men had decided that this noisy duck should be called the Old-squaw.

Of course it was insulting: "This duck makes a lot of noise, like an old Native woman." But for a century, no one challenged it in a formal way. As a preteen birder, I was as clueless as everyone else; I noticed the name was odd, but I never thought about how offensive it was. Finally in the 1990s, biologists working in Alaska pointed out their awkward position of asking Native communities to help with conservation plans for a duck that had the ugly word "squaw" in its name. They petitioned for a change. In July 2000, the checklist committee announced they would accept a formal change to Long-tailed Duck, since that was already in wide use in Europe. But they pointedly "declined to consider political correctness alone in changing long-standing English names of birds."

Now, nineteen years later, Robert Driver was asking them to rename

McCown's Longspur. The reasoning could have been labeled "political correctness," and again the checklist committee declined to consider it; the proposal failed, seven votes to one, with one abstention. "I don't feel it is the Committee's mission to serve as an ethics or investigative committee," one member commented. "Judging historical figures by current moral standards is problematic, unfair to some degree, and rarely black-and-white," wrote another. "I am hesitant to change English names because of changing views of appropriate behavior," said a third. The rejection of the proposal was published in July 2019. That could have been the end of it.

But it wasn't. The world of birding and ornithology had been changing, and the committee's decision ran into a buzz saw of opposition. The opposition was broad-based, too. A petition urging the committee to reconsider soon gained hundreds of signatures, and the signers included many of the younger leaders in the field, including avid birders, newly minted PhD ornithologists, and early-career professionals. Members of the newer generations weren't going to accept a bird name they now regarded as a Confederate monument.

For his part and to his credit, the chair of the checklist committee, Dr. Terry Chesser, took the longspur petition seriously. He worked with Robert Driver to draft a new proposal, it passed in 2020, and the erstwhile McCown's Longspur was officially renamed Thick-billed Longspur.

It didn't stop with John McCown, though. Young birders began pointing out that other people for whom birds had been named also had dubious backgrounds—Townsend, for example, had robbed the graves of Native Americans—and they floated the idea that all eponymous bird names should be changed. A new movement, Bird Names for Birds, began to take shape. Naturally the concept soon got dragged into the "Right vs. Left" culture wars by people with no interest in the birds themselves. (I made a mild comment about the subject in an interview on public radio, and I was attacked on a right-wing fringe website: "This leftist loon wants to cancel birds!") Most senior ornithologists were cold to the idea of changing eponymous names, but the American Ornithological Society eventually set up an advisory committee that began, at a cautious pace, to consider what to do about the question.*

During this time, the National Audubon Society began struggling with the legacy of their namesake. The history of John James and his family as enslavers had been known all along, but it gained urgency in the push to make the environmental movement more inclusive. To their credit, the society's leaders asked Dr. J. Drew Lanham to weigh in. Lanham is a Black ornithologist, birder, writer, poet, and admired thinker (and a dear friend of mine); from his unique perspective, he wrote a clear-eyed, hard-hitting essay, "What Do We Do about John James Audubon?" It was published in their magazine, posted prominently on their website, and linked to their brief biography of the artist in their online gallery of his paintings. And the society's leadership began exploring the radical question of removing Audubon's name from the name of their organization.

Not surprisingly, that question led to bitter debate that has continued even as I write this. Some have countered with the examples of George Washington and Thomas Jefferson—each of whom enslaved more people than Audubon ever did, and for longer periods of time, and each of whom had more of a negative impact on Native American cultures. Should we reexamine their memorials as well, and if we don't, are we employing a double standard? I can't pretend to have any answers. But I think it's good that we, as a society, are beginning to ask these questions.

Out on the high plains in 1843, John James Audubon did not know the still-unnamed longspur was somewhere nearby. At Fort Union, at what would be the border between North Dakota and Montana one day, he could not have known that he was poised on the boundary between distinct eras in history.

---

*In November 2023, the leadership of the AOS surprised almost everyone by announcing a plan to phase out *all* eponymous names of birds in North America, gradually replacing them all with more descriptive names. Debate about this has been intense, and continues as this book is going to press.

At that time and in that place, there was no open conflict between white European-Americans and Native Americans.* There had been some before, and there would be plenty later; but in 1843, the region that would become western North Dakota was still relatively peaceful. John McCown was then a young second lieutenant in the U.S. Artillery and had not seen much action, although he would be involved in attacking the Seminole and other Native groups later. Sitting Bull, later to be a spiritual and military leader of the Lakota, was a twelve-year-old boy living with his family near the Yellowstone River. Crazy Horse and George Custer were both only about three years old; it would be another thirty-three years before they would meet at the fateful Battle of the Greasy Grass—or, as the losing side called it, the Battle of the Little Bighorn.

Audubon himself was seldom affected by any of the "Indian Wars" that raged across North America for centuries. He arrived in eastern Pennsylvania and then in northern Kentucky long after the Native populations had been cheated or beaten out of their claims to the land, and in his travels elsewhere, he was never close to active zones of conflict. He spent some time with Shawnees and Osages and admired their skills, but most of the time he didn't think about Native Americans at all.

Apparently he didn't think much about Black Americans either. By the 1840s, calls for the abolition of slavery were becoming impossible to ignore, and would lead to a bloody Civil War two decades later; but he had sold the last of his slaves long before and had moved to New York, where slavery was outlawed, in 1841, and after that he seems to have ignored the subject. As for equal rights for women, the concept would have been considered absurd in his day, and the movement for equality

*However, that summer there was conflict farther west on the Missouri between U.S. fur traders and the Blackfeet. Audubon had considered going west from Fort Union, to get closer to the Rocky Mountains, but news of the hostilities dissuaded him. Friction with the Blackfeet had begun years earlier. In 1806, returning from the Pacific, Meriwether Lewis had shown uncharacteristically bad judgment after encountering a party of Blackfeet in what is now western Montana. The Blackfeet, who had gotten along well with British fur traders before that, developed a grudge against the United States that would last for decades.

would not accelerate in a serious way until years later. Audubon could float on a layer of white male privilege, untouched by any social movement, as long as he remained focused on his birds and mammals and other aspects of natural history.

I can imagine Audubon casting a lingering, longing gaze toward the West before he turned to start the long trek downriver to the civilization of the East Coast. His last adventure was coming to an end; he would never see the Rocky Mountains or the Pacific Ocean. Within a couple of years, with his eyesight beginning to fail, he would put down his brushes for the last time and leave the tasks of illustration to his sons and collaborators. Gradually he would slip into dementia. When friends brought him news of new discoveries, new birds being found out at the frontier, he could only stare without comprehending. More and more people were entering ornithology, carrying the study of birds to new heights, but he would not be climbing with them.

Of course, we can't know what was happening inside his mind in those last years. But I would like to think that his thoughts grew quieter and he gained an inner peace. That the raging fires of his ambition and pride and hunger for knowledge would have straightened into a single pure flame in the new stillness. And in that stillness, he might have come to feel a deeper empathy for all life and especially, finally, for his fellow humans. All of them. This is just wishful thinking, but I can't help myself; I have to hold out for that hope of redemption.

Interlude:
Channeling the
Illustrator

Vision Impossible

It had been an absurd idea, doomed to failure from the start. I had said to myself: *Well, I've done some bird drawings in the past. I'll just learn to copy the style of the most famous bird painter in history, and try to produce works that equal his.*

Did I succeed? Of course not. Why would I have expected to? Copying a genius is a fool's goal. Try to write like Shakespeare and you may come up with flowery phrases, but you won't write *King Lear.* Win the Meryl Streep look-alike contest, and it won't suddenly give you brilliant acting skills. Study and practice on the electric guitar long enough and you might be able to play "For the Love of God" just like Steve Vai, but you won't write a composition like that. It's never that easy, and legends are never so easily duplicated.

Oh, I had tried. For months I had studied and analyzed Audubon's works. I had put away the oil paints I'd grown accustomed to using, bought large sheets of watercolor paper, found reference materials and drawn feather-by-feather birds, struggled with transparent watercolors

Six owls by John James Audubon. This was one of Audubon's least successful compositions, both artistically and scientifically. The two birds at left are both Burrowing Owls, but Audubon initially thought they were two different species. The one at top center is a Little Owl, from Europe, mistakenly thought to be from Canada. The two at top right are Northern Pygmy-Owls, while the bottom right bird is a Short-eared Owl. Audubon painted only the six owls, and his engraver, Robert Havell Jr., furnished the dead-stick perches and the background for the final plate.

and pastels and a mix of media . . . all to no effect. My pseudo–John James bird portraits never would be mistaken for work by Audubon.

It was tempting to compare my results to his least successful compositions. Here we go, plate 432 in *Birds of America*: six owls, two sitting awkwardly on bare ground, four on those generic dead sticks, all with rather dumb expressions on their faces. In this case Audubon drew the dumb owls and Robert Havell Jr. provided the ground and sticks. Maybe my best portraits were as good as this? Maybe.

But the comparison was pointless. Audubon's reputation was built on his best work, not his worst. And his best work is phenomenal.

Most of his images show the same visual genius. Look at his portrait of the Osprey, flying, carrying a fish in its talons. It's as simple as could be, just the lone bird with its fish against a white background, with some plain water and low hills far behind. It's even set up to be a scientific illustration, positioned so that we can see most of the underside of one wing and most of the top side of the other, for maximum information value. And yet the design is stunning, beautiful in its fine detail and beautiful in its overall simplicity.

After a while, my attempts to analyze Audubon started to feel embarrassing. I had looked at the spacing of elements, angles of lines, juxtaposition of colors, and everything else I could think of, as if I could reduce his work to mathematical formulae. I thought of a passage from *A Moveable Feast*, in which Hemingway quotes Gertrude Stein about a painter she didn't like:

> "I call him 'the Measuring Worm,'" she said. "He comes over from London and he sees a good picture and takes a pencil out of his pocket and you watch him measuring it on the pencil with his thumb. Sighting on it and measuring it and seeing exactly how it is done. Then he goes back to London and does it and it doesn't come out right. He's missed what it's all about."

Likewise, I had missed what it was all about. Audubon's compositions came from an inner vision, not from some calculated formula of design principles. Yes, he was a terrible person in many ways—an enslaver, a white supremacist, a scientific fraud—but there was still some beautiful place inside him that could produce gorgeous works of genuine art, even as he continued striving to beat out his rivals by painting more different kinds of birds.

I don't idolize Audubon as some have done in the past, and I certainly don't seek to be like him; his character flaws, like his bird portraits, are too gigantic to ignore. But can we still admire the magnificent works of art? Can we separate the art from the artist, or the product from the producer, in any arena? How should we think of a man who wrote inspiring words about all men being created equal, and all men having a God-given right to liberty, while enslaved men were toiling away on his plantation—can we still celebrate the Declaration of Independence? We would need a certain level of maturity, as individuals and as a society, to recognize great deeds while fully acknowledging the flaws of those who did them. Audubon is not a hero to me, not a role model. But I don't advocate for throwing his artwork away.

I am putting away the attempt to copy his artistic style, though, and for good. It was an interesting experiment, but it's over. It reminded me that to have any hope of creating real art, I must try to bring out my own inner vision, rather than trying to steal someone else's. It's time for me to break out the oil paints again, and go back to attempting portraits of eagles, cranes, macaws, and other big birds, rendered with less feather detail and more shadow and light. My results won't be as artistic as Audubon's, I'm sure, and they certainly won't ever be as famous, but they'll be my own.

---

opposite page: Osprey by John James Audubon. Some of Audubon's portraits, like this one, are very simple, and others are extremely complex, but they typically display a genius for pleasing compositions.

Fish Hawk.
FALCO HALIÆTUS.

13

The Search Never Ends

It must have been a bittersweet moment for John James Audubon when his little expedition pushed off from Fort Union on August 16, 1843, to begin the long trek back to the East Coast.

Of course he missed his beloved Lucy, after being away for months. Maybe he missed some of the comforts of his new Hudson River estate. But he had to have realized that this expedition was his last adventure, and that it was winding down. As their flat-bottomed Mackinaw boat surged down the Missouri, every mile took him farther from the allure of the wild frontier, and closer to the civilized and settled and ordinary. His own age of discovery was coming to an end.

The group did find one undescribed bird on the run downriver. On September 7, at a camp in what would be South Dakota today, they heard the two-note cry of an unfamiliar nightbird. John Bell managed to shoot a specimen; Audubon studied the soft-feathered, mottled brown bird and decided it was new. He called it Nuttall's Whip-poor-will, in keeping with his trend of naming species for his friends, and because Thomas Nuttall had told him of a bird like this in the West.* Today the American Ornithological Society calls it the Common Poorwill.

*Oddly, Audubon had already introduced the name "Nuttall's Whip-poor-will" four years earlier, in the last volume of *Ornithological Biography*. "According to my friend Mr Nuttall, there exists in the Rocky Mountains a species of *Caprimulgus* scarcely half the size of the Whip-poor-will. It was frequently seen by him, often within a few feet, but was not procured, probably because he is not in the habit of carrying a gun on his rambles."

Was it really a "new" species? Well, no. Various Native peoples had long known this bird all over the western reaches of this continent, and had applied their own names to it. As throughout this book, any mention of discovery of a new or undescribed bird has to carry an implied asterisk: this was new to the written record of Western science, or to the strict canon of the Linnaean system, but it might have been well known already to other cultures.

Whether we regard the poorwill as a discovery or a belated rediscovery, this was the last time Audubon would participate in such. The formal description of the novel nightbird would be published in 1844, in the seventh and final volume of the Royal Octavo Edition of his *Birds of America*, along with four other new birds (and six that he thought were new, but weren't) from the Missouri River expedition. With that, he closed the book on his contributions to ornithology.

When the group left the upper Missouri, they left some possibilities behind—some undescribed birds they had missed. One was the Thick-billed Longspur I discussed in the preceding chapter. Another was a much larger and more conspicuous creature. The Western Grebe, a flashy black-and-white waterbird with a far-carrying cry, was a species that made a big impression on me during my own first visit to that general region at the age of nineteen. How did Audubon's party miss it? Perhaps they didn't happen to visit the shallow lakes where the grebes were breeding, and they might not have seen any migrant Western Grebes on the river itself. But if they had, they could have begun the process of untangling two separate grebe mysteries that, between them, span more than three centuries.

To understand, we have to begin with a different large species, the Great Crested Grebe. A slender, long-necked swimmer, as big as a medium-size duck, this grebe is well known all over Europe, with noisy pairs nesting on marshy lakes and ponds, flocks wintering on larger lakes and coastal waters. It was among the first batch of familiar European birds that Linnaeus named in 1758. Subsequent explorations found that it was also widespread across Asia, Africa, and Australia.

But not the Americas. There is no evidence that the Great Crested Grebe has ever occurred in the New World. To Audubon and his contemporaries in the mid-1800s, that would have been a shocking assertion, because they all "knew" it was a part of our avifauna.

The seeds for this confusion were planted as far back as the 1570s, when a Spaniard named Francisco Hernandez traveled through Mexico. Bucking the trend of the time, he wasn't after gold or conquest; he wanted knowledge, especially about plants and animals. The results of his journey, published many years later, included a waterbird he called Acitli. (In a surprising show of respect for Indigenous peoples, he used local Nahuatl names for many creatures.) The Acitli, a long-necked bird with webbed feet, could have been practically anything. But when John Ray edited and published Francis Willughby's *Ornithology* in England in 1678, he included the Acitli and suggested it was probably the same bird as the Great Crested Grebe.

A century later, the French scientist Buffon—who had angered Americans, from Thomas Jefferson on, by asserting that creatures west of the Atlantic were inferior to those of Europe—made the same claim. Writing in 1781, he stated confidently that the Acitli of Hernandez was the same as the Great Crested Grebe, a resident of both Europe and North America. And why not? Various large birds, from Ospreys to Mallards, were already known to live on both continents. And after all, this was just America, that vaguely inferior land. Buffon probably assumed that a slightly-less-great version of this great European grebe could live there.

In the early 1800s, Alexander Wilson didn't include any grebes in the volumes of *American Ornithology* completed before he died. But Charles Bonaparte, picking up on Wilson's work in the 1820s, wrote that Great Crested Grebes were found in the northern part of the continent: "rare in the middle states, and only during winter; common in the interior, and on the lakes." In the following decades, every major work on North American birds included this grebe. As late as 1872, ornithologist Elliott Coues reported that the Great Crested

Grebe was found in "N. Am. at large; U.S. in winter, but not nearly so common as [the Red-necked Grebe]." Not until the 1880s did ornithologists admit they could not confirm even one valid North American record.

Although several authors mentioned Great Crested Grebes on this continent, Audubon's account is the most intriguing. His painting of the species, done in England in the 1830s, was based on specimens borrowed from British naturalists. But his lengthy text in *Ornithological Biography* conveyed a sense that he was quite familiar with the bird:

> This beautiful species returns from its northern places of residence, and passes over the Western Country, about the beginning of September. . . . They pass swiftly through the air, at a height of about a hundred yards, in flocks of from seven or eight to fifty or more, proceeding in a loose body, and propelling themselves by continued flappings, their necks and feet stretched out to their full length. I have observed them thus passing in autumn, for several years in succession, over different parts of the Ohio, at all hours of the day. . . . I never saw this species near the sea-coast, where, on the contrary, I have met with the Red-necked Grebe.

He describes how Great Crested Grebes swim and dive, how they take off from the water, and how he had caught them on fishing lines. It's a bizarre amount of detail for a bird that wasn't there.

Some have accused the artist of making up all these details. Given his history with other birds, that is quite possible, but it may not be the whole explanation. During his time in "the Western Country," in Kentucky and on early treks down the Mississippi, he was operating with scant access to reference materials. Many, many birds he saw must have been left unnamed, or only provisionally identified at the time. Later, thinking back on flocks he'd seen flying south or swimmers he had caught on fishing lines, he could have decided they

Great Crested Grebes, winter plumage *(left)* and breeding plumage *(right)*, by John James Audubon. In the early 1800s, naturalists assumed this bird was widespread in North America, but it wasn't; this is strictly an Old World species. Audubon made this portrait around 1835 while in England, basing it on borrowed specimens.

were Great Crested Grebes, since everyone "knew" that species was around.

Three members of the grebe family—Red-necked, Horned, and Eared Grebes—are widespread across both Europe and North America. The Red-necked Grebe is only a little smaller than the Great Crested, and probably was mistaken for it by some American naturalists.

But another potential source of confusion, especially deep in the interior, was the Western Grebe. It's another large, long-necked species that was still undescribed in the 1840s. There's no indication that Audubon saw it on his Missouri River trip, although he passed through a considerable region where it's a common summer resident today, and his notes mentioned seeing "grebes" at least once. Had he seen a Western Grebe, he might have just assumed it was the Great Crested Grebe.

Red-necked Grebe, Horned Grebe, Eared Grebe, Great Crested Grebe: all are named for adornments they wear in breeding plumage, when all have crests and feather tufts and rich colors about the head and neck. In nonbreeding plumage, during fall and winter, all lose the ornamentation and become plain whitish below, from chin to belly, and dark gray to blackish on the upperside. That simple bicolored theme applies to the Western Grebe all year, since it shows hardly any seasonal change.

When George Lawrence described the Western Grebe in 1858 (fifteen years after Audubon left the upper Missouri), he assumed the specimens in front of him must all be in winter plumage. Lawrence was sure that, like other grebes, this species must molt into fancier feathers in the spring: "judging from analogy, it is fair to infer that in its nuptial attire it makes a grand display." It was several more years before anyone realized this grebe looked essentially the same in all seasons.

In the same publication, Lawrence described a second grebe. Slightly smaller with a little more white on the face, it was otherwise extremely similar to the Western Grebe. Lawrence called it Clark's Grebe. He admitted it was "a near ally" of the Western, but he thought the two would prove distinct once they were observed on the breeding grounds: "As is well known, the distinguishing characteristics are the ruffs and crests with which the head is ornamented in the breeding season." But the Western Grebe and its "near ally" didn't develop any ruffs or crests; they stayed bicolored, and almost identical to each other, all year. As more information came in, as the Western Grebe proved to be common all over the West, scientists concluded that Lawrence had been wrong and that his "Clark's Grebe" must be some mere variation.

By the time the newly formed American Ornithologists' Union (AOU) issued their first official list of North American birds in 1886, they demonstrated their maturity with their sober treatment of grebes. The Great Crested Grebe, after years of false claims, was not included at all. Clark's Grebe was relegated to the "Hypothetical List," and dismissed there as "probably the female" of the Western Grebe. When the AOU released the third edition of their list in 1910, Clark's Grebe had disappeared even from the Hypothetical List, and thereafter it was essentially forgotten for more than half a century.

The year that Audubon died, 1851, also produced some of the last new birds in the east. The first Kirtland's Warbler was collected in Ohio; the Philadelphia Vireo got its formal name. But the frontier was pushing west. That same year in Texas, John McCown shot the longspur that would, for a time, be named after him, and Samuel Woodhouse found the first specimens of a thicket-dwelling sprite, the Black-capped Vireo. Over the following two and a half decades, as white colonists pushed through the Rockies and the Southwest, almost all the remaining undescribed bird species north of the Mexican border would be cataloged and named.

It took a while for leaders in the field to realize it had happened. In 1874, in his "manual of instruction" titled *Field Ornithology*, Elliott Coues wrote: "Keep your gun *always* ready . . . shoot an unknown bird on sight; it may give you the slip in a moment, and a prize may be lost. . . . I should consider a bird new to science ample reward for a month's steady work." But that last statement was already far out of date by the time it was published, and it was absurd when the same text was repeated in later editions. The vast majority of the bird species in temperate North America had been discovered and described, and it was nonsense to think that a person going out collecting for a month could hope to find a new one.

By some measures, 1886 could mark an end point for the age of discovery of birds in the continental United States and Canada. With the formation of the American Ornithologists' Union three years earlier, the new continent had its own professional group for avian science. They had a standing committee on classification of species, and their first formal publication, the AOU *Checklist* of 1886, presented a detailed count of all the birds within their territory. It seemed definitive. That could have been the end of it—implying that species here had been described and cataloged, and now it was time to stop looking for new ones and focus on learning more about these known creatures.

But that wasn't the end. Changes in definitions, changes in understanding, and changes in methods would keep the age of discovery alive.

In the first century after Linnaeus, from the 1750s to the 1850s, the focus had been on finding new species. That term had been only vaguely defined; the species was just a distinct kind that would breed true: The offspring of robins would grow up to be robins. Simple enough—and if some other kind of bird looked different from the robin, it must be a distinct species. How different did it have to be? Well, different enough to satisfy whoever was doing the naming. When it was assumed that each kind was the unchanging product of creation, variations within species seemed unimportant.

Those variations drew more attention after Darwin published *On the Origin of Species* in 1859. Now they meant more. Species could change over time, and they could vary by geography, so now regional differences could be interpreted in a new light.

The 1886 AOU list, for the first time, made extensive use of the category of subspecies. These were regional populations within a species that looked distinct at the core of their breeding range, but that might intergrade with other subspecies where their ranges met. They were recognizable forms that hadn't evolved far enough to be considered full species. The AOU put this category to work on some vexing and subtle birds. Explorers pushing west in the mid-1800s had found

Song Sparrows, Fox Sparrows, Hermit Thrushes, and others that looked somewhat different from those in the East, and many of these had been described and named as new species. After consideration by the AOU's checklist committee, these were recast in lesser roles: seven subspecies of Song Sparrows, four of Fox Sparrows, three of Hermit Thrushes, and so on. The approach made it possible to treat natural diversity in a manageable way.

The subspecies designation was useful for well-marked geographic forms, but as you might guess, the concept was eventually abused and overused. The drive to discover and name new forms was just too strong to resist. By the end of the nineteenth century, any claim of a new species in a well-explored region would be viewed skeptically. But for a purported new subspecies—or a new "race," as they were often termed—the standard of proof was more relaxed. Sure, this population nesting here, near the southern Atlantic Coast, averages a little smaller and darker; go ahead and name it as a new race. And on to the next one.

For would-be discoverers who had missed the scientific gold rush for species a century earlier, suddenly there was a whole new world to conquer. New names for subspecies proliferated like starlings, especially in the early decades of the twentieth century. At least fifty-two races of Song Sparrows were named. (Admittedly, this sparrow shows a lot of regional variation across its broad range, but a careful modern assessment put the number of subspecies at twenty-four.) For the Common Yellowthroat, that little black-masked warbler of open marshes, ornithologist Harry Oberholser recognized twenty subspecies just within the state of Texas. (More recent treatments put the number at a dozen or fewer for the entire continent.) Other widespread birds were subjected to similar levels of over-splitting.

For a while, peaking in the 1930s, birders also embraced the idea of subspecies. Birding was growing as a hobby, while diverging from the science of ornithology; but amateur birders hoping to build up their life lists would count any named subspecies in their totals. Most subspecies were too similar and subtle to be identified in the wild, so birders relied on the principle that every race separated out geographically in the breeding season. They could check off a dozen races of Horned Larks just by driving around the United States in summer. Hmm, here in the Sacramento Valley this must be the subspecies *rubea*, the Ruddy Horned Lark, even though it looks nearly the same as the California Horned Lark we ticked yesterday in the San Joaquin Valley. Whatever. Understandably, this kind of thing wasn't very satisfying. By the 1950s, birders had largely given up on tallying these local geographic races and were counting their lists solely on the basis of full species.

By the 1950s, ornithologists, too, were generally showing less interest in subspecies. The science had moved on from the descriptive phase to focus on behavior, ecological requirements, and more technical aspects. Detecting and naming a new subspecies no longer carried much prestige. A new species certainly would make headlines, but no one expected to find one of those—not in temperate North America or Europe, at least.

In 1957, the American Ornithologists' Union published the fifth edition of their AOU *Checklist of North American Birds*. At the time, most professionals would have said this seven-hundred-page tome was close to the final word. They would have predicted that few, if any, new bird species remained to be discovered north of the Mexican border.

They would have been wrong. Today the AOU has become the AOS—American Ornithological Society—and now they keep their bird list online, updated annually, rather than printing the occasional heavy volume that would promptly be out of date. And as I write this, the current list recognizes no fewer than thirty-seven birds in the continental U.S. and Canada that were *not* regarded as full species in the 1957 edition.

That figure doesn't include the many birds added to the list for other reasons. It doesn't include tropical species, like the Buff-collared Nightjar and Rufous-capped Warbler, that have expanded their ranges northward from Mexico. It doesn't include the scores of migratory Asian birds that have strayed off course to Alaska in the spring or fall, or rare seabirds that have been found with better exploration offshore. It doesn't include non-native species that have been accidentally introduced, such as many parrots, parakeets, and others in Florida. No, these are thirty-seven birds that have been here all along, but weren't recognized as full species until recently.

That would have seemed a spectacular haul to Wilson, Audubon, Nuttall, and their ilk, especially so long after they had scoured the continent. Thirty-seven new species! All have been officially recognized since 1973. I was a teenager in the 1970s and already an avid birder, so I have watched this development as it unfolded. These "new" birds all represented a new and different kind of discovery. Instead of trekking through wilderness to seek some bright bit of feathered novelty, the modern discoverers have lived adventures of perception, examining the birds that were already known, but seeing them in a new light.

Take the "rediscovery" of Clark's Grebe. When we left it a few paragraphs ago, this bird was in limbo. Described and named in 1858 at the same time as the Western Grebe, it had been promptly doubted. Early publications of the AOU had relegated Clark's to the "Hypothetical List," and later editions had scrubbed it altogether. Nowhere in the seven hundred pages of the 1957 AOU *Checklist* was there any hint that Western Grebes showed any variation, or that such a bird as a Clark's Grebe had ever been proposed.

As late as the 1970s, none of the bird field guides or other standard references hinted at it, either. After all, its differences were slight. Compared to the Western Grebe, Clark's had white coming up a little higher on the face, and a brighter yellow bill. You wouldn't see these points unless you were looking for them. An experienced birder could identify a Western Grebe at a glance, so there was no reason to look more closely.

In the mid-1970s, as an obsessed birder just out of my teens, I had moved to Tucson. I wasn't enrolled at the University of Arizona, but I spent countless hours reading in their science library. And in 1977, two items I read converged with one experience in the field to give me a new appreciation for grebes.

First, on the recommendation of birding genius Ted Parker, I read Ernst Mayr's *Populations, Species, and Evolution*. This book, published in 1970, gave a masterful overview of what was then the latest thinking on the Biological Species Concept, on how species evolve and how they should be defined. I read it carefully and slowly, considering how it applied to birds I knew. Just four years earlier, in 1973, the AOU's checklist committee had published some changes in classifications. The eastern Myrtle Warbler had been merged with the western Audubon's Warbler, despite their visible differences, into one species called the Yellow-rumped Warbler; while the Boat-tailed Grackle of the Southeast would be regarded as a separate species from the Great-tailed Grackle of the Southwest, despite their similarities. The scientists looked beyond mere appearances to consider how these populations interacted (or didn't) where their ranges came together. Ernst Mayr's book helped me understand the reasoning behind these changes.

The second revelation came from the library's collection of the *Living Bird*, which the Cornell Lab of Ornithology was then publishing as an annual. Each issue had a variety of semi-technical articles, written by scientists but geared toward serious amateurs. The 1965 volume had carried a piece titled "The Color Phases of the Western Grebe" by Robert Storer, a leading ornithologist with an interest in the grebe family. He began: "It may come as a surprise to many that there are two color phases in a bird so well known as the Western Grebe." Indeed, it probably was a surprise to almost everyone who read the article. Storer referred to the birds with more white on the face—the ones George Lawrence had described as Clark's Grebe—as the "light phase," and the typical dark-faced Western Grebe as the "dark phase."*

The interesting quality about these color forms, Storer wrote, was their strong tendency to mate with their own kind. At the Bear River waterfowl refuge in Utah in 1963, where dark birds had outnumbered light ones by almost eight to one, he had observed only 4 mixed pairs. By contrast, he had seen 14 pairs of light birds and 109 pairs of dark birds. He discussed this odd phenomenon at length, but never suggested the two could be distinct species.

---

*Reflecting how the language of science changes, the term "phases" for such color variations has fallen out of favor, and they're more likely to be called "morphs" today.

When I read the article, though, more than a decade later and just after reading Mayr's book about species and evolution, I was struck by those numbers. Surely, I thought, regardless of what we call these birds, they were functioning as separate species at that spot. If they were breeding side by side without mixing, wasn't this worth pursuing?

I had a chance to pursue it at the end of that summer. Friends and I went birding at Lake Havasu, a reservoir that stretches for miles along Arizona's western edge, renting a couple of motorboats so we could cover more of the lake. Western Grebes were known to nest in the marshes there, so I suggested we should look for these light and dark morphs, or whatever they were.

My friends were among the sharpest birders in the Southwest, but they had never heard of variations in Western Grebes. They thought I was joking. I was still a kid, remember, and I had a reputation as a punster and joker. Light morphs and dark morphs on a black-and-white bird? They laughed at the idea.

But out on the lake, paralleling the edge between tall green marsh grass and blue water, we began seeing Western Grebes—graceful, long-necked swimmers, gleaming in the Arizona sun—and seeing two distinct kinds. Some had the black of the head spreading down to below their eyes, and their bills were a dull greenish yellow. Some had white from the cheeks extending up above their eyes, and their bills were a brighter orange yellow. The difference was obvious once we looked for it. My friends stopped laughing and started focusing. Unlike the situation Robert Storer had reported in northern Utah, here the light-faced birds were at least as numerous as the dark ones. And—when we saw pairs, they were two of a kind. Two dark birds or two light birds. Furthermore, some grebes still had small downy young from late-summer nesting attempts, and those of the light birds seemed whiter than those of the dark-faced pairs.

This revelation was exciting. We felt as if we were on the edge of something significant and new. And we almost were. But at that moment a doctoral student from Utah State, John Ratti, was finishing a three-year study of this phenomenon. Ratti had reams of observations

Clark's Grebe *(left)* and Western Grebe *(right)* by Kenn Kaufman. When Audubon drew illustrations of grebes, they were shown with every feather neatly in place and clearly outlined. When you see grebes in the wild, in the water (where they spend virtually all their time), their feathers always look disheveled, not neatly arranged. For my illustration of Western and Clark's Grebes, I compromised, going for something in between Audubon's orderly feather details and the way the birds actually look in life. These two grebe species are so similar that the differences between them were largely ignored for more than a century after their discovery.

involving thousands of grebes in multiple states, and he confirmed that the overwhelming majority of pairs were two of a kind: two dark birds or two light birds. Mixed pairs were rare, and mixed pairs with broods of young were even harder to find. When Ratti published the results of his research in 1979, he quoted Ernst Mayr's work and pointed out that the "color phases" of Western Grebes appeared to meet the definition of biological species. And if they were distinct, he wrote, then the light-faced birds already had a name, because they matched the description of *clarkii* that George Lawrence had published in 1858.

Naturally, ornithologists and birders took notice, but the suggestion wasn't accepted right away. More research was needed. Another graduate student, Gary Nuechterlein, was already working on these grebes, and he documented differences in their voices: both had reedy, grating calls, but the double note of the dark-faced birds (*krrek kreek!*) was replaced by a drawn-out single note in light ones (*krrreeek!*). The grebes responded to playbacks of their own type. Observations and studies all over the West confirmed that the two forms mated preferentially with their own kind everywhere. Eventually a team studied the DNA of these two and found that they differed as much, genetically, as any two closely related species of grebes.

In 1985, with an abundance of evidence at hand, the checklist committee of the AOU determined that the Western Grebe and Clark's Grebe were two distinct species, just as George Lawrence had suggested 127 years earlier.

This is how the discovery of bird species works now in North America. It's a team effort, and this has been true for practically all thirty-seven birds afforded full species status since 1957. It doesn't rest on visible differences that would show up in museum specimens. Instead, each step forward is based on other factors, including careful studies in the field, observations on how birds choose their mates, analysis of their voices and how they react to the voices of others, and often deep studies of their DNA.

To me, that doesn't make it any less exciting—I would say it adds to the excitement, because so many more people can take part in the discovery, directly or at least vicariously.

Naturalists in the early nineteenth century never would have considered separating a species just on the basis of voice. That was part of the reason they had so much trouble with the little Empidonax flycatchers, which all have distinctive voices but look so devilishly alike.

Audubon got as far as describing a species he called Traill's Flycatcher, and showing how it was different from what he called the Small Green Crested Flycatcher (Acadian Flycatcher), but then he ran out of patience with the group. His protégé, Spencer Baird, described two more species, the Least Flycatcher and Yellow-bellied Flycatcher, by collecting and comparing long series of specimens in the 1840s. For the next century, it was accepted that these four—Traill's, Acadian, Least, and Yellow-bellied—were the only Empidonax flycatchers in the East. Western members of the group were more complicated, but at least the eastern "Empids" were understood.

Or were they? In the 1920s, as an intense teenage birder eager to make his mark in the field, Roger Tory Peterson listened to the songs of Traill's Flycatchers. These birds had short, sneezy songs, and a superficial description of their sounds might have applied to any individual. But with a close listen, some birds sang a three-noted *feeBEEEoh*, with the accent on the second syllable, while others emphasized the first of just two syllables: *FITZbew!* Peterson had heard the first type in upstate New York and the second type nearby in Ohio; but in 1931, on a return visit to his hometown of Jamestown, New York, he heard singers of each theme. If the song types could be found together in the breeding season, it suggested they were more than mere regional variations.

In the following decades, many people—scientists and amateurs alike—struggled to figure out these flycatchers. Gradually it became clear that all those in the far north were of the three-note song type, while two-note singers were widespread farther south, but there were places where the two lived side by side with no intermediate sounds. Searchers noticed that two-noted birds tended to build smaller, more compact nests, while those of the three-noted birds were often larger and more loosely built. The two-noted singers often chose slightly drier habitats. Three-noted singers were slightly more greenish in color. But museum ornithologists of the old school resisted the idea of designating species when the evidence was still mostly audible, not visible.

Not until 1973 did the checklist committee of the AOU finally recognize the split. The more southerly, two-noted singers—the ones Audubon had described as Traill's Flycatchers after finding them in Arkansas—would be called Willow Flycatchers. The more northerly, three-noted singers became Alder Flycatchers. Half a century on from that 1973 decision, these two are well known to North American birders, who recognize them by both songs and callnotes. Birders have documented their geographic ranges, including places where one species is expanding farther into the range of the other, perhaps displacing it. No one now questions the value of diagnosing these flycatchers by sound.

Many other species "splits" of the last half century have depended heavily on voices. A variable little nocturnal flier was called the Screech Owl for many years, even though everyone knew it sounded different east and west of the Great Plains; in 1983 it was split into the Eastern Screech-Owl and Western Screech-Owl. Birders had long noted that Brown Towhees, large sparrows of the Southwest, had a different song in California than they did from Arizona to Texas. Eventually it turned out they also differed genetically, so in 1989 they were split into the California Towhee and Canyon Towhee. The Whip-poor-will chants its name in the woods at night, but alert birders noticed that it sounded different in the mountains from Arizona southward than it did in northeastern forests. Further studies found these populations also differed in some markings, in their DNA, and even in the color of their eggs, and in 2010 they were recognized as two species, the Mexican Whip-poor-will and Eastern Whip-poor-will.

Even meadowlarks got split. One prize of Audubon's 1843 trip up the Missouri River was confirmation that the meadowlark there sounded different from eastern ones, as Lewis and Clark had noted years earlier; Audubon had named it as a new species. As late as 1886, some considered the Western Meadowlark just a subspecies, but later studies proved it was distinct. However, when I lived in Arizona in the late twentieth century, we were aware that a population of "Eastern Meadowlarks" in desert grasslands also sounded slightly different from those in the East, and looked slightly different as well. Eventually, the young ornithologist Johanna Beam led a study of genetics and vocalizations in these birds; as a result, the southwestern birds were recognized as a separate species, the Chihuahuan Meadowlark, in 2022.

These were all team efforts, looking at multiple lines of evidence about particular birds. With enough study, they all led to clean splits, widely accepted. But not every case is so clear-cut. An ongoing saga, messy and controversial but fascinating, involves the Red Crossbills of North America.

Crossbills are small, sociable finches, named for the oddly twisted tips of their mandibles. Their specialized bill shape allows them to pry open the cones of pines, spruces, and other conifers, extracting the seeds that would be hard to reach for most birds. Conifer trees tend to be irregular in their reproduction, growing major cone crops in some years but not others, so crossbills tend to be nomads. Their flocks range widely throughout regions of evergreen forests to go wherever fresh cones happen to be abundant, and when enough food is available, they may build nests and raise young at almost any time of year.

The Red Crossbill had been considered the most widespread species, irregularly common in conifers over much of the northern hemisphere. I'd seen Red Crossbills for the first time as a boy in Kansas, and had watched them clambering about, like tiny parrots, on treetop pine cones in a local park. When the flock flew from one grove to another, they were easy to follow by their sharp *klip-klip-klip* callnotes. They were common one winter and I was surprised when they didn't show up at all the following year, but that is their way.

In the years since I had seen them many times, in many places: in forests from Maine and eastern Canada to southeastern Alaska; at high elevations in the Rockies and the Appalachians; in the mountains of southern Arizona and southern Mexico. Brick-red males and yellow-green females, with stubby shapes and flocking behavior and especially those sharp callnotes, it seemed they always would be easy to identify.

For scientists trying to classify subspecies, however, Red Crossbills in North America were far from easy. They could be divided into groups by size, bill shape, and overall color, but these groups didn't match up to geography. A subspecies is supposed to have its own exclusive breeding range, overlapping with other races only in the nonbreeding season. But different types of Red Crossbills might show up anywhere, at any season. Large, heavy-billed birds and small, thin-billed birds might wander into the same forest to breed at different times . . . or even at the same time. The usual approaches to defining subspecies just wouldn't work.

Several experts tried. I witnessed one of the final attempts around 1980, when I was studying specimens of sandpipers in the collections of the Smithsonian in Washington. Allan Phillips—one of the last of the old-school museum ornithologists—was visiting at the same time, and he had laid out several trays of crossbill skins to examine. Wiry and energetic, he was moving specimens from one tray to another, measuring a beak here and a wing there, making pencil notations on the specimen tags. When I stopped to watch, Phillips looked irritated but then launched into a mini-lecture about subspecies, talking fast, interspersing his sentences with a fizzing laugh.

Every previous ornithologist had been wrong about Red Crossbills, he said, including himself. The defined subspecies were all wrong. But he was going to get them right this time. Just a few more specimens, and he was sure everything would fall into place.

It occurred to me later that I'd been granted a glimpse of history. Phillips might have been Spencer Baird—working among the cabinets of this same museum a century earlier, focusing on series of specimens arranged before him. Phillips was a genius in his own way, but he wouldn't succeed this time. In the case of Red Crossbills, specimens wouldn't be enough. Any more progress would require more modern methods. When those methods were applied to crossbills, beginning in the 1980s, the results changed our views of these birds.

A graduate student named Jeffrey Groth decided to study Red Crossbills that ranged through upper elevations of the southern Appalachians. He knew voices were important to these social finches, so as part of his research, he recorded their callnotes. All gave the familiar *kip-kip-kip* calls while perched and in flight. But as he listened closely, Groth detected two different tones to these calls. Some birds made hard, clipped notes. Others sounded lower, huskier, and longer. It was a subtle difference, but analysis showed it was real. Keeping some in cages for a while, Groth found that every individual stayed consistent in call type. And—there were physical differences. The crossbills with the second call type were larger, with larger bills.

And they separated out completely. Both call types of Red Crossbills were flying around the southern Appalachians in separate flocks, nesting in the same general regions, but there were no intermediates between the types. They were behaving like distinct species.

The news captivated me and my friends, because we had a new attitude: *If they operate as full species, that's what they must be.* But the Red Crossbill story immediately got better. Jeffrey Groth extended his studies beyond the Appalachians, and other researchers began focusing on this complex, actively recording the voices of crossbills everywhere. Within a few years, our views of these birds had changed radically. At least ten types of Red Crossbills ranged across North America; their callnotes were their most diagnostic features, but they also varied in bill size, preference for certain trees, and distribution.

It was soon apparent that these types didn't match up to existing subspecies names, so we just labeled them with numbers. Type 3 was small-billed and usually fed on hemlock seeds in the Pacific Northwest, but flocks sometimes moved east to the Great Lakes and New England. Types 2 and 5 were both large-billed and both were common in the Rockies, but Type 2 preferred ponderosa pine there and readily adapted to other trees while occurring all over the continent, while Type 5 focused on lodgepole pine and Engelmann spruce, and was less likely to wander east. Type 10 keyed in on Sitka spruce, while Type 4 was focused on Douglas-fir. And so on. Every time Red Crossbills invaded a region—as happened often in winter, sometimes at other seasons—serious birders would strive to record their callnotes.

As I write this, more than thirty years after Jeffrey Groth's epiphany in the Appalachians, we have vast amounts of data, but scientists are still grappling with how to interpret it. Only one call type has been formally recognized as a distinct species. The crossbill researcher Craig Benkman noticed that Type 9 was never found away from two small mountain ranges in southern Idaho. Investigating, he found these birds were adapted to a variety of lodgepole pine growing only there. Other Red Crossbill types would pass through those mountains but wouldn't stay, and wouldn't interbreed with the local birds. After years of studies (including genetic analysis), the former Type 9 was accepted in 2017 as a full species, the Cassia Crossbill.

Then, to add a wrinkle to the story, this supposedly sedentary bird was recorded in July 2021 in central Colorado. Birders found many more in Colorado the following year, and an earlier recording from 2012 turned up. These sites are more than four hundred miles from the known range in Idaho, across vast open stretches of desert and plains.

Does this mean the Cassia Crossbill is not a good species after all? No—but it does suggest we still have a lot to learn. It also reflects the nature of current progress on questions like these. Figuring out species status is a collaboration involving many people, including both professional scientists and serious amateur birders.

Discovery is now a shared experience, and the circle of sharing has grown wider. Defining a new bird species today in the United States or Canada must involve some genetic data, and only professionals have access to labs for analyzing the DNA. But once that species is defined, serious amateurs have the initiative to survey birds in the field, everywhere and all the time, detecting things like incursions of odd Red Crossbill call types. The vast community of birders now plays a major role in mapping out where every bird species lives.

A century ago, something like a report of the first Northern Wheatear for Pennsylvania fit right in with other things published by the

American Ornithologists' Union. Today, such a note might be published by the American Birding Association. Professional ornithology has shifted to more highly technical issues, and the legions of amateur birders have taken up the slack of tracking the geographic range of every species. And that's a topic that's heating up. Bird distribution has always changed over time, but recently the pace has accelerated, with species rapidly appearing in (or disappearing from) large regions.

I thought about that on a March day when David Muth and I trekked around New Orleans. Visiting sites and habitats that Audubon would have explored two centuries earlier, we saw many birds that simply were not present in his day. Some were species that had been introduced into eastern North America intentionally (European Starling, House Sparrow) or unintentionally (House Finch, Eurasian Collared-Dove). Others had arrived on their own. Cattle Egrets were unknown in North America before the 1950s, having crossed from Africa to northeastern South America in the late 1800s and then spread north. White-winged Doves formerly had a limited range in Texas and the Southwest, but they're now common across the Gulf Coast to Florida, and north in the interior to Nebraska. What would Audubon think of these changes? He still might overlook the Neotropic Cormorants that have spread eastward here from their stronghold in southwestern Louisiana (as he probably did in Texas in 1837). But he certainly would notice the flocks of noisy, colorful Black-bellied Whistling-Ducks, which were specialties of southernmost Texas before they began a massive range expansion just a few decades ago.

And I suspect he would be most intrigued, as I was, by a Limpkin that flapped across a pond at Bayou Sauvage just east of the city. "Yes, we have a resident population now," David told me.

The Limpkin explosion—there's no other word for it—has been one of the most remarkable events in North American birding in the twenty-first century. It has energized birders and would-be discoverers across half the continent.

This unique swampland bird, like a small brown crane with large white spots, had always been a rare and local denizen of Florida.

Audubon wrote in 1838 that the Limpkin (which he called the Scolopaceous Courlan) seemed entirely confined to the Florida Everglades. That still would have been a fair generalization 170 years later. Although Limpkins are widespread in the American tropics, here in the United States they were restricted to the Florida peninsula through the early 2000s. A few might edge into southern Georgia, but only very rarely would a single bird wander farther north. Audubon thought it odd that they weren't more widespread, but inadvertently he revealed why their range was so restricted: "The Everglades abound with a species of large greenish snail, on which these birds principally feed." That dependence on large apple snails (genus *Pomacea*) had always limited their numbers and range.

But as I described in chapter 7, an exotic apple snail, accidentally released into Florida a couple of decades ago, has become abundant there, changing the dynamic in the swamps. It pulled the local population of Snail Kites back from the brink of extinction, and it led to an extraordinary population growth of Limpkins.

How much have their populations increased? It's impossible to census a non-flocking swamp bird in a place like Florida, but we can glean hints from the results of the annual Christmas Bird Count at Gainesville. In the northern part of the peninsula, north of the main historic range of the species, Gainesville recorded an average of fewer than two Limpkins per year between 1990 and 2011. Then the number started to climb. They hit 66 Limpkins in 2015, and in 2018 the total was 540! Numbers have fluctuated since then, but have stayed up in the hundreds. This is just within one circle with a diameter of fifteen miles. Extrapolating across the state of Florida, the total increase must have been staggering.

Also staggering has been the outpouring of records to the north and west of Florida. When the population was lower, there were hints the species could stray far on occasion. Single birds had reached Maryland and Virginia, and even islands off eastern Canada. But such occurrences were extremely rare. In the decade between 2000 and 2010, only *one* Limpkin was found north of Florida. Just one individual. Most birders assumed we would never see one outside the core Florida range.

Limpkin, adult, by John James Audubon. Until very recently, the range of this
tropical bird in the United States was strictly limited to Florida. Audubon may
have seen this species when he visited Florida in 1831 to 1832, but his writings
about it seem intentionally vague. His portrait of a Limpkin, probably painted in
Charleston around 1836, was actually based on a specimen from South America;
the form found in Florida has a different pattern, with much more white spotting
on the body and wings.

That assumption began to change rapidly around the end of 2017, a year that saw Limpkins scattered around a few sites in South Carolina, Georgia, and Alabama. Right at the end of December, four birds were found south of New Orleans. In 2018 a few were near New Orleans all year, and one appeared in Maryland for the first time in forty-seven years. Then 2019 produced one in Illinois and at least three in Ohio—first records for both states—and two in Virginia, plus too many to count across the South. By 2021 they were all over the New Orleans area and elsewhere in southern Louisiana and were beginning to breed there, and others had shown up at various points in southeastern Texas. That year also saw records in Maryland, Oklahoma, Arkansas, Illinois, and as far north as Minnesota.

Then came 2022, and it was just ridiculous. Kansas had its first record—and then at least another eight individuals at scattered points. Missouri had its first record—followed by at least another nine. There were first records followed by multiple others in Wisconsin, Michigan, Iowa, and Indiana, and single firsts for Kentucky and New York. And 2023 was more extreme. Limpkins established firsts (and then additional records) for Colorado, Pennsylvania, and Ontario. During the single month of July, Limpkins were reported from more than sixty-five sites across Louisiana and eastern Texas, often with pairs or family groups at each site. So many were scattered across Tennessee, Arkansas, and Missouri that compilers stopped trying to keep track of total numbers. During the months of August and September 2023, Limpkins were found at fourteen different sites in Wisconsin, thirteen in Illinois, and ten in Ohio.

Birders were ecstatic. It was just too amazing that a "Florida specialty" might show up near Niagara Falls, or north of Minneapolis, or in the shadow of the Colorado Rockies. We were all exulting on social media about "Hot Limpkin Summer," cheering each other on. The vagrant waders could appear in any spot that had water, from major wildlife refuges to tiny creeks and ponds, so everyone could get in on the search. Anyone had a chance to be a discoverer—if not of a first state record, then of a first for the county, first for the year, first for this local park.

This is how we do things now. Serious birders have such a network of communication that we can track avian events as they unfold, and then go out to add our own observations to the accumulated data. Limpkins provided the most explosive such event recently, but we've also tracked the more gradual range expansions of other birds. We track the unpredictable flights of irruptive species, too. Whenever an invasion of Red Crossbills begins, we know about it right away, and we go out to record their callnotes to see which types are involved. When new species are recognized, as when the Chihuahuan Meadowlark was split from the Eastern Meadowlark in 2022, we go out to explore the boundaries of their geographic ranges.

In bird study, as in almost every other pursuit of knowledge, discovery has become a shared experience, a group adventure, a team effort. But hasn't that been true through most of recorded history? We remember Neil Armstrong as the first man to reach the moon, but he got there as the result of teamwork by thousands. We speak of explorers like Magellan or Cook as if they had explored alone, but they sailed with full crews and with the backing of wealthy patrons—and most of the places they "discovered" were already inhabited.

Likewise, most who have explored the worlds of natural history have been embedded in networks of shared information. Mark Catesby, seeking new birds in the Carolina backcountry in the 1720s, benefited from several previous publications—and from the deep knowledge of the Cherokee and Chickasaw hunters who let him join their treks. Carl Linnaeus, setting up his system of classification from the 1730s to the 1760s, built on a foundation of knowledge about plants and animals that had been developing for two millennia. Alexander Wilson, preparing to publish his *American Ornithology* in 1808, found that he was largely compiling information already gathered by Catesby, Bartram, Jefferson, the Peale family, and others. Audubon, for all his travels two decades later, introduced only a handful of genuine species to Western science, and most of those involved collaboration with Bachman, Harris, or others.

We could say that discovery, for an individual, is an elusive myth.

But I prefer to see it the opposite way. I think we can all make discoveries, every day. At a deep level, I believe that something new to us, personally, can be just as important as something that's new to everyone. When I was a boy, whenever I saw a new bird for the first time, I would say that I had discovered it. Recently I have gone back to framing life that way again.

And I was blessed to see someone else making such a discovery not too long ago. On a hot summer afternoon I was walking alone at Bartram's Garden, just outside Philadelphia. I was contemplating the epic explorations of birdlife that had taken place on this same ground—by a young William Bartram in the 1750s and beyond, and by an eager Alexander Wilson in the early 1800s. As I came around a bend in the wide woodland trail, I paused because some people were stopped in front of me, staring off to the side.

I guessed they were a family: two young adults with two little girls, both surely under the age of ten. What had caught their attention was a songbird, a little smaller and slimmer than a robin, hopping about on the ground just a few feet away.

The bird wasn't colorful—plain gray with a black cap, and a little rusty brown under the tail—but it was full of personality, jaunty and self-assured, peering this way and that, hopping even closer, flipping its longish tail up and down. Then it paused and cocked its head, peering straight at them with one beady black eye, and let out a *Meeyyewww*, exactly like the cry of a small cat. The two little girls gasped and looked at each other, mouths open in surprise, and the smaller one clapped her hands together and giggled.

These children had just made an amazing discovery: the Gray Catbird. Maybe they would follow up and learn its name, but even if not, in this moment it was a source of surprise and wonder. A wave of emotion caught me as I remembered how I had discovered this bird, too, when I was about that age. "In the beginner's mind there are many possibilities. In the expert's mind there are few." Reason enough for us to hold tight to that sense of the beginner's mind forever if we can.

I backed away and went down a different path, leaving this young family to their adventures. *This is what matters*, I said to myself. We may remember those who found creatures considered new to science, but the magic happens on the personal level, when they are new to us. And the potential for such finds is always there. Miracles wait for us around every corner.

The quiet afternoon seemed alive with possibilities. I set off down the trail, eyes open wide, hoping to make discoveries of my own.

Further Reading

Works published in the 1700s and 1800s by Linnaeus, Mark Catesby, Alexander Wilson, Charles Bonaparte, and many other important historical characters are now available online through the Biodiversity Heritage Library. Here are some more recent sources of information.

General

Farber, Paul Lawrence. 1982. *The Emergence of Ornithology as a Scientific Discipline: 1760-1850*. Dordrecht, Holland: D. Reidel Publishing.

Weidensaul, Scott. 2007. *Of a Feather: A Brief History of American Birding*. New York: Harcourt.

John James Audubon and His Works

Butler, Charles T., editor. 2018. *Audubon's Last Wilderness Journey: The Viviparous Quadrupeds of North America*. Auburn: Jule Collins Smith Museum of Fine Art, Auburn University.

Heitman, Danny. 2008. *A Summer of Birds: John James Audubon at Oakley House*. Baton Rouge: Louisiana State University Press.

Herrick, Francis H. 1917. *Audubon the Naturalist: A History of His Life and Time*. New York: Appleton.

Logan, Peter B. 2016. *Audubon: America's Greatest Naturalist and His Voyage of Discovery to Labrador*. San Francisco: Ashbryn Press.

Low, Suzanne M. 2002. *A Guide to Audubon's* Birds of America. New Haven and New York: William Reese Company and Donald A. Heald.

Patterson, Daniel, editor. 2016. *The Missouri River Journals of John James Audubon*. Lincoln: University of Nebraska Press.

Rhodes, Richard. 2004. *John James Audubon: The Making of an American*. New York: Knopf.

Tyler, Ron. 1993. *Audubon's Great National Work: The Royal Octavo Edition of* The Birds of America. Austin: University of Texas Press.

Alexander Wilson

Burtt, Edward H., Jr., and William E. Davis, Jr. 2013. *Alexander Wilson: The Scot Who Founded American Ornithology*. Cambridge, MA: Belknap Press of Harvard University Press.

Cantwell, Robert. 1961. *Alexander Wilson: Naturalist and Pioneer*. Philadelphia and New York: J. B. Lippincott.

Hunter, Clark, editor. 1983. *The Life and Letters of Alexander Wilson*. Philadelphia: American Philosophical Society.

Other Individuals and Miscellaneous Topics

Blunt, Wilfrid. 2001. *Linnaeus: The Compleat Naturalist*. Princeton, NJ: Princeton University Press.

Greenberg, Joel. 2014. *A Feathered River Across the Sky: The Passenger Pigeon's Flight to Extinction*. New York: Bloomsbury.

Lindsay, Debra J. 2018. *Maria Martin's World: Art & Science, Faith & Family in Audubon's America*. Tuscaloosa: University of Alabama Press.

McBurney, Henrietta. 2021. *Illuminating Natural History: The Art and Science of Mark Catesby*. London: Paul Mellon Centre for Studies in British Art.

McDermott, John Francis. 1951. *Up the Missouri with Audubon: The Journal of Edward Harris*. Norman: University of Oklahoma Press.

Miller, Lillian B., editor. 1983, 1988, 1992, 1996. *The Selected Papers of Charles Willson Peale and his Family*. Four volumes. New Haven: Yale University Press.

Stroud, Patricia Tyson. 2000. *The Emperor of Nature: Charles Lucien Bonaparte and His World*. Philadelphia: University of Pennsylvania Press.

Wagner, David J. 2008. *American Wildlife Art*. Seattle: Marquand Books.

Acknowledgments

When I mentioned the idea for this book to my longtime agent and friend, Wendy Strothman, she pointed out that it had more potential than I had considered. As I delved into the subject and as we discussed it periodically over the next five years, the project became far more challenging than I'd envisioned—but also, ultimately, far more interesting and rewarding.

To research this book, I had to read thousands of pages of publications from the 1700s and 1800s. A few years ago, that would have required access to rare-book rooms at major universities or museums. But I was able to find everything I needed through a remarkable online resource called the Biodiversity Heritage Library, hosted by the Smithsonian Institution. If I needed to check something published by Linnaeus in 1744 or by Bonaparte in 1828, with just a few clicks I could be viewing scans of the actual pages. I can't overstate the importance of this collection, which deserves the support of everyone interested in the natural sciences.

Another remarkable resource was the recent work of Matthew R. Halley. A genius in multiple arenas, including ornithology and history, Halley has been revising our understanding of Audubon, Wilson, Peale, and others through intensive research since about 2010. His many published papers altered my outlook on every aspect of this story, and he generously shared unpublished material and reviewed a couple of my chapters for accuracy. Any remaining errors are my responsibility, of course.

The New-York Historical Society owns almost all the watercolors from Audubon's *Birds of America*, and while the originals are locked away for preservation, their website carries scans of them along with extensive notes. I made major use of this online collection. Their museum staff kindly sent me even higher-resolution scans of a few, allowing me to compare fine differences between the originals and the engraved versions. The Houghton Library at Harvard University has a collection of some of Audubon's earliest drawings, as well as early material from other naturalists, and I often referred to the online scans of these.

Also valuable for me have been short essays by Rick Wright, most of them on his modestly titled blog, *Birding New Jersey*. An expert field ornithologist, linguist, and historian, Wright frequently explores episodes in the history of bird study, and his essays have led me to a number of obscure sources that I might have missed otherwise.

In addition to persons mentioned in the text of this book, some individuals shared valuable information when I visited key sites. These included Dave Finders and Sawyer Finn at the Fort Union Trading Post National Historic Site, North Dakota; Paula Reich at the Toledo Museum of Art in Ohio; Kim Staub at the Historic Wyck House in Philadelphia; Heidi Taylor-Caudill at the John James Audubon State Park Museum, Henderson, Kentucky; and Jason Weckstein at the Academy of Natural Sciences of Drexel University, Philadelphia.

Other people who helped me with information or support in a variety of ways included Paul Baicich, Edison Buenaño, Jeff Cox, Victor L. Emanuel, Gabriel Foley, Douglas Wayne Gray, Stephen Carr Hampton, Brian Kennedy, J. Drew Lanham, David Muth, Lee Nellis, Jane Patterson, Ian Paulsen, Jordan Rutter, David Sibley, Margy Trumbull, Ava Valentino, Karen Zach, Jeffrey W. Zipkin, and the crew at the Wild Brew coffee shop in Oak Harbor, Ohio.

In finalizing this book itself, it was my privilege to work with the professionals at Avid Reader Press/Simon & Schuster. Ben Loehnen is renowned as a legendary editor, but he's also an expert birder, so his suggestions and edits improved every aspect of this book on multiple levels. Carolyn Kelly expertly (and patiently!) guided me through the logistics of text and illustrations. My thanks also to others on the Avid Reader/S&S team, including Jofie Ferrari-Adler, Meredith Vilarello,

Rhina Garcia, David Gee, Caroline McGregor, Katya Buresh, Alison Forner, Clay Smith, Jessica Chin, Allison Green, Robert Sternitzky, Ruth Lee-Mui, and Paul Dippolito.

As always, I'm deeply grateful to Kimberly Kaufman, my wife, partner, and best friend. Her unwavering support, even when thoroughly immersed in her own important work, would be unbelievable to those who don't know her. This is the most challenging book I've ever tried to write, and without Kimberly, it wouldn't have been possible.

Image Credits

The historical images in the text are all old enough to be in the public domain, and of those, the Audubon prints are now available from innumerable sources. For the others, I relied on the online Biodiversity Heritage Library, which includes materials donated by other collections, as listed below.

Page 35 (terns): Contributed by Smithsonian Libraries and Archives.

Page 38 (Golden Eagle): Contributed by Harvard University, Museum of Comparative Zoology, Ernst Mayr Library.

Page 47 (Carolina Parakeet): Contributed by Smithsonian Libraries and Archives.

Page 58 (Orchard Orioles): Contributed by Smithsonian Libraries and Archives.

Page 95 ("Little Thrush"): Contributed by Smithsonian Libraries and Archives.

Other images: My original painting of the Snowy Egret, on page 70 and in the color insert, is now in the permanent collection of the Leigh Yawkey Woodson Art Museum in Wausau, Wisconsin, and is reproduced here with permission.

My drawings of the Snail Kite (page 226) and Thick-billed / McCown's Longspur (page 328), both repeated in the color insert, are partly based on photographs by Brian E. Small (www.briansmallphoto.com). My drawings of the Western Sandpiper (page 245) and Baird's Sandpiper (page 252), both repeated in the color insert, are partly based on photographs by Brian L. Zwiebel (brianzwiebelphotography.com). We bird illustrators frequently base our work on photos, and if those photos are not our own, I believe we should always credit the sources and offer to pay for their use.

Index

Abbot, John, 60n
abundance, 283–92
Academy of Natural Sciences, 67, 137–41,
    144–45, 147, 149, 152, 154–55, 162,
    294, 309
American Birding Association, 312–13,
    324–25, 361
American Fur Company, 316, 317
American Ornithological Society (formerly
    American Ornithologists' Union), ix,
    23, 182, 186–88, 270, 327–29, 340,
    347, 361
    checklists of, 327–32, 346, 347–51, 354,
    356
American Ornithology (Bonaparte), 141
American Ornithology (Wilson), 3, 4, 6,
    55–62, 65–67, 86, 97, 98, 113, 125,
    127–28, 139–42, 144, 145, 161, 166,
    172, 206, 212, 233, 235, 236, 238,
    240–42, 264n, 300, 304, 365
    Orchard Oriole in, *59*
    Ord and, 67, 140, 158, 159, 241, 246,
    295–96
American Philosophical Society, 138,
    140
American Revolution, 40, 50, 83, 153
Arctic Zoology (Pennant), 96
Aristotle, 28
Atkins, J. W., 188
Audubon (magazine), 68, 69, 282
Audubon, Jean, 113–14, 131, 132, 134
Audubon, John James, 1–15, 67, 72–73,
    100, 105, 113–15, 128–29, 139, 141,
    162, 196, 228, 284, 296–97, 309, 310,
    327, 332–34, 350, 365
    Academy of Natural Sciences and,
    144–45, 147, 152, 154
    American Black Duck and, 268–70,
    269
    American Golden-Plover and, 286–87
    Bachman and, 184–85, 191, 365

Bank Swallow and, 288–89, 304
"Bird of Washington" of, 148–53, *151*,
    156–57, 161, 223, 302, 322
Birds of America, see Birds of America,
    The
birth of, 113–15, 131, 132, 134
Bonaparte and, 143, 144, 156–57
Boone and, 83n
Carolina Chickadee and, 305–6, 308
Carolina Parakeet and, 317–18
Clapper Rail and, 286
classification systems and, 300–301
death of, 162, 191, 346
in England, 152–53, 166–67, 184,
    315
eponymous names given to species by,
    121n, 179–80, 322–23
family origins of, 113–15, 131–36
in Florida, 4, 201, 207, 211–24,
    214, 217, 219, 227, 268, 270, 272,
    363
flycatchers and, 145–48, 156, 302,
    355–56
Harris and, 137, 144, 154, 156, 263,
    365
Harris's Hawk and, 137, 154–56
in Kentucky, 83–86, 98, 105, 115,
    130, 146, 149, 180, 287, 315, 317,
    343
King Rail and, 306, 308
in Labrador, 1–2, 4–7, 9, 10–14, 76, 166,
    183n, 272, 274, 278, 305, 314
last years of, 334
Lehman and, 201–2
Limpkin and, 362
Martin and, 202, 259
Mason and, 115, 118, 119, 121, 201,
    202, 259
migrations and, 264–66
Missouri River trip of, 9, 10, 166,
    310–11, 314–24, *321*, 341, 356

About the Author

KENN KAUFMAN, now a legend among naturalists, burst onto the birding scene as a teenager in the 1970s, hitchhiking all over North America in pursuit of birds—an adventure chronicled in his cult-classic book *Kingbird Highway*. After several years as a professional tour leader, taking birding groups to all seven continents, he transitioned to a career as a writer, illustrator, and editor. He has authored or coauthored thirteen books, including his own series of Kaufman Field Guides, and his paintings have been juried into prestigious wildlife art exhibitions. Since the 1980s, he has been an editor and consultant on birds for the National Audubon Society. Kenn is a Fellow of the American Ornithological Society, a recipient of the Eisenmann Medal from the Linnaean Society of New York, and the only person to have received the American Birding Association's lifetime achievement award twice. He lives in Oak Harbor, Ohio, with his wife, Kimberly Kaufman, also a dedicated naturalist.